RAF Meteor Jet Fighters in World War II

An Operational Log

Hugh Harkins

RAF Meteor Jet Fighters in World War II

An Operational Log

A CENTURION BOOK

© Hugh Harkins 2013

ISBN 13: 978-1-903630-22-8

ISBN 10: 1-903630-22-3

First Published in the United Kingdom 2013

The Author is identified as the copyright holder of this work under sections 77 and 78 of the Copyright Designs and Patents Act 1988.

Published by Centurion Publishing, PO Box 3268, United Kingdom, G65 9YE

Cover design ©Centurion Publishing & Createspace

Page layout, concept and design © Centurion Publishing

All rights reserved. No part of this publication may be reproduced, stored in a retrieval system, transmitted in any form, or by any means, electronic, mechanical, or photocopied, recorded or otherwise without the written permission of the publishers.

Dedicated to the memory of my parents

Table of Contents

Introduction   5

Chapter One: Gloster E.28/39 – The Pioneer   6

Chapter Two: Gloster F.9/40 – Progenitor to the Meteor   25

Chapter Three: Gloster Meteor F Mk.I/III/IV   35

Chapter Four: Other Jet Aircraft Developments - Allied and Axis   59

Chapter Five: The Battle of the Bombs - The V-1 Campaign   87

Chapter Six: Chronology of 616 Squadron Meteor Operations during the Flying-Bomb Campaign – 12 July - 3 September 1944   134

Chapter Seven: No.616 Squadron Chronology of Operations 4 September 1944 – 31 January 1945   165

Chapter Eight: The Second Diver Campaign and Operations with Second Tactical Air Force - No. 616 Squadron Operations 1 February 1945 – 29 August 1945   179

Chapter Nine: The End of the War in Europe and after - Formation of other jet fighter squadrons.   209

Appendices   215

Bibliography   265

Glossary   269

Introduction

The advent of the gas-turbine engine pioneered in the late 1930's by Frank Whittle in Britain and Germany's Dr Hans von Ohain, and its subsequent development into operational jet-propulsion units led to the introduction of a new breed of combat aircraft in the last year of World War II. While Germany developed, built and flew many jet powered aircraft during the war, with several of these subsequently entering operational service, only a handful of allied jet designs actually flew before the war's end. Of these, only the Gloster Meteor twin-jet fighter actually entered service; No.616 Squadron becoming the first jet powered squadron in the world to be declared operational. In many respects, 616Squadron gained this accolade on paper only, as some German Units were operating jet powered aircraft in contested air defence zones prior to the Meteor being declared operational.

Flying their first operational sorties against V-1 Flying Bombs on 27 July 1944, the Meteor was at the time being operated on an ad hoc basis, as a direct response to the V-1 attacks against southern Britain. The Squadron did not fully relinquish its Spitfire VII's until 13 August 1944, the date on which the last operational Spitfire mission was flown.

The Meteor I was flown operational against the V-1 from late July 1944 until early September that year, following which it entered an intensive period of training through February 1945, by which time the Squadron had been transferred to the 2nd Tactical Air Force for operations on continental Europe supporting the allied armies advancing towards the German hinterland. A handful of aircraft began operating from Belgium from early February 1945, albeit in a non-operational role. The rest of the Squadron, which had been temporarily transferred back to RAF Fighter Command, commenced flying Anti-V-1 operations from early March 1945, until the 19th of that month, after which it reverted back to 2nd Tactical Air Force, flying out to Belgium on the 31st of the Month. The Squadron commenced operational missions as part of 2nd Tactical Air Force on 1 April, flying air defence and reconnaissance/ground attack sorties until the war in Europe ended, flying its last operational sorties on the 4 $^{May\ 1945}$. By this time 504 Squadron was on the strength of Fighter Command, with several other squadrons commencing conversion to the Meteor III before World War II ended. Within weeks of the war's end the Meteor IV, which had flown on 15 August, captured with Word Speed Record with an average speed of 606 mph.

Chapter One

Gloster E.28/39 – The Pioneer

The Gloster E.28/39 was Britain's first jet powered aircraft, known by the Air Ministry as the Gloster-Whittle E.28/39.

Whittle wrote post war, "I first started thinking about the general subject in 1928, in my fourth term as a Flight Cadet at the R.A.F. College, Cranwell… but it was not until eighteen months later, when on an Instructors Course at the Central Flying School, Wittering, that I conceived the idea of using a gas turbine for jet propulsion. I applied for my first patent in January 1930." Whittle submitted this idea to the Air Ministry, but was met with general disinterest, as it was thought that the developmental difficulties would be too great with the level of technology available at the time. Having the Air Ministry door shut, Whittle tried in vain to interest private industry as the general opinion of the Air Ministry was also prevalent in private industry in regards to using a gas turbine for jet propulsion. Losing hope of being able to get funding to test the idea, Whittle continued with paper plans for the next several years, when he was approached by a pair of ex RAF officers while he was on a posting as an Engineer Officer at Cambridge. These individuals, Mr. R. D. Williams and I. C. B. Tinlimg, suggested to Whittle that he try to push the project forward and Whittle agreed. It is a point of interest to note that Whittle's 1930 patent had by this time lapsed through non-payment of fees.

Modest funding was eventually secured, allowing Whittle and his business partners to form Power Jets Ltd in March 1936. It should be noted that the Air Ministry had a concern in Power Jets from the start, with a number of shares that were "allotted" to Whittle being "held in trust", by the Air Ministry.

In June 1936, Power Jets contracted the British Thomson-Houston Company to manufacture the Whittle engine, minus the combustion chamber, instruments and a number of accessories. This first practical application of Whittle's gas-turbine jet was designed as a simple "single-stage centrifugal compressor with bilateral intakes, driven by a single-stage turbine... Combustion was to take place in a single combustion chamber through which the working fluid passes from the compressor to the turbine." While this engine was being designed, Power Jets conducted combustion experiments at facilities provided by the British Thomson-Houston Company with apparatus supplied by Laidlaw Drew and Company. These tests were conducted until Whittle was convinced that he had the necessary data to design the combustion chamber, a contract for which was then placed with Laidlaw Drew and Company.

When Whittle's Course at Cambridge was completed the Air Ministry authorised him to remain there, which was described by Whittle as being "a device to enable me to continue work on the engine", allowing more time to be spent at the British Thomson-Houston plant in Rugby, where his engine was being built.

On 12 April 1937, the W U (Whittle Unit) was run for the first time, resulting in the unit almost being blown apart. However, intermittent testing of the engine continued until 23 August 1937. From these rudimentary tests it became clear to Whittle that the "combustion problem" had not been solved "and that the compressor performance was far below expectations", although Whittle was convinced that the testing had been "sufficiently encouraging to show that we were on the right track." Once testing had ended on 23 August, the team set about a complete reconstruction of the engine, which was conducted by the British Thomson-Houston Company, with the rebuilt engine ready for testing by 16 April 1938, and from this date until 6 May of that year, testing continued, again on an intermittent basis. However, on this date the engine suffered extensive damage during a turbine blade failure and was allocated to be rebuilt for a second time to continue testing at a later date. This second series of testing had again left Whittle feeling the combustion problems had still not been solved. The cost of the second reconstruction of the Whittle Unit was born by the Air Ministry, and the engine was ready to begin testing by the end of October 1938, continuing on an intermittent basis until February 1941, when a further turbine blade failure damaged it so severely that it was considered irreparable. This pioneer gas turbine jet engine had served the development team well, with an enormous volume of data being gathered from the tests, which would be incorporated into future jet engine designs.

One of the most important aspects of the WU tests was that by early 1939, the Air Ministry had come around to the possibilities of the jet engine, and that far from being a long-term research project as they had initially considered it; Whittle's design, it was thought, could form the basis for a practical jet powered aircraft in the near future. Consequently, on 12 July 1939, the Air Ministry awarded Power Jets Ltd a contract to develop a flight capable jet engine, in addition to agreeing to purchase Whittle's experimental jet engine and bear the costs of testing.

While Whittle was pushing his W.1 Gas Turbine, Gloster Aircraft was designing the twin-boom F.18/37, but had plenty of spare design capacity available. Whittle had visited the Gloster Works on 29 April 1939, along with Wing Commander J.H. McC Reynolds, the Air Ministry Overseer, the Air Ministry's permanent presence at Gloster's, where they Met George Carter and several others including some of the test pilots that would be instrumental in flight testing the future Gloster jet powered aircraft. He had previously met Carter and one of the pilots, Jerry Sayer and was also known to Summers.

Left: The exhaust end of the Whittle W.1, the first flight rated jet engine built in Britain. **Below left:** This view shows the gearcase of the later W.1A engine, which introduced some improvements over the W.1.

This particular visit had been arranged at the behest of the Air Ministry, which had looked on Carters F.18/37 design as being the most suitable then available for incorporation into the new jet enterprise. While Whittle briefed Carter on the jet engine, Carter Briefed Whittle on the F.18/37 and showed him the mock-up.

Ironically, and often sidelined from history is the fact that there are claims that Carter himself was previously involved in gas-turbine technology development, apparently working on the idea in the 1920's. He was enthusiastic to hear about Whittles progress in jet-engine developments. However, the claims that Carter had previously worked on Gas-turbine technology do not appear to be supported by documentary evidence. The claim that he had patented a gas-turbine design around 1911-12 is not supported by records as such a patent cannot be found in Carters name.

As Gloster's Chief Designer, George Carter was invited to observe Whittle's Gas turbine running at Lutterworth, in the hope that this would persuade Glosters to accept responsibility for designing an aircraft to be powered by a developed variant of the Whittle gas-turbine.

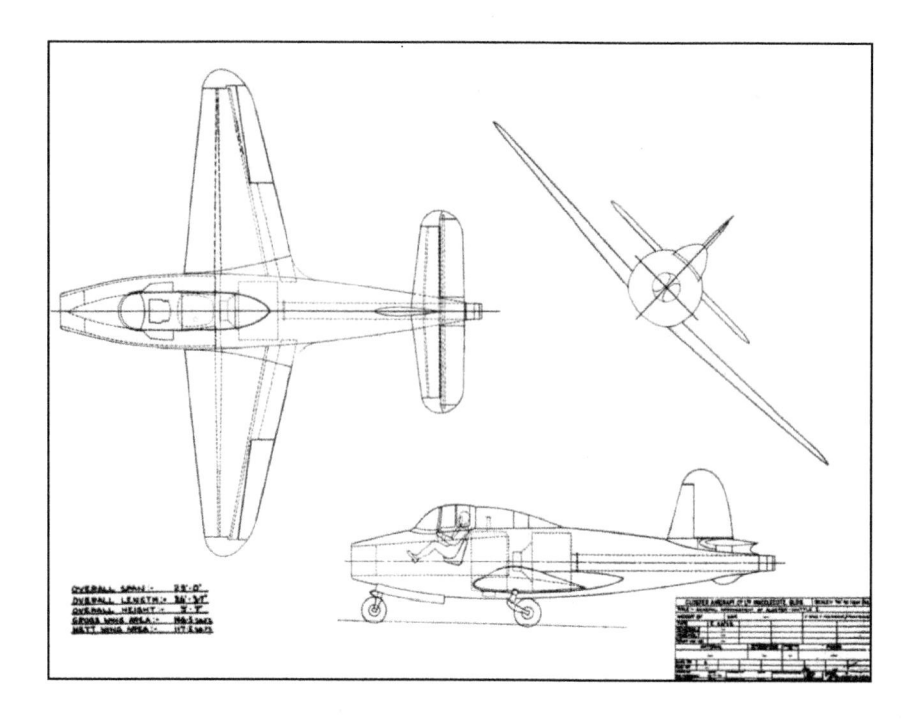

Three-view general arrangement of the final configuration of the Gloster E.28/39. The specification details are overall span 29' 0"; overall length 26' 0.27"; overall height 2' 0.7"; gross wing area 146.5 sq ft; net wing area 117.5 sq ft. Glosters

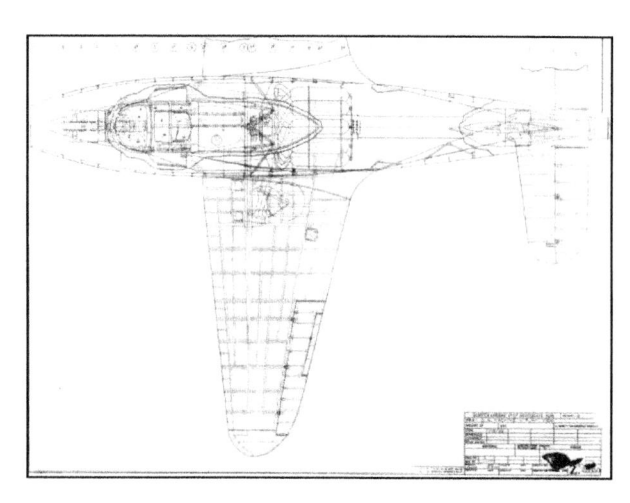

Left: Plan view of the Gloster E.28/39 dated August 1940. Glosters

Although not entirely impressed, as later writings would confirm, Carter was aware of the potential breakthrough Whittle's outstanding achievements in Gas-turbine technology could bring. On the other side of the coin, being brought on-board this bold venture was a gift Gloster's could not ignore as it had little in the way of confirmed design work on its books at the time.

Carter would later write "My introduction to the jet engine took place in September 1939, when asked by the Air Ministry if we would take on the job of designing a jet-propelled aeroplane." He continued that he went to see Whittles "Jet engine at work. After some preliminary talk and a look over a few of the drawings, we went along to the test bay and I had my first sight of a gas-turbine-cum-jet-propulsion unit. It seemed to me to be a quaint sort of contraption – rather on the rough and ready side – and by no means the kind of thing to inspire confidence as prospective power installation."

"It started working with a characteristic muffled thud as the fuel mixture was ignited, and was quickly speeded up to register a modest amount of thrust, which to the best of my recollection was about 400 lb. Some parts of the engine casing showed a dull red heat, which combined with an intensely-high pitched volume of noise, made it seem as though the engine might at any moment disintegrate in bits and pieces."

Carters report to Glosters stated "We went to the test bed and watched a run. The intensity of the noise was just about the limit. Some parts of the engine glowed a dull red colour. It seemed to me that I had never seen a more unpromising contraption to be asked to put inside an aeroplane. If, however, so much could be accomplished under the rudimentary conditions obtaining at Lutterworth, it was not difficult to foresee immense possibilities for future development."

The contract for the development of the E.28/39 was officially awarded to the Gloster's on 3 February 1940. George Carter was the chief designer of the E.28/39, although there was obviously co-operation in the design from Power Jets, developers of the planned jet engine, headed by the designer Frank Whittle. The aircraft was, first and foremost, a simple test-bed aircraft for testing the Whittle jet engines then being developed. However, it was also to have the potential for development into an operational fighter. Part of the contract award stated that the primary function of the aircraft was to "flight test the engine…", but the aircraft design "will be based on the requirement for a fixed gun interceptor…" Of course, these requirements for an operational aircraft would be severely constrained by the aircraft's size and weight, which were themselves constrained by the limited power output of the early jet engines being designed to power it. The provision for armament of a developed variant was not required for the two development aircraft ordered, although the space and weight required for these operational items were to be included in the development aircraft design.

The aircraft's very small size and limited weight constraints, imposed by the potential power plants, meant that the weight for armament would have to be kept as light as it was deemed operationally possible. This armament would consist of 4 x 0.303 in machine guns with provision for 2,000 rounds of ammunition. This was inferior to the armament of the latest British fighters being produced at the time, with the standard on the Hawker Hurricane I and Supermarine Spitfire I being eight x 0.303 in machine guns, and harked back to the obsolete Gloster Gladiator bi-plane fighter, which was armed with only four machine guns. Furthermore, the RAF was at the time looking at provisioning 20 mm cannon to arm its latest fighters. The contract stipulated a maximum speed of at least 380 mph, which was superior to in-service fighters at the time.

As previously mentioned, the aircraft, which was designed to be small and lightweight, was basically a low set wing monoplane, featuring a single vertical tail and fabric covered rudder. The tricycle undercarriage was very short, with the aircraft sitting very low on the ground. This was possible because there was no requirement for propeller ground clearance as in a conventional aircraft. The telescopic strut nose-wheel unit was steerable and retracted rearward when the aircraft was airborne, with the main single-wheel undercarriage units retracting inward toward the fuselage. All three undercarriage units were equipped with brakes. The engine was housed in the fuselage with the cockpit ahead of it and the air intake in the nose. Fuel was housed in an 81 gallon tank, which was mounted between the cockpit and the engine, in an area between the two air intake ducts. There were a number of configurations for dealing with the jet exhaust, but the one chosen was a simple jet pipe coming from the engine, exhausting through the pipe at the extreme rear of the fuselage. The fuselage itself was of circular, all-metal semi-monocoque construction, with a light alloy stressed skin. The main-planes, which tapered in chord and thickness, were basically of two-spar construction with a stressed skin covering. They were attached to the fuselage at the centreline. The ailerons were fabric covered. The split-trailing-edge flaps were hand operated by a pump in the cockpit. Two types of wings were designed for the E.28/39's, the NACA 23012 Section and the EC 1240 'High Speed' Section wing. The tail unit consisted of the tail-plane and fabric covered rudder and elevators.

In early 1940, it had become clear to the Air Ministry that there was a reasonable hope that a jet powered fighter could be brought into operational service during the course of the war. This assumption led to a number of steps being taken. The first of which was authorisation for Power Jets to proceed with development of more advanced jet engines, particularly the W.2. The Gloster Aircraft Company was eventually contracted to build the F.9/40, which emerged as the Meteor prototype. The British Thomson-Houston Company and other companies were contracted to manufacture gas turbine jet engines and Power Jets was to be designated as a Research and Development organisation and that other companies and organisations employed in the research, development and building of jet engines and jet powered aircraft should be supplied with the information and drawings they required from Power Jets.

The E.28/39 aircraft commenced constructed at Gloster's experimental and development facility at Hucclecote, but the first aircraft was eventually moved to a facility of Regent Motors in Cheltenham, as this site was considered to be less vulnerable to enemy bombing raids. During one such air raid, an incendiary bomb had come close to destroying the aircraft, with only 15 feet or so saving the aircraft from such a fate.

The design drawing and construction of the flight capable jet engine ordered by the Air Ministry was sub-contracted by Power

Jets to the British Thomson-Houston Company. Although the contract had been for a flight engine only, during the manufacturing process it was found that some components of the engine, which had been designated W.1 (Whittle 1), were considered not to be airworthy. These, along with some spare components were used to build a non-flight rated engine designated W.1X.

On completion, the W.1X did not meet expectations, but was considered to be a huge advance over the original experimental WU. Bench tests on the W.1X provided valuable data, which resulted in some modifications being made to the W.1 flight engine during manufacture.

Once completed, the W.1 engine was subjected to a "25 hour special category test to clear it for flight" and was installed in E.28/39 W4041/G for taxi trials in April 1941, with the first engine run of the installed engine being conducted on 6 April, and the following day the first tentative taxi tests were conducted, during which the aircraft left the ground "for a short straight hop." Further taxi trials were conducted the following day, with the aircraft conducting three runs, leaving the ground briefly on each run, with various altitudes and distances of around 6ft and 100-200 yards respectively. It was concluded that the aircraft needed a run of 600-700 yards to leave the ground. Although these brief periods in the air can be classed as flights, the aircraft's officially recorded first flight took place at Cranwell on 15 May 1941.

The flight rated W.1 was cleared for 10 hours flying time when it was installed in the E.28/39 W4041/G in preparation for the aircrafts first flight. The aircraft was then prepared and transported by road to Cranwell, where it had been decided that the first flight would take place, as this particular site had a long runway with wide open spaces. Further taxi trials were conducted at Cranwell on 14 May.

The first flight on 15 May 1941 was witnessed by Whittle, Carter and other personnel from Power Jets, Ltd, and the Gloster Aircraft Company. Unfavourable weather delayed the first flight until the evening, when Gloster's Chief Test Pilot Jerry Sayer taxied the aircraft out to the runway around 7.40 pm. The cockpit hood remained open as Sayer powered the engine up to 16,500 rpm as the aircraft was held at the end of the runway facing into a westerly wind. The brakes were released and the aircraft appeared to accelerate very quickly, rising into the air on this historic first flight of a British turbojet powered aircraft. At the time of the first flight, which lasted 17 minutes, it was thought that this was the first flight of a jet powered aircraft anywhere in the world as there was no knowledge of Germany's Heinkel 178 flight in 1939, or indeed the Italian flight the following year.

The initial flight test program was completed in fourteen days, during which around ten hours of flight time was accumulated in some 15 flights. During this phase of testing the aircraft had reached an attitude of some 25,000 ft and an IAS of 300 mph. The small 81 gallon fuel capacity proved capable of allowing an endurance of up to 56 minutes, depending on flight profiles.

The control characteristics of the aircraft were considered to be generally good. However, it was pointed out by Sayer that no more than 2-g could be applied due to stress considerations with the compressor casing of the W.1 engine.

Power Jets were busy developing more powerful engines to follow the W.1, among which was the W.2, a variant of which, the W.2B was being developed by Rover with co-operation from Power Jets. In early 1940, the Rover Car Company embarked upon development work of Power Jets engine designs with a view to fielding a production turbojet engine. This company would be responsible for introducing the change from 'reverse-flow' to the 'straight-flow' combustion and Rover development of the Whittle engine designs resulted in the W.2B/23, which was developed into the production variant known as the W.2B/23 Welland I, which would power the early production Meteors (Britain's first operational jet fighter aircraft) as well as a number of the F.9/40's (prototypes of the Meteor).

In summer 1941, a United States government and military delegation of three was in the UK and were taken on a tour of the

Gloster factory on 28 July, at which time a formal request by the US was issued for specifications and drawings of both the Gloster E.28/39 and F.9/40. Within 11 days the British government had agreed to the requests, which effectively launched the American jet fighter program, which without access to British data and hardware would have been left more-or-less dead in the water. The British governments willingness to supply what were closely guarded secrets stemmed from Prime Minister Churchill's desire to appease the US government, firstly to ensure the supply of lend-lease materials and secondly in the hope that the US would soon join in the Allied war effort against the Axis powers of Italy and Germany. In the event, even after the Japanese attack on Pearl Harbour on 7 December 1941, the US refrained from joining in the European war and only found herself at war with Germany after the latter declared war on the US on 11 December 1941.

As well as the aircraft technical details, complete drawings of the W.2B and the actual W.1X non-flight rated engine were sent to the US in autumn 1941. A variant of the W.1, designated Type I-A was built by General Electric and this was used to power the Bell XP-59, America's first jet powered aircraft, which conducted its first flight on 1 October 1942. Often ignored is the fact that Major General Harry Hap Arnold, Chief of the US Army Air Corp was informed of British progress in jet engine development as early as September 1940. Arnold was reported as being "shocked" by the progress of Britain, which combined with reports that Germany was also working on this revolutionary new power application, resulted in him ordering an enquiry into why the US was so far behind. Arnold was also present for the E.28/39's early taxi trials and "was absolutely stunned by how far the British had advanced." It would later be accepted in official documents that the United States lagging so far behind Great Britain and Germany in regards to jet propulsion was the "most serious inferiority in American aeronautical development which appeared during the Second World War."

A

SECRET
GLOSTER AIRCRAFT CO. LTD.

TEST FLIGHT REPORT No.: 1

PILOT P.E.G. Sayer.

Type of Test: 1st Flight. General Experience of the type.
Date and Time of Start 15.5.41.   1940 hrs.   **Duration** 17 mins.

AIRCRAFT: Type and No. E.28/39. W.4041.
Type of Undercarriage Dowty nose wheel type. All retractable.
Other Features Main wheel lever suspension type. Nose wheel strut type.

AIRSCREW: Type and No. No airscrew fitted with this method of propulsion.
Dia.:
Pitch Setting Fine .... Coarse
Ground Clearance Flying Position .... Tail on Ground

ENGINE: Type and No. Whittle Supercharger Type W.1.
Reduction Gear
R.P.M. O.G. Fine Pitch 16500 Take-off.   Coarse Pitch
Boost O.G.
Type of Air Intake
Radiator Stbd radiator blanked off. Port radiator in circuit.
Other Features

WEIGHTS CARRIED: Petrol Paraffin. 50 galls.   Oil 1 gall.
Cooling Liquid 3.5 galls. water.
Total Weight 3441 lb. estimated from Tare C.G.
C.G. Position .284 A.M.C. U/C Down. .297 A.M.C. U/C Up calculated from (Tare C.G.)
Loading Sht. No. 142   Date 7.5.41.

MARKS:
Exhaust System
Cooling System
Oil System
Guns and Mountings
Bombs and Racks
Sights
Nav. and Ident. Lamps
Aerial
Fairing
Type of Cockpit Heating
Pilot Position & Type

Nose wheel leg total travel 12" as against 10" on original nose wheel leg fitted for taxying trials at Brockworth. Static travel 6" instead of 7" on the first leg.
Nose wheel strut pressure reduced from 140 lbsq.in. to 115 lbsq.in. Tyre pressure reduced from 35 lbsq.in. to 20 lbsq.in.
Steering on nose wheel 11° either side of the centre line. Brakes on all three wheels.

TEST INSTRUMENTS:
Ican. Altimeter No.: .... Calibrated
A.S.I. Instrument No.:
R.P.M.
Boost Gauge
Air Temp.

GLOSTER AIRCRAFT CO. LTD.
PHOTOCOPY REF No. 12457   Signature of Pilot ...Sayer...

A grainy copy of the original pilots report on the first flight of E.28/39, W4041/G. Gloster Aircraft Company

Following its first series of test flying the E.28/39 was grounded to receive modifications, which included fitting An 860 lb static thrust W.1A engine, which was basically a modified variant of the W.1, incorporating some features developed for the W.2B, allowing them to be flight tested in the E.28/39. Other modifications included the aircraft being fitted with the EC 1240 'high-speed' wing, which replaced the NACA 23012 wing.

With the new engine installed, W4041/G commenced a second series of flight tests at Edgehill, Warwickshire, on 16 February (also reported as 4 February) 1942. From the 6th or 7th flight of this test series, the W.1A began to produce some problems, with the wrinkling of the exhaust cone as well as the turbine clearance dropping below the required safety limits. However, Power Jets introduced fixes to these problems and flight testing re-commenced within ten days. During the eighth flight of the series on 24 March 1942, Sayer was commencing an ascent on a planned climb to 30,000 ft when he encountered serious engine vibrations, resulting in the flight being cut short and the aircraft returning to Edgehill. The post flight inspection found that a turbine blade had broken. The aircraft resumed flying on 2 June, but lost power at altitude, and the aircraft returned to the airfield. The aircraft again re-commenced flight testing on 6 June 1942, with Sayer climbing to 30,000 ft in a time of 28 minutes, following which he commenced a level speed run. Some two minutes into this run, Sayer felt a roughness, followed by a complete power failure. Sayers report stated that a "forced landing was carried out from 30,000 ft on Edgehill Aerodrome and no damage was done to the airframe." This incident had a major bearing on the development of the W.2B engine planned for installation in some of the F.9/40 prototypes. The report went on to conclude that the engine failure had been caused by "Oil starvation to the gearbox and front and rear bearings. The oil in the feed pipe congealed and so restricted the oil flow to these parts. Some rapid development is required on the oil system to overcome this trouble, followed by more high-altitude flight trials, particularly as the installation on the F.9/40 is even more exposed than on the E.28/39."

A modified W.1A was supplied by Power Jets, featuring an oil system modified to prevent the problem of freezing while at high-altitude. With this new engine, W4041/G was cleared for flight again and flew on 27 September 1942. This flight had to be terminated prematurely due to oil pressure problems and the aircraft landed back at Edgehill, suffering slight damage to the port under-wing skin surface when one of the wing-tips struck the ground during landing. A few weeks later the test program received another setback when Sayer was killed while flying a Hawker Typhoon. Sayer had been conducting practise airfield attacks with an RAF pilot, but both aircraft failed to return and it was concluded that they must have collided. The task of flying the E.28/39 now fell to Sayers assistant test pilot, Michael Daunt, who conducted his first flight in the E.28/39 once the aircraft had been repaired, on 6 November 1942. The aircraft was transferred to Farnborough for testing modification to the fuel system before it was handed over to the R.A.E. (Royal Aircraft Establishment) for further flight testing.

Development of the planned production engine, the W.2B, was stagnating during late 1942 and into early 1943. This lack of progress would eventually lead to the decision for Rover to relinquish its part in the jet engine development, which would now be taken over by Rolls Royce, with this decision actually being taken informally over a lunch meeting. Once Rolls Royce took over design responsibility of the W.2B things began to move quickly. Instead of small groups of people working here and there on various aspects of the engine as had been the case with Rover, some 2,000 personnel were now allocated, with the aim of getting the engine development ready for production as quickly as possible. It is generally accepted that Rovers involvement in the W.2B engine added up to two years onto the development of the engine, although the company was responsible for many of the more outstanding features of the power plant. While Whittle was no doubt pleased with this new energy that would inevitably result in a reliable production standard jet engine, he could have been under no illusions that he had now lost control over the future of British turbojet development and production. Power Jets was simply far too small to compete with the giant that was Rolls Royce, and from this point would have to take a back seat. Accepting the inevitable, Whittle told Hooker of Rolls Royce that he would stand back and leave the final development of the W.2B to them, while Power Jets would concentrate on improvements for future engines such as the W.2/700, which was developed from the W.2/500.

Around the time that the W.2B was being taken over by Rolls Royce the second of the two E.28/39 aircraft, W4046/G was entering the scene. As Gloster's Chief test pilot, Daunt was preparing for the first flight of the Gloster F.9/40, WG206/G, the task of flying the second E.28/39 was allocated to another Gloster test pilot, John Grierson, who took the aircraft aloft on its maiden flight on 1 March 1943. Over the next fortnight, some 13 flights were logged in the aircraft, which was powered by a 1,200 lb W.2 engine. Post war, Grierson wrote of this aircraft, "The E.28 is a most pleasant little aeroplane to handle, particularly on account of the excellent field of vision from the pilots seat, and because the ailerons, the most difficult controls to design and the ones of greatest importance from the point of view of manoeuvre, seem to have set a new standard of lightness and positiveness…"

The W.2 engine was replaced by a Rolls Royce built W.2B/23, which was rated at 1,526 lb static thrust, and the first flight with this power unit installed took place on 16 April 1943. The next day W4046/G flew from Edgehill to Hatfield, where it was demonstrated to VIP's, which included the Prime Minister, Winston Churchill, as part of a larger demonstration of new aircraft types. For the 70 mile flight to Hatfield, the E.28/39 was escorted by two Spitfires and a single Hawker Typhoon, all fully armed. Such were the security measures for this flight that permission had to be granted from Fighter Command, only after an all-clear had been obtained that no enemy aircraft were over the areas to be flown. After take-off the pilot quickly left the Spitfires behind and the Typhoon was only just capable of keeping up, requiring maximum cruising power to do so. Two days later the E.28/39 was flown by Daunt on a demonstration for the Prime Minister and officers from the Air Staff. This was done with a cloud base of only around 600 ft and the demonstration flight, which lasted some six minutes, included a high speed dash across the airfield at a speed of 400 mph. The other aircraft being demonstrated included Spitfires and Mosquito's, the fastest of which were about 50 mph slower than the E.28/39 at sea level. The demonstration fully impressed the Prime Minster, who apparently asked why Britain did not have squadrons of jet fighters in service. In any case, the demonstration to the highest authority in the land all-but guaranteed the funding required for the F.9/40, Meteor and de Havilland E.5/42 Spider Crab, which led to the Vampire F Mk. I fighter.

The first E.28/39, W4041/G, in flight, while being operated at RAE Farnborough. RAE

A sideline to history is the fact that Whittle, the inventor of the jet engine in Britain was not present, apparently not even invited to this important demonstration. This was evidence of the changing winds, in which Rolls Royce and not Whittle's Company, Power Jets, had pushed into the premier position of producing Britain's production standard jet engines. By this time, early 1943, the best that Power Jets could hope for was that Rolls Royce would take on production of a variant of the Whittle W.2/500 or /700 to power the Meteor after around 100 or so production Rolls Royce W.2B/23 Welland I engines had been produced. However, Rolls Royce was busy developing its planned successor to the Welland in the shape of the W.2B/37 Derwent I engine. This power plant would incorporate a number of features developed for the

W.2/500, while Whittle's competition against the W.2B/37 was the W.2/700.

The return flight to Edgehill was flown at an altitude of 6,000 ft, with the engine at approximately 14,000 rpm, allowing the aircraft to cruise at 260 mph IAS. The pilots of the escorting Spitfires apparently commented that this cruising speed seemed to be rather high for the Spitfire at this altitude. A short time later, W4046/G went to Farnborough for testing. It was now powered by a new W.2B rated at 1,526 lb static thrust. Flight testing at Farnborough with this engine allowed the aircraft to be flown at 466 mph, the fastest speed attained by the aircraft.

W4046/G was lost on 30 June 1943, after the ailerons froze when the aircraft was flying at 37,000 ft while in a climb. The aircraft entered an inverted spin from which it was not recovered leading to the pilot, Squadron Leader D. Davie, bailing out at around 33,000 ft and the aircraft crashing. The loss of this W.2B powered aircraft saw the burden of W.2B flight testing fall on those F.9/40's so powered.

Another test pilot who flew W4046/G was John Crosby Warren, who would unfortunately be killed when he crashed in one of the F.9/40 Meteor prototypes in 1944. Crosby commented of the E.28/39, "There seems to be no sign or sound of aerodynamic burble under any engine conditions up to 360 mph..." he continued "... the ease with which the aircraft slides through the air is amazing." He noted that "For ordinary flying it may be necessary to provide flaps which can be operated at higher speeds than those normally fitted to conventional engine (airscrew) machines, to enable pilots to lose speed more easily." This would later prove to be the case as speeds of jet powered aircraft continued to increase.

Meanwhile the first E.28/39 was still being flown. On 23 May 1943, W4041/G flew powered by a Whittle W.2/500 rated at 1,620 lb static thrust. Of this engine, test pilot Michael Daunt commented that it was "the smoothest unit that this pilot has had the pleasure of flying." On 4 June 1943, W4041/G attained a speed of 360 mph while in a dive. On 23 June (also listed in some reports as 24 June) 1943, during engine development testing at Barford St John's, W4041/G, flown by Grierson, attained an altitude of 42,170 ft. The following day, John Crosby Warren flew the aircraft in a flight which concluded the Gloster flight trials.

W4041/G is seen during flight testing late in the program with modifications, most notable of which is the incorporation of end-plates to the horizontal tails. Royal Aircraft Establishment

From April 1944, the aircraft began flying powered by a W.2/500 rated at 1,760 lb. By this time Power Jets had been nationalised; the decision being taken in January 1944 and implemented from February that year. Rolls Royce was given an assurance that this nationalised company would not be directly competitive with private industry, effectively safeguarding future production of the W.2B/37 Derwent engine.

W4041/G was used for a series of other trials by various test agencies during 1944, 1945 and 1946. Trials continued with the high speed wing and the aircraft was dispatched to Farnborough where it was equipped with end-plate fins designed to counter instability. Its last flight test program involved flight tests at High Mach Numbers with the high-speed section (EC 1240/0640) wing. The test flights were to be repeated with the aircraft fitted with the conventional section (NACA 2212) wing, but the program was curtailed as the aircraft was required for "exhibition" and the Pioneer of Britain's jet powered aircraft was retired for display at the Science Museum, South Kensington on 27 April 1946.

Pilot reports had described the aircraft as good at aerobatics, with no real problems during manoeuvring. Other reports showed that it was a "very clean aerodynamic design". However, it was ultimately not suitable for development into a front line fighter, not least because of its very small size, with a weight in the order of 4,000 lb or so depending on configuration, but it paved the way for the F.9/40 Meteor and other jet aircraft that followed; a fitting legacy for the aircraft known as the Pioneer.

Chapter Two

Gloster F.9/40 - Progenitor to the Meteor

DG202/G was the first of the eight F.9/40 prototypes. It was powered by two W.2/23 engines, which would be further developed into the W.2B/23 Welland I, which would power the first production variant, the Meteor F Mk. I. MAP

The F.9/40's and Meteor I/III's were of all-metal stressed-skin construction. The fuselage was assembled in three main sections. The rear section consisted of the one-piece tail-plane, tail-plane elevators, vertical tail, fin top and the two-piece rudder. The ailerons were carried on the outer wing sections. The centre section housed the fuel tanks, main undercarriage units, rear fuselage and air brakes to aircraft so fitted. The forward section housed the 4 x 20-mm Hispano cannon armament, two on each side of the fuselage ahead of the cockpit, ammunition bays and nose undercarriage unit. The non-steerable nose wheel unit retracted rearwards to be housed in the forward fuselage.

The centre section included the wings, which included the flaps and ailerons located on the outer wing section. The wings also housed the main undercarriage units and the engines, which were housed in nacelles built around the wings. The extreme wing tips of the aircraft were designed to be detachable.

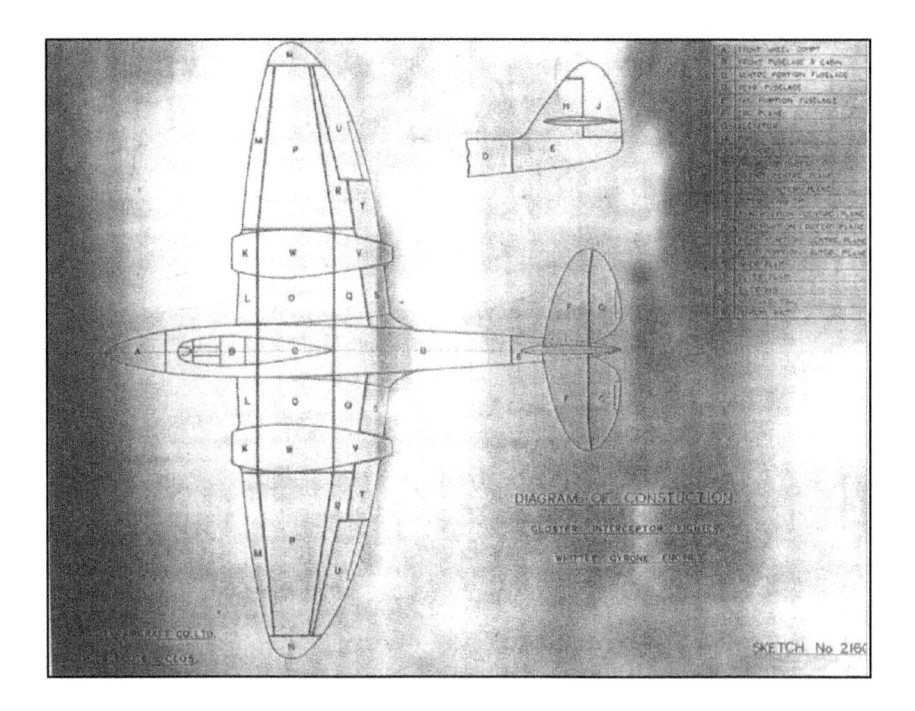

This early plan and horizontal tail view shows a design dated April 1940. This aircraft is referred to as the 'Gloster Interceptor Fighter, Whittle Gyrone engines'. This was a very early configuration for the F.9/40, but shows the basic thinking of what the design should look like. Gloster Aircraft Company

The high set position of the tail-plane was brought about by the desire to move the tail unit out of the jet streams. The 'acorn' fairing, which is located on the tail fin, is reminiscent of that seen on previous high set tail plane fighters like the Westland Whirlwind and later seen on the Westland Welkin. The rudder was split into two sections, with both of the resultant elevator sections being fitted with a trim tab, with another located on the lower rudder section.

On 7 February 1941, the Ministry of Aircraft Production (MAP) ordered twelve F.9/40 prototypes of the Gloster-Whittle twin-engine jet powered fighter, with serials DG202 - DG213 being allocated. The order also included the building of jigs and manufacturing tooling to enable an eventual 80 aircraft per month to be manufactured, and in August that year a production order for 300 aircraft was placed. These production variants of the F.9/40's were to have a wing span of 43 ft, and it was decided to power the aircraft with two Whittle W.2B turbojet engines (to be built by Rover), with a planned thrust of 1,640 lb each. With this thrust it was hoped for a maximum speed of at least 440 mph and for the aircraft to be capable of climbing to 30,000 ft in around 24 minutes.

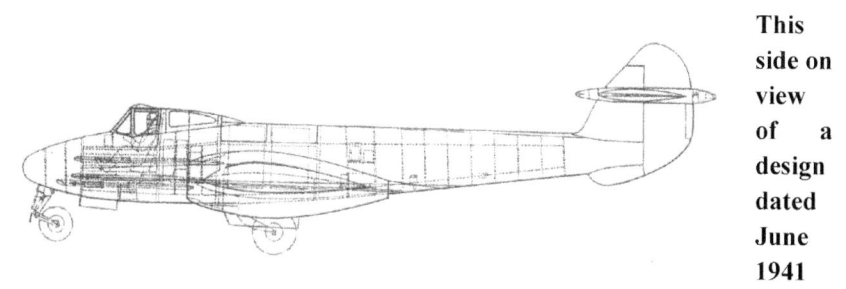

This side on view of a design dated June 1941 shows an aircraft more reminiscent of what the F.9/40's would emerge as. This design, however, has a six cannon main armament, which would be cut down to four for the Meteor. Gloster Aircraft Company

It was initially hoped for the new jet fighters to enter service around the end of 1942 or early in 1943. While this schedule appeared at best optimistic, it proved to be impossible in light of the delays and problems suffered in development of a suitable engine; the W.2B/23 Welland I being selected as the engine for the production variant. In November 1941, the W.2B had been de-rated to 1,000 lb static thrust and the same month saw the order for 12 F.9/40 prototypes reduced to six aircraft, but this was later increased again to eight, DG202/G - DG209/G. The aircraft had the additional 'G' suffix applied at the end of their serial numbers indicating that they were 'high security' and were to be guarded at all times when the aircraft were on the ground, as was the case with the E.28/39's. At the time of the order the aircraft was unofficially called the 'Rampage', but this name was dropped and the name 'Meteor' was allocated by MAP in February 1942.

Initially all twelve of the then planned F.9/40's were to be powered by the W.2B. However, delays with this engine scrapped the plans to deliver all the aircraft by March 1942. This serious delay with the delivery of W.2B engines, combined with the apparent lack of co-operation shown by the manufacturer, Rover, resulted in the customer looking at other options. On 2 March 1942, the Power Jets variant, on which the W.2B was based, known as the W.2/500, was selected as a possible alternative to the W.2B. This new design progressed quickly and in May 1942, amid added frustration at the delays with the W.2B, the decision was taken to power some of the F.9/40 prototypes with alternative engines to speed up development.

Construction of the first of the F.9/40's, DG202/G, commenced at Gloster's plant in Brockworth in autumn 1941, and the aircraft was completed in June 1942. Wing stiffness testing had been completed by the 26th of that month and a day later fuel flow testing was completed as the aircraft was prepared for its first ground run, conducted on 29 June at Glosters Bentham plant. For this test a pair of 'ground only' Rover assembled W.2B/23 engines – which had been de-rated to 1,000 lb thrust – were used. These ground run only engines were not certified for flight, owing to un-reliability of turbine blades.

Following the ground runs, the wings of DG202/G were removed and the aircraft was transported by road to RAF Newmarket Heath, near Cambridge on 2 July 1942, for more ground engine running and aircraft taxi tests, the latter commencing on 10 July on Newmarket Heaths 9,000 ft runway with F/Lt P.E.G. Sayer in the cockpit. This series of high speed taxi trials was conducted with the fuel tanks half full and the aircraft actually lifted off the ground some six feet into the air following a 1,100 yard run. Following these initial runs the trials were halted while problems with the undercarriage were addressed, resuming again on 18 July after a fix, which included fitting wheels and tyres designed for the Hawker Typhoon.

By mid-August 1942, the taxi trials had been completed, the engines removed and the aircraft was eventually stored in a MAP hanger at Newmarket Heath while it awaited the delivery of flight ready W.2 jet engines, which were much delayed. One of these engines had blown up during bench testing.

The first of the F.9/40 prototypes to fly was actually the fifth prototype, DG206/G, which conducted its maiden flight on 5 March 1943. This aircraft was powered by a pair of Halford H.1 engines. It is seen here in 1944. MAP

Delays with flight ready engines meant that DG202 would not be the first F.9/40 to fly, this accolade going to the fifth prototype, DG206, construction of which was completed in August 1942. This aircraft was to be powered by two Halford H.1 engines, each rated at 1,500 lb (680 kg) static thrust. The first run of a Halford H.1 engine took place on 13 June 1942, and even at this early stage it was expected that the developed H.1 could eventually achieve 3,000 lb static thrust, but it was eventually concluded that this thrust rating would require installation of a larger turbine.

Although all prototypes were officially designated F.9/40, some documentation referred to the various aircraft with a last letter donating the type of engine that they were powered by, with DG206/G, therefore, sometimes having the designation F.9/40H. In the case of this aircraft a different designation may well have been warranted as the aircraft fuselage was wider than the other F.9/40 prototypes by 15 inches. This was necessitated for various reasons such as a differing wing span of 44 ft 3 in. DG206/G was also equipped with a clear view canopy.

DG206/G was transferred to RAF Cranwell, Lincolnshire by road as it was from here that the first flight was scheduled to take place. On 3 March, this aircraft conducted taxi runs and a few brief seconds of flight, while at a weight of 11,500 lb. The official first flight of an F.9/40 took place on 5 March 1943, when the aircraft lifted off from Cranwell's runway powered by two de Havilland H.1 engines, with Michael Daunt at the controls.

During flight testing, yaw encountered at speeds over 200 mph IAS resulted in modifications being incorporated to the rudder design. The aircraft was then transferred by road to Newmarket Heath, where it re-commenced flight testing on 17 April 1943. On 28 May, DG206/G flew from Newmarket Heath to land at Barford St John, near Bradbury, Oxfordshire.

A short time after the first flight of DG206/G, production of the W.2B engine began, resulting in preparations for DG202/G's long awaited first flight. On 22 May 1943, this aircraft was transported by road from Newmarket Heath to RAF Barford St John near Bradbury, from where it was to make its first flight. However, there were further delays and the aircraft remained firmly grounded for the next few months undergoing modifications. During this time, some items were removed from the aircraft and allocated to other F.9/40 development aircraft, further delaying its maiden flight.

The fourth F.9/40, DG205/G was the next aircraft to fly when it conducted its maiden flight from Barford St John on 23 June (some reports state 12 June) 1943, powered by two W.2B/23 engines. This aircraft was used for testing by Gloster's and at Hatfield before being lost when it crashed at Moreton Valence, near Gloucester on 27 April 1944.

DG202/G eventually conducted its first official flight on 24 July 1943, powered by a pair of W.2B/23 engines (which had been installed in the aircraft in June) with Daunt at the controls for the six minute flight. Two days later, the aircraft was flown on a 27 minute flight by John Crosby-Warren, whom was again at the controls for flights on three successive days before July was out. These test flights were used to check engine handling and aileron characteristics among other tests, accumulating some

117 minutes, during which time the maximum altitude attained was 29,000 ft. During this early period of flight testing most flights were of only around 20 minutes or under duration.

During August 1943, DG202/G was grounded for modifications, being fitted with the tail-plane vertical fin 'acorn' fairing by the 18th. The aircraft was also fitted with new B.23 variants of the engine after they were delivered to Barford St John on 30 September, being certified ready for flight from 12 October. On 17 October, the aircraft was moved to Moreton Valence where it was to resume flight testing as the Barford St John site was due be closed.

The second prototype, DG203/G, conducted its maiden flight from Moreton Valence on 9 November 1943, powered by two W.2/500 engines. This aircraft was used for development flight testing of the W.2/500/700 engines. After its flying career was over it was allocated ground instructional serial 5926M.

The third prototype, DG204/G, unofficially known as the F.9/40M, was powered by two Metropolitan Vickers, Metrovick F.2 axial-flow turbojet engines, which were housed in under-wing nacelles, hung under the wings in a similar fashion to that seen on the German Me.262 jet powered fighter. Like DG206, this aircraft, which, commenced taxi trials at Barford St John on 3 August 1943, received extensive modifications to the wings and engine nacelles to allow the installation of its Metrovick F.2 engines. Delays with the engines (the original engines had to be sent back to the manufacturer) delayed the aircrafts first flight, which occurred at Farnborough on 13 November 1943. It was employed on engine development testing at Farnborough, but crashed on 1 April 1944.

The seventh prototype, DG208/G, was fitted with a modified tail fin, rudder and dive brakes and conducted its maiden flight on 24 January 1944.

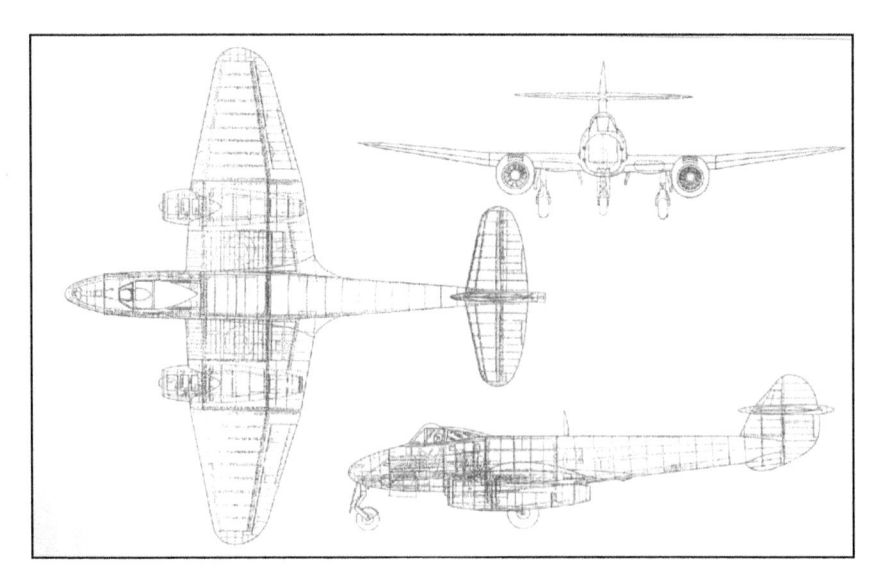

Top: The Metrovick F.2 powered aircraft required a number of modifications. Most obvious from this general arrangement drawing are the adoption of nacelles for the engines, which are slung under the wings. Gloster Aircraft Company. **The only aircraft so configured was the third F.9/40, DG204/G above.** MAP

When Rolls Royce took over responsibility for the Rover Brunswick jet production faculties and overall management of the W.2B program in early 1943, new life was breathed into the program and the company quickly began production of the W.2B/23 engine, which was then rated at 1,400 lb static thrust.

The seventh prototype, DG208/G, was fitted with a modified tail fin, rudder and dive brakes and conducted its maiden flight on 24 January 1944. MAP

Development of the W.2B/23 now progressed quickly and the engine was performing well going into January 1944.

The first prototype, DG202/G, was allocated for development of the W.2B/23 Welland I engine, which was being developed from the W.2B/23 development engines. It flew, powered by a pair of W.2B/23c engines, at Rolls Royce Hucknall on 6 November 1943 and twenty five hours of testing with these engines was conducted at Hucknall and the Rolls Royce airfield at Church Broughton, including engine restart, engine surge and fuel consumption testing before the aircraft was returned to Gloster's for an overhaul in January 1944. On completion of the overhaul, the aircraft was flown to the Rolls Royce airfield at Balderton in a 25 minute flight. Further testing was conducted at Balderton before the aircraft returned to Church Broughton for another series of flight testing on 28 April 1944, by which time the first of the Meteor F Mk. I production aircraft was flying.

On 13 December 1944, DG202/G was taking off on a test flight when its port engine exploded, resulting in considerable damage to the engine nacelle and centre and outer wing sections. By this time the aircraft had accumulated around 367 flying hours on development testing, paving the way for the introduction to service of the Meteor F Mk. I production variant. The aircraft was eventually repaired and integrated into the Meteor development program again, which included aircraft carrier suitability tests in 1945, before being grounded and stored in September that year.

In August 1943, the eighth F.9/40, DG209/G, was fitted with a modified centre section and used for development of the W.2B/37 Derwent I engine, which would eventually power the Meteor F Mk. III, for which this aircraft had effectively become the prototype. The W.2B/37 was developed from the W.2B/23 Welland I and Whittle W.2/500 and the aircraft flew with two of these units installed on 18 April 1944. The aircraft was allocated to Rolls Royce for engine trials at Hucknall before being struck of charge and scrapped at Farnborough in July 1946.

The increasing frustration at the delays with the W.2B had resulted in the decision to power the sixth F.9/40, WG207/G, with Halford H.1 engines, with the go-ahead being given in September 1942. This aircraft effectively became the prototype of the Meteor II, which at the time was planned to be the main production variant. MAP had ordered 100 production H.1 engines on 8 August 1942, by which time two engines were running. These engines were to be built by de Havilland. Equipped to act as the de-facto prototype of the Meteor F Mk. II, powered by two 2,700 lb (1225 kg) static thrust de Havilland H.1B Goblin turbojet engines, DG207/G conducted its maiden flight from Moreton Valence on 24 July 1945. However, no production contract was awarded and the Meteor II fell by the wayside.

Chapter Three

Gloster Meteor F Mk.I, III & IV

EE212/G was the third production Meteor F Mk. I. The aircraft is seen in flight over southern England in 1944. MAP

The available power output of the early jet engines combined with the Meteors high weights meant that the first production variants would have limited performance compared with planned future variants. Engine thrust was the key to performance and development continued to produce high power outputs, requiring larger turbines. These engines developments emerged as the W.2B/37 Derwent and the Power Jets W.2/700. Other higher thrust engines were also in development such as the Rolls Royce B.41 Nene. However, the initial service variant of the Meteor would be handicapped by its lack of power; the price of getting the aircraft into service in the summer of 1944. From May 1944, the W.2B/23 Welland I was cleared as suitably reliable for operational service and deliveries of new production standard engines commenced. Around this time, the Welland was also conducting its first 500-hour run test. This was not initially planned at that time, but rather a 100 hour test was continued to reach 500 hours. Following this test, clearance for the Welland was increased from the previous 80 hours to 180 hours between overhauls for service engines.

The first production Meteor F Mk. I, EE210/G, conducted its maiden flight on 12 January 1944. In February that year the aircraft was sent to the United States, where it was adorned with USAAF markings. MAP

The Rolls Royce W.2B/23 Welland I was developed from the early Rover W.2/23 engines, development of which was taken over by Rolls Royce in early 1943. The Welland I was the initial service variant of the W.2B. Rated at 1,600 lb static thrust at sea level, this engine powered the Meteor F Mk. I and the first 15 Meteor F Mk. III's. Rolls Royce

Twenty Gloster Meteor F Mk. I (Gloster designation GA. 41) with serial numbers EE210/G – EE229 had been ordered on 8 August 1941, under contract A/C 1490/41. On 13 June 1943, it was decided to power the Meteor F MK. I with the W.2B/23 Welland I engine, now under the wing of Rolls Royce, who had energetically set about getting the engine up to production standard.

The Meteor I was little more than an interim variant designed to get the aircraft into squadron service. These aircraft received only small changes to the airframe compared with the standard F.9/40 prototypes like DG202/G that they were based on. These changes included fitting a clear view canopy and installation of items of operational equipment, not least of which was the armament.

The first Meteor I, EE210/G, conducted its first flight on 12 January 1944. In February, this aircraft was sent to the United States where it was based at Muroc Army Air Force Base for flight testing with USAAF (United States Army Air Force) markings. As part of this technology transfer exchange, a Bell XP-59 had been delivered to the UK and flown at Moreton Valence in September 1943. The XP-59 was the US's first jet powered aircraft, designed around two I-A turbojets, which were basically American built variants of the British W.1, plans of which had been sent to the US as early as August 1941. In truth, the UK had nothing to learn from the XP-59A, which would be classed as completely unsuitable for service as a combat aircraft. However, the technology transfer deal had niceties that had to be observed. While the US was the beneficiary of the deal, there remained an uneasiness within the high commands of the USAAF, particularly with Hap Arnold, who were extremely sensitive to the fact that the US had been left behind in this important knew field of aviation technology. There can be little doubt that transfer of the first Meteor I to the United States would have caused some delay in the service entry of the Meteor, however, small.

As previously mentioned, the Meteor I was always intended as an interim model while a main production variant was developed. Its performance was well below that achieved by later variants like the Derwent powered Meteor III and IV. However, in regards to maximum operational speeds, the Meteor I was way ahead of any other Allied operational fighter when it entered service in July 1944. The best of the piston-engine fighters then available simply could not match the Meteor I at the lower operating altitudes that it was employed in, mainly countering German V-1 Flying Bombs at altitudes of between 1,000 and 4,000 ft. The aircraft was, however, very short on endurance and its rate of climb fell well below that achieved by the best of the piston-engine fighters then available.

The following figures are taken directly from official evaluation and operational performance documents:

Meteor I – rate of climb at 10,000 ft is 2,500 FPM (ft per minute), which compares poorly with the 4,500 ft FPM of the Spitfire XIV, 3,600 FPM of the Mustang III and 2,900 FPM of the Tempest V. At 15,000 ft the Meteor I narrows the gap slightly with 2,250 FPM compared to 3,700 FPM of the Spitfire XIV, 3,000 FPM of the Mustang III and 2,750 FPM of the Tempest V.

It is in maximum speed that the Meteor I left its piston engine rivals behind. At 10,000 ft, the maximum speed figure of 430 mph of the Meteor I was higher than the 405 mph of the Spitfire XIV, 403 mph of the Mustang III and 402 mph of the Tempest V. At 15,000 ft the Maximum speed figures are 436 mph for the Meteor I, 415 mph for the Spitfire XIV, 425 mph for the Mustang III and 411 mph for the Tempest V.

As can be seen from the above figures, in regards to operating speeds, the Meteor I was faster than the best of the piston engine fighters then available. At sea level the speed advantage was just as marked, with the Meteor I able to comfortably exceed 400 mph, with 410 mph being the norm, an achievement that none of the piston engine fighters were able to emulate. During the Anti-Diver campaign the Meteors superior speed at low altitude was demonstrated on a number of occasions when Meteor I's intercepted, overhauled and shot down V-1 flying bombs at speeds in excess of 400 mph, after Tempests V's and Mustangs III's had been forced to break off through an inability to overhaul the Divers.

The 330 gallon internal fuel gave the Meteor I/III an endurance of approximately 45 minutes. Endurance of the Meteor III would be substantially increased by the addition of external fuel tanks, but although wind-tunnel tests and flight trials were conducted during 1944 and 1945, these did not appear in time to be used operationally before the war in Europe ended in May 1945.

No.616 Squadron was chosen to be the first squadron to equip with the new jet fighters. This unit was operating Supermarine Spitfire VII's from RAF Culmhead as part of No.10 group. The first 2 Meteor I's were delivered to the Squadron from Farnborough on 12 July 1944, and these were transferred to RAF Manston, Kent on 21 July, followed by the remainder of 616 Squadron with their Spitfire VII's. A few days later five more Meteors were delivered, giving the squadron its first operational jet fighters as the two delivered earlier in July, were non-operational. With this limited jet capability the Air Marshal Hill Commanding ADGB decided to employ them in the campaign to counter the German V-1 Flying Bomb attacks, which had commenced in June. Consequently, a Meteor Flight was formed within 616 Squadron, which flew its first operational sorties on 27 July, while the remainder of the Squadron remained operational on Spitfire VII's. The delivery of a few more aircraft, combined with additional pilots being cleared for operational flying on the Meteor, saw the Spitfire VII's retired in August, with the last operational Spitfire sorties by the Squadron being flown on the 13th of that month.

No.616 Squadron continued to fly the limited number of Meteor I's until February 1945, with the last sorties being flown on the 18th of that month, following which the Squadron was equipped exclusively with Meteor III's.

The Meteor I was also operated by the Conversion Unit at Colerne, where they were used to convert No.504 Squadron to Meteors from March 1945 and 74 Squadron from May 1945. These squadrons, however, would not operate Meteor I's, being equipped with Meteor III's during conversion.

Meteor F Mk. I EE214/G in flight over southern England in 1944 was, along with EE213/G, one of the first two Meteor F Mk. I's delivered to No. 616 Squadron when the aircraft arrived at RAF Culmhead from RAE Farnborough on 12 July 1944. MAP

The Trent Meteor in flight. MAP

Several Meteor I's went straight into the development program without entering squadron service, while others were allocated to various research and development programs following service with 616 Squadron. A Meteor I powered by W.2B/23c engines conducted static longitudinal stability trials in 1944, another was trialled with W.2/700 Batch III engines in July 1945 and a Meteor I conducted Mk. 2 and Mk3G IFF (Identification Friend or Foe) trials in 1945.

A Meteor III fitted with W.2B/37 Derwent I engines at the A&AEE at Bascombe Down in March 1945. MAP

EE211/G went to RAE Farnborough and was fitted with the long-chord engine nacelles. EE212/G went to RAE Farnborough. EE215/G (possibly EE214) was used for trials with the ventral fuel tank. EE215 was transferred to Power Jets Ltd, where it was employed in development work on a re-heat system. EE219 was modified with two auxiliary fins fitted to the tail-plane, as well as having the ventral bumper removed for its use in directional stability trials. EE223/G was used by Rolls Royce for engine development, becoming the first Meteor I to be powered by the W.2B/37 Derwent I engine housed in the short-chord engine nacelle. EE224 went to the A&AEE (Aeroplane and Armament Experimental Establishment), and was converted to take a second seat, for which the ammunition bay was removed. After conversion, this aircraft became the first two-seat Meteor post-war.

Following service with No.616 squadron, where it had accumulated around 80 hours flying, the 18th production Meteor I, EE227, was transferred to RAE Farnborough where it was allocated to directional stability trials; requiring the top of the fin and rudder to be removed. This aircraft was returned to Meteor I standard before being moved to Rolls Royce Hucknall in February 1945 as an engine test-bed, being fitted with a pair of RB.50 Trent propeller driven turbines, which were fitted with five bladed 7-ft 11-in diameter propellers. After conversion this aircraft became known as the 'Trent Meteor', the world's first turboprop powered aircraft, flying for the first time in this guise at Church Broughton on 20 September 1945, with Eric Greenwood at the controls. The Trent turboprop was developed from the W.2B/37 Derwent I by introducing reduction gearing and a duel-shaft, which drove the five bladed propellers, which spanned 7 ft 11 in (2.41 m). The span of the propellers necessitated modifications to the undercarriage, mainly in the form of introduction of a longer span undercarriage leg.

The first production Meteor III EE230/G at Bascombe Down, Wiltshire, prior to delivery. This aircraft was powered by the W.2B/23 Welland I engine used in the Meteor I. MAP

Meteor F Mk. III

Weight problems with the planned Meteor F MK. II led to its cancellation, therefore, 230 of the Meteors originally ordered in August 1941 were to be delivered as Meteor F Mk. III's, which was to be powered by the more powerful W.2B/37 Derwent I engine as well as introducing a number of other changes including a new sliding canopy, a strengthened airframe able to take the higher stresses associated with the increased speeds of jet powered flight and slotted air brakes.

General arrangement of *Meteor* MK. FIII. Standard case tested.

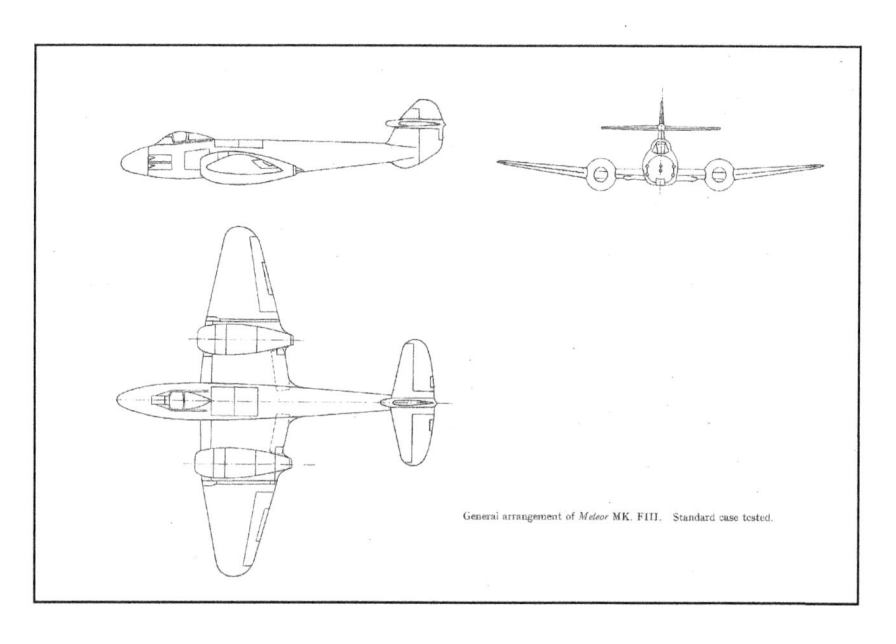

General arrangement three-view drawing of the Meteor F Mk. III.
Aeronautical Research Council

Design work on the W.2B/37 Derwent I commenced in April 1943. A test-engine had been built by July and shortly afterwards testing commenced. By November, it had completed a 100-hour test run at a thrust of 2,000-lb. The flight testing of the engine, which began in April 1944, was with engines rated at 1,800 lb static thrust, with an engine weight of 920-lb. Engine testing continued with further 100-hour run tests leading to a 500-hour run test being completed. This engine was designated B37 Derwent Series I. The Series II engine increased thrust to 2,200 lb, while the Series IV engine increased thrust further to 2,400 lb. The Series III Derwent was an experimental engine not intended for service use.

Development of the airframe was ahead of engine development resulting in the first 15 Meteor III's being powered by the lower thrust W.2B/23c Welland I that had powered the Meteor I. With these engines installed, the first Meteor III, EE230 conducted its maiden flight in September 1944. The 16th Meteor III, EE245, was the first Meteor III powered by the Derwent I engine.

Meteor F Mk. III EE249/G at Bascombe Down in March 1945 prior to delivery to No. 616 Squadron. MAP

The performance of the first 15 Meteor III's, which were powered by the W.2B/23c Welland I, rated at 1,600 lb Static Thrust, was almost identical to the Meteor I. The main difference being that some of the operational limitations of the Meteor I were removed with the Meteor III. At sea level, speed was 410 mph, rising to 430 at 10,000 ft, 440 at 20,000 ft, 445 at 30,000 ft and 437 mph at 40,000 ft. Rate of climb was more or less the same as the Meteor I at 3,150 ft per min at sea level dropping to 2,500 ft per minute at 10,000 ft, 2,000 at 20,000 ft, 1,300 at 30,000 ft and 400 at 40,000 ft.

When powered by the W.2B/37 units rated at 2,000 lb Static Thrust the performance of the Meteor III increased markedly, with a sea level speed of 465 mph, rising to 476 mph at 10,000 ft, 483 mph at 20,000 ft, 484 mph at 30,000 ft, then dropping to 466 mph at 40,000 ft. Rate of climb was also largely increased over that of the Meteor I and W.2B/23 powered Meteor III's, with a sea level climb rate of 3,975 ft per minute, dropping to 3,250 ft per minute at 10,000 ft, 2,500 ft per minute at 20,000 ft, 1,700 ft per minute at 30,000 ft and 750 ft per minute at 40,000 ft. However, the early Derwent I engines were rated at considerably less than the 2,000 lb static thrust. Development of the early Derwent I's was pushed to give 1,800 lbs static thrust, corresponding to a sea level sped of 435 mph, rising to 465 mph at 30,000 ft.

As can be seen from these various engine and performance figures, the first of the Derwent I powered Meteor III's were not capable of producing the 2,000 lb thrust that is often quoted. Correspondingly they were capable of 435 mph at sea level and 465 mph at 30,000 ft, significantly lower than the speeds of 450+ mph at sea level and 493 mph at 30,000 ft often quoted.

In the weeks following the end of the war in Europe, the performance of the Meteor was significantly increased as more powerful Derwent engines became available. The increased thrust of the Derwent I was pushed to 2,200 lb allowing a sea level speed of 485 mph, increasing to 503 mph at 30,000 ft. This was increased again to 2,400 lb giving a sea level speed of 505 mph, rising to 520 mph at 30,000 ft. However, the original short engine nacelles of the Meteor I/III, subjected these aircraft to a speed limitation of 500 mph (indicated up to a height of 6,500 ft), reducing proportionately to 300 mph (indicated) at 30,000 ft. To overcome this, various new engine nacelles were designed, leading to the long nacelle introduced in summer 1945, which in turn led to the Meteor IV powered by the Derwent V engine, which made its first flight on 15 August 1945, the day the war in the Far East effectively ended when Japan agreed to ceasefire terms leading to the final surrender on 3 September that year.

In the immediate Post war years the Meteor F Mk. III (later re-designated Meteor F.3) would form the backbone of RAF Fighter Command. RAF

Meteor III EE455 was one of the last 15 production aircraft delivered with the long-chord engine nacelles developed during the war and subsequently fitted to the Meteor F Mk. IV. MAP

Production of the Meteor III (later F.3) stretched to 210 aircraft; EE230/G - EE254, EE269 – EE318, EE331 – EE369, EE384 – EE429, EE444 – EE493. These aircraft were manufactured in five different sub batches from 1944-46; many built post war. The last 15 Meteor III's were modified with the long-chord engine nacelles flight tested on Meteor I EE211/G.

Large numbers of Meteor III's were incorporated into various test and development programs, many post war. These included the following:
Meteor III EE291 was utilised in 1945 for exhaust reheating trials and EE232 was used for night flying trials in June 1945. In September 1945, a standard Meteor III conducted tropical trials at Khartoum, Sudan. Among the tests carried out was the creation of an artificial sand-storm, by running the engines of an Avro Anson positioned ahead of the Meteor. Extreme weather trials were continued later in the year when in December 1945, Meteor III, EE331 conducted severe cold weather trials at Edmonton, Alberta, Canada. This aircraft was nominally placed on the strength of the RCAF (Royal Canadian Air Force). EE338 had its armament of four 20 mm cannon removed from the nose and the space used for installation of a camera suite for testing. EE246, EE338 and EE416 were used on ejection-seat testing with Martin

Baker. EE389 was used for air to air refuelling trials with a nose mounted re-fuelling probe, which hooked into a basket trailed by a converted Lancaster, G-33-2. EE395 was sent on a tour of New Zealand in late 1945, being allocated the new serial NZ6001, being nominally on the strength of the RNZAF (Royal New Zealand Air Force). It was later given serial INST 147, becoming a ground instruction aircraft at Hobsonville, New Zealand. EE445 was fitted with a Griffiths wing and used for boundary layer control tests. EE337 and EE387 were used on deck landing trials aboard the Fleet Aircraft Carrier HMS *Implacable*. In 1948, EE337 had been converted to act as a naval Meteor, powered by the Derwent V engines of the Meteor IV, which bestowed upon the aircraft a very high rate of climb. EE457 was one of the Meteor III's fitted with long-chord nacelles. The 71st Meteor III went to Rolls Royce Hucknall for engine development testing powered by Derwent I's. Following some 250 hours flying it was sent to the Central Gunnery School.

Although they never met in combat, it is inevitable that the Meteor III is compared to its wartime rival, the Me.262. The Meteor III had a higher profile drag compared with that of the Me.262. This was principally caused by the Meteors higher wing drag, in turn caused by the Meteors lower wing loading, which corresponded to lower maximum speeds compared to the Me.262. After a series of trials with the Me.262 at RAE Farnborough in 1945, it was determined that with engines of equal thrust the Meteor III would be 20 mph slower than the Me.262. On the plus side for the Meteor III, the lower wing loading gave it better take off performance, including a shorter take off run, and better manoeuvrability compared with the Me.262.

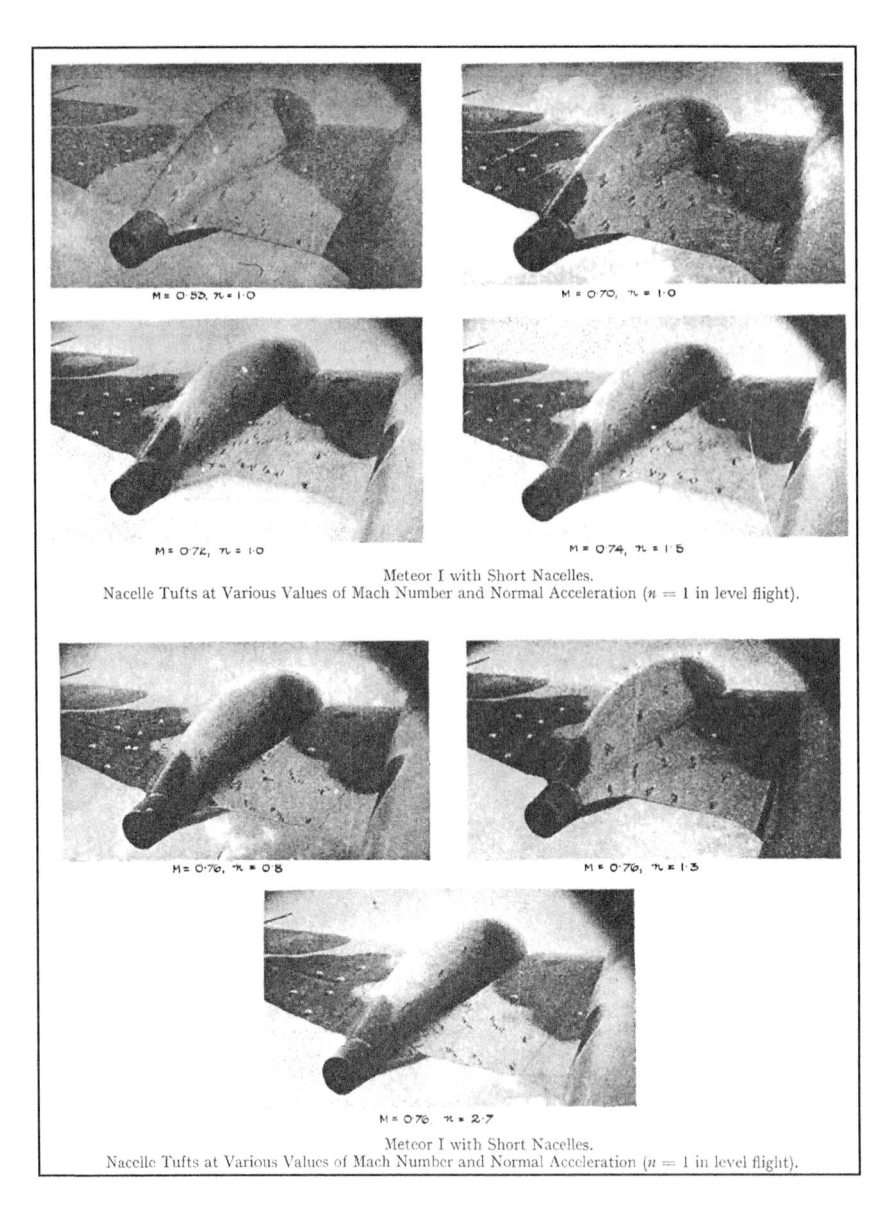

Meteor I with Short Nacelles.
Nacelle Tufts at Various Values of Mach Number and Normal Acceleration ($n = 1$ in level flight).

Meteor I with Short Nacelles.
Nacelle Tufts at Various Values of Mach Number and Normal Acceleration ($n = 1$ in level flight).

This page and the following two pages show diagrams from Aeronautical Research Council Report 2222, detailing research carried out by the second production Meteor I, EE211/G in development of the long-chord engine nacelles, which led to the Meteor F Mk. IV. At the bottom of the following two pages photographs show Meteor I, EE211/G fitted with the long-chord engine nacelles. Aeronautical Research Council

$M = 0.70, n = 1.0$

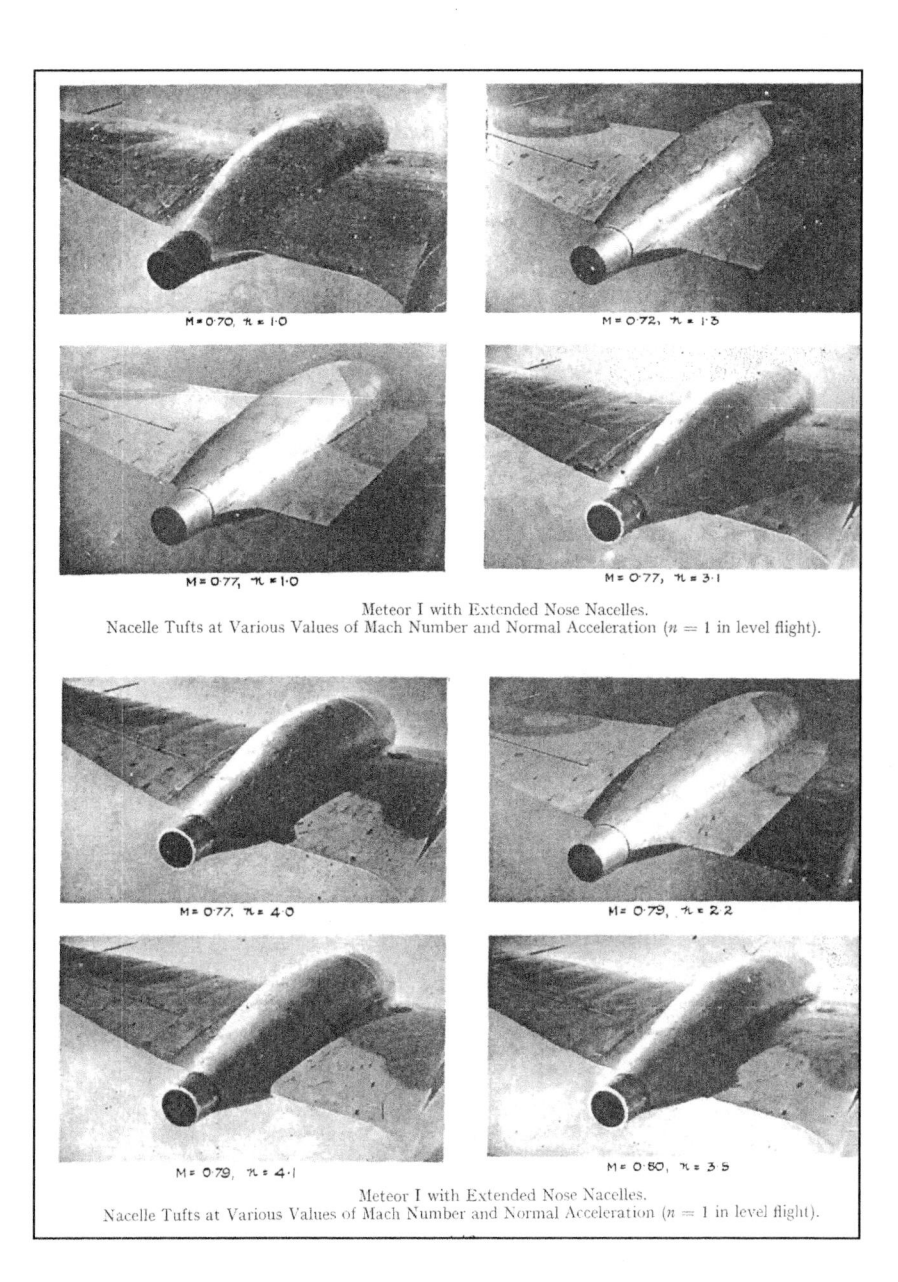

$M = 0.72, n = 1.3$

$M = 0.77, n = 1.0$

$M = 0.77, n = 3.1$

Meteor I with Extended Nose Nacelles.
Nacelle Tufts at Various Values of Mach Number and Normal Acceleration ($n = 1$ in level flight).

$M = 0.77, n = 4.0$

$M = 0.79, n = 2.2$

$M = 0.79, n = 4.1$

$M = 0.80, n = 3.5$

Meteor I with Extended Nose Nacelles.
Nacelle Tufts at Various Values of Mach Number and Normal Acceleration ($n = 1$ in level flight).

M = 0.72, n = 0.6

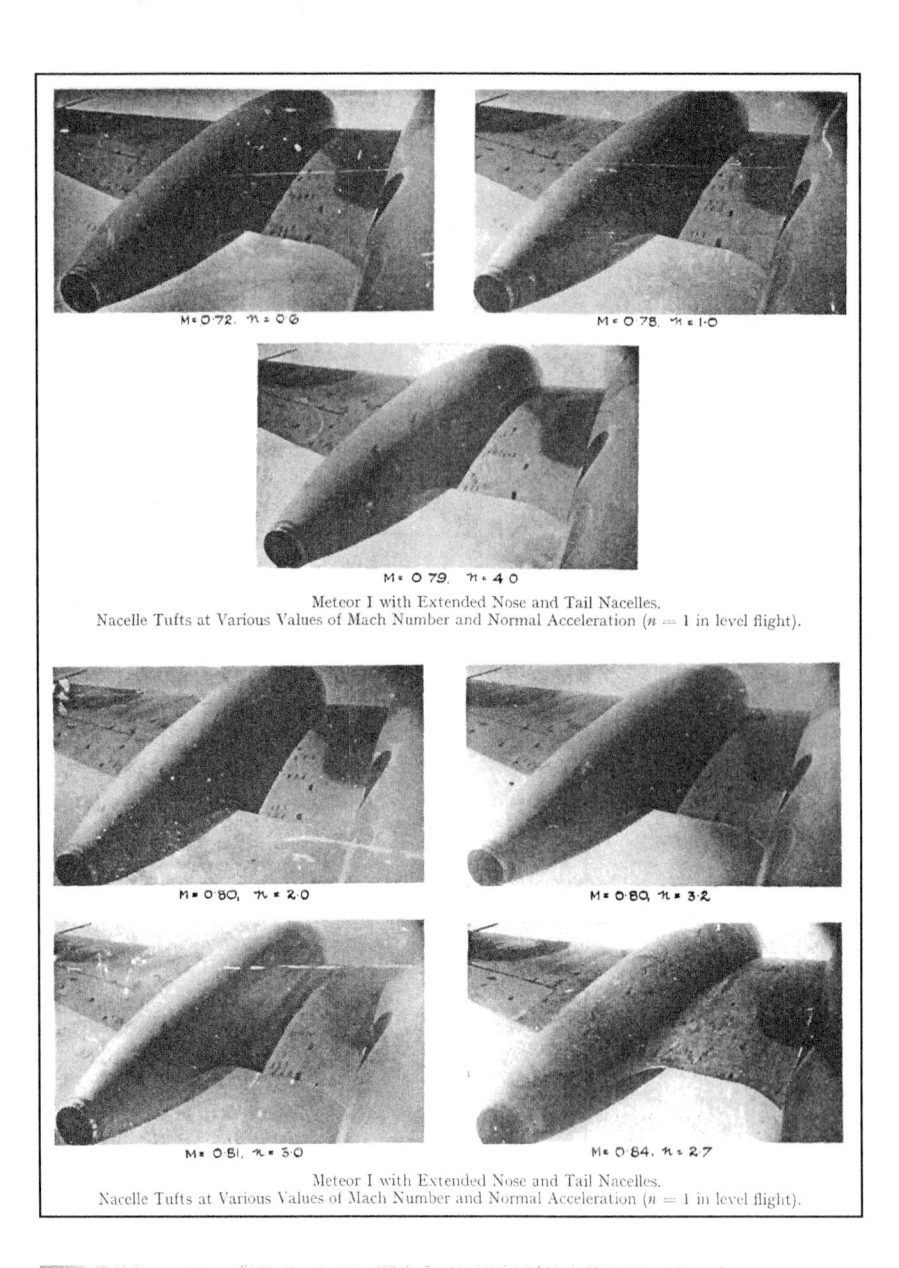

M = 0.78, n = 1.0

M = 0.79, n = 4.0

Meteor I with Extended Nose and Tail Nacelles.
Nacelle Tufts at Various Values of Mach Number and Normal Acceleration ($n = 1$ in level flight).

M = 0.80, n = 2.0

M = 0.80, n = 3.2

M = 0.81, n = 3.0

M = 0.84, n = 2.7

Meteor I with Extended Nose and Tail Nacelles.
Nacelle Tufts at Various Values of Mach Number and Normal Acceleration ($n = 1$ in level flight).

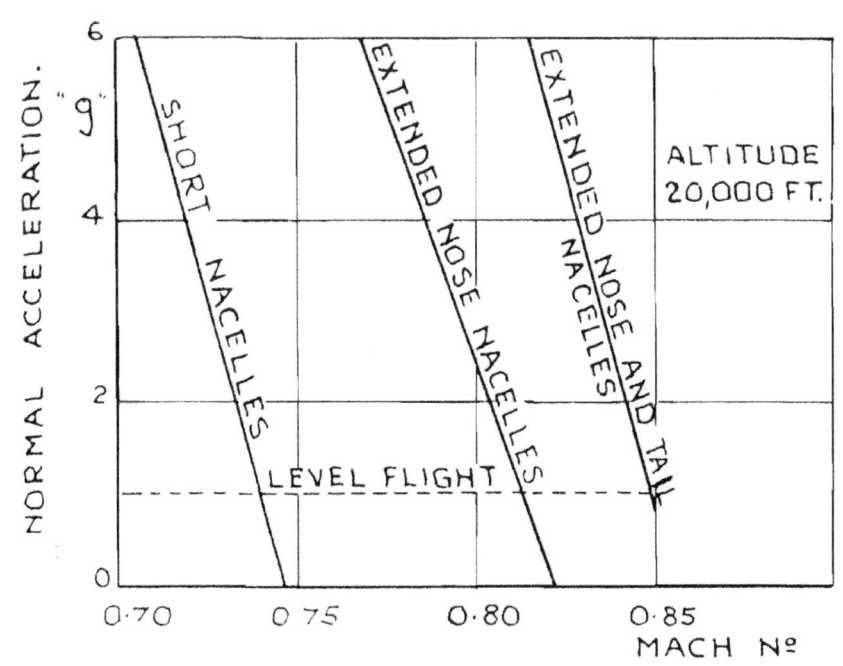

Mach Number and Normal Acceleration for
Onset of Buffeting with Different Nacelles—Meteor.

The table below is taken from information in Aeronautical Research Council Technical Report R & M No. 2791

Leading Particulars of Meteor III

Wing:		
Gross Area	S ft sq	374
Wing span	b ft	43
S.M.C.	c ft	8.71
Wing root chord ft		11.68
Wing aspect ratio		4.94
Wing body setting	deg	1.0
Dihedral		
Centre-plane spar datum		0 deg 52 ½'
Outer-plane spar datum		6 deg 0'
Tail Unit:		
Tail-plane area ft sq		61
Tail-plane incidence (short nacelles)		0 deg
Fin and rudder total area ft sq		42.4
Rudder total area ft sq		19.0
Fin arm		23.0 ft
Fin volume coefficient		0.059
Other particulars:		
Actual weight of aircraft		11,000 lb.

The following is taken from the Air Ministry Meteor III performance card dated 21.3.45 (Note: The Meteor III's deployed on operations in 1945 were not equipped for the carriage of bombs.)

WEIGHTS	
Maximum lb.	13,342
Mean lb.	11,950
Light lb. oil	
(No fuel/Bombs or ammunition)	
Tare lb.	
DIMENSIONS	
Span ft	43
Gross wing area sq. ft.	374
Length ft.	41' 5"
Height ft. (Tail-down)	13
Crew	1
PERFORMANCE.	
Take-off over 50 ft. (Max wt.) yards	1,000
Landing over 50 ft. (Light wt.) yards	740
Service ceiling (Max wt.) ft.	45,000
Service ceiling (Mean wt.) ft.	46,000
Maximum speed M. (mean wt.) mph	485
S. (mean wt.) mph	493
CRUISING SPEED	
At 30,000 ft. Most economical mph	350
At maximum weak mixture power mph	415
TIME TO 30,000 ft. (max wt.) mins	11.5
Performance figures are for cause (a)	
First few engines will give 2,000 lb. S/T (Static Thrust)	
By autumn, 1945, will give 2,400 lb. S/T	
ARMAMENT.	
GUNS.	
Bore	20 mm
No.	4
Rounds per gun	180
Position	Forward of wings Body in side of nose
MAXIMUM ALTERNATIVE BOMB LOADS.	
Fuselage lbs.	0
Wings lbs.	2,000 lb (2 x 1,000 lb)

The following table is taken from RA.E. Tech. Note No. F.A. 235/5

Aero. 1706

Dated October 1945

Analysis of Aircraft Drag

Aircraft Component	Meteor III	Me 262	He 162	Ar 234
Wings	28.0	20.3	8.7	29.5
Tail-plane	12.0	7.1	3.0	9.3
Fuselage	11.0	10.4	6.0	11.4
Nacelles	12.0	15.0	5.0	15.0
Cabin	1.5	2.0	1.5	2.0
Guns	4.0	3.0	2.0	-
Pitot	0.5	0.5	0.5	0.5
Miscellaneous (Interference etc.)	3.0	8.0	7.0	10.5
Total	72.0 lbs.	66.3 lbs.	33.7 lbs.	78.2 lbs.
	At 100 ft/sec	100 ft/sec	100 ft/sec	100 ft/sec

Meteor IV

As previously noted, the short engine nacelles of the Meteor I/III, subjected these aircraft to a speed limitation of 500 mph (indicated up to a height of 6,500 ft, reducing proportionately to 300 mph (indicated) at 30,000 ft. To overcome this, various new engine nacelles were designed, leading to the long nacelle introduced in summer 1945, which in turn led to the Meteor IV powered by the Derwent V engines, which conducted its first flight on 15 August 1945, the day the war in the Far East effectively ended when Japan agreed to ceasefire terms leading to the final surrender on 3 September that year.

The pinnacle of wartime allied jet fighter development, the Meteor IV, which was powered by two Rolls Royce Derwent V engines, was capable of far greater speeds compared to the Meteor III. At sea level, the Meteor IV was capable of 585 mph and at 30,000 ft it could attain 560 mph. These speeds were attained due to the wartime development that led to the change from short-chord to long chord engine nacelles.

The following is a summary of development testing on a Meteor I, which led to the introduction of the long-chord engine nacelle, instrumental in pushing the operational speed of the Meteor close to 600 mph. This summary is extracted from the Ministry of Supply, Aeronautical Research Council Report No.2222

'The Meteor I is a single-seat fighter powered by two Rolls Royce W2B/23 jet propulsion engines. For some of the high speed flight tests made at the R.A.E., the engines were replaced by W.2/700 units in order to give better performance at high altitudes. Tests on this aircraft have been made with three alternative types of nacelles. The short nacelles, which are fitted on standard Meteor I aircraft, gave buffeting and high drag at Mach numbers above about 0.74. To reduce buffeting and the drag the nacelles were modified, first by extending the nose, and later by extending both the nose and the tail. In this form the external shape of the aircraft is very nearly the same as that of the Meteor IV.'

'The Meteor which was used for high-speed flight tests was not fitted with cannon, but appropriate ballast was installed to compensate for this. The aircraft was fitted with specially strengthened wings and metal covered ailerons. For the earlier tests the rudder and elevator were both fabric covered, but in later tests the fabric covered elevator was replaced by a metal covered one in order to reduce the stick forces required at high Mach numbers.'

'At the R.A.E. no specific measurements of maximum lift coefficient have been made at high Mach numbers, but during diving tests for the investigation of drag and longitudinal trim, pull outs have been made at fairly high normal accelerations. For example on a Meteor with long nacelles a pull-out has been made at 3g… at an altitude of 30,000 ft. and a Mach number of 0.84. In this case there was some buffeting, but there were no indications that the maximum lift coefficient had been reached.'

'On the Meteor I with the original short nacelles, the nacelles caused a breakaway of flow on the upper surface of the wing at high Mach numbers, giving a nose down trim change. On the model with extended nacelles (or without nacelles), the changes of pitching moments on the wing and body, and downwash at the tail, were very small at all Mach numbers up to 0.82. The nose-up trim was apparently due to *reduction* of the incidence for no lift at high Mach numbers, instead of the increase usually found on other models.'

'*Effects of Nacelles.* – For an engine nacelle mounted on a wing, compressibility usually produces a considerable increase of drag, beginning at a lower Mach number than that at which the wing drag starts to rise. The Mach number at which the nacelle drag starts to increase can be raised by increasing the fineness ratio of the nacelle. In addition to these drag changes, a nacelle whose centre line is above or below with wing chord line had important effects on the lift and pitching moment of the wing at high Mach numbers.'

'It was found that the drag of the original nacelles started to rise fairly steeply at a Mach number of about 0.65. Also, buffeting had been experienced in flight at Mach numbers above about 0.74, and it was suspected that this was caused by separation of flow near the nacelles. High speed tunnel tests were therefore made for the purpose of improving the nacelle design. Observation of surface tufts on the model in the tunnel showed signs of flow separation at the rear of the nacelle, even at low Mach numbers. As the Mach number increased above about 0.6 the separation, as shown by disturbance of the tufts, spread forward on the wing and became more severe. This separation probably explained the drag rise at a comparatively low Mach number and also the buffeting which had been experienced in flight. Measurements of pressure distribution on the original Meteor nacelle showed that sonic velocity would be reached locally in the nacelle-wing junction at a Mach number of about 0.675. Since the nacelle drag starts to rise at a lower Mach number than this, the separation is probably caused more by the steep adverse pressure gradient in the nacelle-wing junction than by shock waves.'

'Extending the nose and tail of the Meteor nacelles to increase the fineness ratio gave a considerable reduction of the drag at high mach numbers, and also reduced the flow separation. This improvement had been confirmed by flight tests. It is interesting to note that measurements of pressure distribution on the nacelle with extended nose and tail (70) showed that, for wing incidences greater than 1 deg., the critical Mach number (at which sonic velocity was first reached locally) was less than for the original nacelle, and even at lower incidences the critical Mach number was only slightly greater than for the original nacelle. Thus the critical Mach number, defined as the Mach number at which local sonic velocity is first reached, does not give a reliable indication of the improvement due to lengthening the nacelle.'

The Meteor IV, despite retaining the basic Meteor III airframe, albeit strengthened and with the new long-chord engine nacelles, introduced a quantum leap in performance over the Meteor III. For a standard service Meteor IV, the new Derwent V was rated at 3,500-lb static thrust at sea level. This gave the aircraft a speed of 585 mph at sea level and 560 mph at 30,000 ft. These speeds made the Meteor IV the fastest fighter of World War II, although it was not in squadron service, which would be delayed as drawbacks were introduced following the end of the war. The Meteor III with Derwent I's rated at 1,950 lb could reach 30,000 ft in 11.5 minutes and had a service ceiling of 45,000 ft, while the Meteor IV could reach 30,000 ft in around 5 minutes and had a service ceiling of 44,000 ft, although later figures of 50,000 ft would be quoted.

Although the aircraft flew before the war's end, it would not enter service until 1946, the wartime urgency having been left behind with the dark days of the war. However, the aircrafts massive leap in performance over any other type flying at the time meant that the aircraft would make a huge impact on the aviation World in the weeks following the end of the war.

Although retaining the name Derwent, the Series V engine was more or less a new engine, but retaining the 43-in maximum diameter. The thrust rating was almost doubled over the early Derwent I and this great leap in power output led to plans to use the Meteor in an attempt on the World Speed Record. While a new record was almost a formality, as the previous record had been unofficially broken many times during the war, the aim of the record runs was to extend the record by as much as possible. Two Meteor IV's, more or less representative of the planned service variant, minus operational equipment, were allocated to the 'High-Speed Flight' to prepare for the attempt on the World Absolute Speed Record, which, before the war had been set at an average of 469.2 mph (755.138 km/h) by Germany's Messerschmitt 209V.

In the weeks prior to the record breaking runs, Meteorological and other Meteor aircraft had flown over the Herne Bay Course over the North Sea many times, but on the morning of 7 November 1945, less than three months after the end of the war, a new absolute air speed record was set at 606 mph. The record runs with the two Meteor IV's were as follows: Group Captain Wilson; 1st run, 604 mph; 2nd run, 608 mph; 3rd run, 602 mph; 4th run, 611 mph. Eric Greenwood; 1st run, 599 mph; 2nd run, 608 mph; 3rd run, 598 mph; and 4th run, 607 mph. Although four of the runs produced speeds in excess of 606 mph, with the fastest being 611 mph, the average was taken as the record result at 606 mph. The following year the Meteor IV would extend this record to an average of 616 mph, with the fastest run being recorded at 621 mph.

Although the aircraft did not enter operational service until 1946, the prototype had flown on 15 August 1945, allowing the Meteor IV to claim to be a wartime variant and it is rightly included as such in this volume as the major development work that led to this variant was conducted between 1943 and 1945.

This early production Meteor F Mk. IV shows that it was basically an F Mk. III with more powerful engines and the long-chord engine nacelles, the combination of which bestowed upon the Meteor IV a quantum leap in performance over its forebear. The Meteor IV would eventually feature clipped short span wings. MAP

Meteor IV

Maximum weight	13,900 lb
PERFORMANCE.	
Take-off over 50 ft. (max wt.) yards	720
Landing over 50 ft. (Light wt.) yards	740
Landing speed (max wt)	115 mph
Landing speed (light wt)	95 mph
Service ceiling (Max wt.) ft.	50,000
Service ceiling (Mean wt.) ft.	52,000
Maximum speed M. (mean wt.) mph	585
S. (mean wt.) mph	493
CRUISING SPEED	
At 30,000 ft. Most economical mph	350
Range with 275 galls	500 miles
Range with 330 galls	585 miles
Range with 455 galls	820 miles
(These range figures are for an aircraft flying at 30,000 ft and fuel for the climb to this altitude has been allowed for.)	
ARMAMENT.	
GUNS.	
Bore	20 mm
No.	4
Position	Forward of wings Body in side of nose

Chapter Four

Other Jet Aircraft Developments - Allied and Axis

de Havilland F Mk. I single-engine jet fighter in flight. MAP

E.6/41 Spider Crab

Although the E.28/39 remained an experimental design, it paved the way for the introduction of operational jet powered fighters to RAF service. Glosters pushed on with its twin engine F.9/40, which spawned the highly successful Meteor, while other manufacturers joined the jet age. The issuing of Air Staff OR.107 led in time to the issuing of Specification E.6/41 calling for a high performance single-seat, single-engine design built around the Halford jet engine. The specification called for an aircraft with service ceiling of at least 48,000 ft and a minimum required maximum speed of 490 mph at an altitude of 35,000 ft. The need to operate at such high altitudes required the aircraft to be designed with a pressurised cockpit cabin, which was also to be automatic, enabling cockpit conditions consistent with those encountered at 25,000 ft in a non pressurised cockpit, while the aircraft was actually flying at altitudes in excess of 40,000 ft.

de Havilland was tasked to design the E.6/41 and two aircraft were ordered in May 1942, being allocated the serial numbers L2548 and L2551, with a third aircraft with the serial number MP838 ordered in June 1942. de Havilland finalised the design of the aircraft on 8 December that year and by 24 August 1943, the first aircraft, L2548, was ready to commence taxi runs at Hatfield under the power of a Halford designed de Havilland Goblin engine rated at 2,700 lb static thrust.

The design of the E.6/41 departed from conventional thinking, adopting a twin-tail boom and a short fuselage, with the armament and cockpit at the front section and the engine housed in the rear. The single-engine was fed air from intakes which were housed in the wing/fuselage roots. The E.6/41 featured unswept wings fixed toward the rear of the centre nacelle. The exhaust pipe exited the extreme rear of the centre nacelle. The aircraft sat very low on the ground on a tricycle undercarriage due to the lack of need for clearance for a propeller. The Spider Crab prototypes, as the aircraft was then known, were 30 ft 9-in in length, with a span of 40 ft and a wing area of 250.7 sq ft.

Five taxi runs were conducted on 24 August 1943, with the aircraft leaving the ground for around 100 yards on each occasion. These short hops revealed a problem with the rear of the tail boom making contact with the ground on one occasion and coming close to making contact on the other four runs. Modifications were incorporated to the ground angle, increasing clearance, which fixed the problem. The first official flight was conducted on 20 September 1943, during which the aircraft was airborne for 30 minutes. For the most part, the initial flight test was successful. On the negative side, there was an overbalance of the ailerons when the aircraft was flown at speeds in excess of 400 mph IAS resulting in an out of time downward attitude of the left wing requiring modifications to be incorporated to fix the problem. The initial rate of climb was good, as was the handling on take-off.

L2548 received modifications to the fins designed to improve the aircrafts directional stability, following which it was flown again on 3 January 1944. A short time later the aircraft was flown with minor modifications to the intake lips designed to improve the stall problem, which primarily was encountered with practically no warning at a speed of 86 mph.

The second aircraft to fly was the third prototype, MP838, which took to the air for the first time on 21 January 1944, powered by a Halford H.1A engine. This aircraft was tasked with armament trials and was armed with four 20 mm Hispano cannon housed in the underside of the nose. Other testing for MP838 included evaluation of the aircraft's potential as a service fighter for the RAF. This evaluation was conducted at Bascombe Down between 24 May and 23 August 1944, following which the aircraft was moved by road to English Electric at Preston. The results of the trials showed the aircraft to perform favourably compared with existing fighter aircraft. Among the criticism was poor forward and rearward view from the cockpit.

The program suffered a setback, when the first prototype, L2548 suffered an engine failure, causing it to crash on 23 July 1945.

The last of the three prototypes to fly was L2551, which joined the flight test program on 17 March 1944. As with L2548, L2551 was unarmed. This aircraft was modified to represent a planned naval variant; eventually known as the Sea Vampire, with the designation Sea Vampire F.10. Fitted with an arrester hook, this aircraft conducted the first ever landing of a jet aircraft on an aircraft carrier deck, when it alighted on HMS *Ocean* on 3 December 1945.

Vampire F Mk. I

The E.6/41 Spider Crab led directly to the second jet fighter to enter service with the RAF, the de Havilland Vampire. The RAF ordered 120 Vampire F Mk. I fighters on 13 May 1944, to be built at the English Electric works at Preston. The first production F Mk. I flew for the first time at Samlesbury on 20

April 1945, just over two weeks before the end of the war in Europe. The Vampire F Mk. I was a huge improvement over fighters then in service with the Allies, with a maximum speed of 540 mph (869 km/h) at an altitude of 34,000 ft (10365 m). This was in the area of 60 mph faster than the Meteor III, which was credited with a maximum speed of 480 mph (772 km/h) at this altitude, although figures from a number of documents vary this slightly.

The first RAF squadron to equip with the Vampire F Mk. I was No. 247 Squadron, which received its first aircraft at RAF Chilbolton, Hampshire in March 1946. The RAF was by then flying the Meteor F Mk. IV, which was capable of a maximum speed of 585 mph (941 km/h) relegating the Vampire to second place with regards to maximum speed. So fast was the Meteor IV, that a service aircraft, with only minor alterations was able to break the world speed record with a speed of 606 mph in 1945; later increased to 616mph.

Vampire I

The following table is taken from **Aircraft and Armament Experimental Establishment, Bascombe Down Report No. A&AEE/819,a, Vampire F Mk. I TG.274 (Goblin I), Level Speed and Position Error Trials, 9 April 1946.** It shows the maximum level speed together with Mach number and rpm under ICAN conditions for heights from 5,000 to 35,000 ft. for a weight corresponding to 95% of the take-off weight (8,180 lb.).

Height ft.	5,000	10,000	15,000	20,000	25,000	30,000	35,000
TAS mph	495	505	513	520	525	516	505
Mach No.	0.660	0.686	0.710	0.734	0.756	0.760	0.760
R.P.M	10,00	---------	---------	---------	---------	9,900	9,170

No engine surging was apparent throughout the level speed tests.

5.2   Level Speeds. It was noted during the level speed tests at combat engine conditions that above 35,000 ft. it was possible to exceed the aircraft's critical Mach number of 0.76. The highest Mach number obtained during these tests was 0.768 at 36,600 ft., and during this particular speed run the onset of compressibility effects was just noticeable in the form of aileron overbalance.

E.5/42 & E.1/44

A Gloster E.1/44 prototype with a Rolls Royce Nene engine in 1947. MAP

Gloster was also busy with design work for a single-engine jet powered fighter. On 31 January 1942, Gloster's officially entered a proposal for a jet powered single-seat, single-engine fighter. This aircraft was aimed at OR.116 (Operational Requirement 116), which was written as a possible substitute for the F.9/40, should that program suffer insurmountable problems resulting in its cancellation.

OR.116 led to specification E.5/42, which was approved by the Air Ministry on 3 July 1942, with the name Ace being applied to the Gloster aircraft. Due in part to Gloster's high design workload on the F.9/40, the Air Ministry wanted to award the program to Armstrong Whitworth. However, Gloster's eventually managed to convince the Air Ministry that its experience with the E.28/39 and F.9/40 meant it was best placed to be awarded the E.5/42 contract. On 14 August, the Air Ministry announced that the program would stay with Gloster.

Although the program had an 'E' for experimental prefix applied, the program was always intended as a prototype for a possible operational fighter. The design specification was for an aircraft with a top speed of at least 485 mph in level flight at an altitude of 30,000 ft. The aircraft was to be capable of a speed of 550 mph in a dive and service ceiling was to be 47,000 ft or higher. Any service variant that emerged was to be armed with between two and four 20 mm Hispano Mk IV or V cannon.

A contract for construction of three prototypes was awarded to Gloster's on 29 January 1943. These aircraft, which were allocated the serial numbers MM648, MM651 and MM655, were to be powered by the Halford H.1 or H.2 engines rated at 2,300 lb. The specification was finalised on 26 March 1943 and construction of the first aircraft commenced at Gloster' facility at Bentham in November that year.

By early 1944, the program had undergone a number of modifications to the specification resulting in a modified contract being awarded. This still covered the construction of three aircraft; however, the serial numbers were changed to SM801, SM805 and SM809. Another new specification issued on 29 May 1944 became the E.1/44, which had superseded the E.5/42. This design was to be powered by a 5,000 lb Rolls Royce Nene turbojet. British manufactures eventually adopted the SBAC designation numbering system under which the E.1/44 was designated GA.1 Ace. The aircraft was also known as the Wartime Experimental Airplane No.248. The planned first prototype, SM801 was to be a basic development prototype, while the second aircraft, SM805 was to representative of an operational aircraft.

The Gloster Ace was constantly plagued by an ever changing specification, which imposed many delays on the program. A further specification change proved to be so extensive that work on the first two aircraft, SM801 and SM805 was abandoned, although SM809 was able to be proceeded and construction of this aircraft commenced around autumn 1944 under the new designation GA.2, retaining the name Ace. Three additional prototypes were ordered on 26 January 1945, with the serial numbers TX145, TX148 and TX150 being allocated. These aircraft were to be powered by a Rolls Royce Nene 2 turbojet rated at 5,000 lb static thrust.

The program continued after the end of the war, with various changes in specifications, designations, serial numbers and numbers of aircraft ordered. The aircraft that finally flew on 9 March 1948 was much different from the aircraft planned under the original specifications, attaining a maximum speed of 620 mph.

Supermarine 392, E.10/44

Supermarine were heavily involved in the development of the Supermarine Spiteful when on 4 July 1944 the parent company, Vickers Armstrong, sent a letter to MAP proposing a jet-propelled fighter incorporating the new laminar flow wing being developed for the piston engine Spiteful. The proposed jet fighter aircraft was known as the Supermarine Specification 477. Using the same wing as the Spiteful, it was suggested, would allow construction to begin quickly. Supermarine had actually begun design work on the Supermarine 477 in mid-June 1944. While the Meteor I had been handicapped by the low power output of the available engines, the increasing power that was becoming available in various engine developments meant that the Supermarine 477 would be able to be powered by a single engine, namely the Rolls Royce R.B.41. Nene. The aircraft was to be armed with four 20 mm cannon housed in the wings as in the piston engine Spiteful.

MAP almost immediately warmed to the proposal, which would have a greater range than the Meteor or Vampire fighters then in development. On 29 July 1944, Vickers Armstrong was notified of the requirement for three prototypes with an initially planned first flight of 30 March 1945. This resulted in the formulation of OR.182, which led to specification E.10/44 being issued in September 1944. The E.10/44 requirement called for a maximum level speed of at least 550 mph and a service ceiling of 45,000 ft or more.

The order for three prototypes was formalised on 9 September 1944, and the aircraft were allocated the serial numbers TS409, TS413 and TS416 with the designation Supermarine 392. From the start, the program was hampered by a funding shortfall, and while a mock-up was quickly built, work on the three prototypes was slow. Another factor slowing the design work was the loss of the first prototype Spiteful in September 1944. Testing of the laminar flow wing for the 392 could not resume until the second Spiteful prototype flew on 8 January 1945.

Specification E.10/44 was formally issued on 6 February 1945, less than two weeks before Supermarine were ordered to suspend work on programs of low priority and accelerate work on the 392, which at the time was being referred to as the 'Jet Spiteful'.

In summer 1945, various proposals were issued for a jet powered carrier capable fighter, with OR.195 being formally issued on 26 July. From this point on, the 392 was developed more as a naval fighter as the RAF was expressing little interest in the type as the Meteor was beginning to mature into a potent twin engine fighter and the Vampire single-seat fighter was entering production. To this end, the last two of the three prototypes that had been ordered were now to be completed as prototypes of the proposed naval variant. Just over two weeks previous, MAP had awarded a contract for production of 24 pre-production aircraft. This order was broken down as six E.10/44 with serials VH980 - VH985, eighteen E.1/45's, four of these with serials VH987 - VH991 to be built as land based aircraft, while the remaining fourteen aircraft with serials VJ110 - VJ118 and VH995 - VH999 to be completed as naval variants with folding wings and other naval associated equipment. The E.1/45 was allocated the Supermarine designation 398 and was initially known as the 'Jet Seafang', as it featured wings developed from those of the Seafang, which was a naval variant of the Spiteful piston engine fighter. The pre-production order was later cancelled, when the Admiralty ordered 18 Sea Vampire F.20's, a naval variant of the Vampire fighter, in February 1946.

Although the aircraft was designed during the war it did not fly before the end of hostilities in summer 1945. The first prototype, TS409 eventually conducted its first flight on 27 July 1946, and a variant would eventually enter service with the FAA (Fleet Air Arm) with a small number exported.

German Jet and Rocket Aircraft

The Heinkel 178 research aircraft conducted the World's first aircraft flight exclusively under the power of a jet engine when it took to the air on 27 August 1939.

Whittle was not alone in developing jet-powered engines in the 1930's. In Germany, Physicist Dr Hans von Ohain was preparing a jet engine for flight. von Ohain's vision of a jet –powered engine emerged later than Whittles own idea for such an engine, however, Ohain was fortunate that his bureaucratic masters in Germany were more enthusiastic about the prospect of jet-powered high-speed flight than their counterparts in Britain. Consequently, Ohain received the funding and facilities he required to turn the idea into reality, with the first bench-test run of the German jet-unit being conducted around one month before the first run of the Whittle Unit. The German jet-Unit produced a thrust of some 550 lb's and the successful bench-testing led to funding for a flight rated jet engine and a single research aircraft, the Heinkel He.178, to flight test the engine. This, the world's first aircraft to fly exclusively under jet power, conducted its maiden flight on 27 August 1939, powered by a single He S-3b jet-engine rated at 1,100 lb static thrust.

The Heinkel He.178, while designed as an experimental aircraft, was the catalyst that led to the many experimental and operational jet powered aircraft fielded by Germany during the Second World War. Studies of various proposals for single engine and twin engine jet powered fighters were conducted, leading to the He.280 twin jet fighter and the Me.262 twin jet fighter, which would eventually enter squadron service in 1944. As both the He.280 and the Me.262 were reliant on the same engine developments, it is not surprising that their overall size and projected weights were very similar, as was much of the general layout of the aircraft, each having provision for two jet engines low slung on the wings. However, the Me.262 was the more advanced aircraft in regards to design; featuring swept back wings, while the He.280 had more conventional un-swept wings. The Me.262 had a single vertical tail and rudder, while the He.280 featured a twin boom tail.

The He.280 was ready for flight testing in late summer 1940, but as the development of the jet engines was behind that of the airframe, the aircraft, which had been fitted with dummy nacelles, was towed into the air by a He.111 bomber on 22 September 1940. A series of some 40 unpowered flights were conducted over the course of the next six months or so.

The first He.280, V1, conducted its first powered flight on 3 April 1941. It was powered by a pair of jet engines, each developing 600 kg static thrust. The second and third prototypes followed it into the air and a contract for a further six was awarded to Heinkel. The early jet engines, however, proved a disappointment and poor thrust, combined with unreliability saw some of the He.280's being fitted with the so called 'Argus Tubes', housing the pulse jet engine developed for the Fieseler Fi.103, which was being developed at the time. This would eventually enter service as the V1 Flying Bomb, a type, which Britain's first jet fighter would eventually combat in the skies over South East England in summer 1944. Of course, the He.280 flights with the V-1 power plants were also in part aimed at testing the reliability of these units.

Development of the German aircraft designed for flight with jet engines was ahead of the engine development itself. This resulted in the Me.262 making its first flight powered by a single Jumo 210G piston engine housed in the nose. This power plant was initially used in the first of the Me.109 fighters. This flight, under piston power, was conducted on 18 April 1941. The first jet powered flight of a Me.262 took place on 25 March 1942, when the aircraft took off under the power of a pair of BMW 003 turbojets, each developing 460 kg of static thrust. The first flight of the prototype Me.262 fitted with Jumo 004 engines took place on 18 July 1942 and the second and third aircraft to fly, V2 and V4, were powered by these engines when they made their respective maiden flights on 1 October 1942 and April 1943.

The unreliability of the HeS 8 engines of the He.280 saw this aircraft eventually powered by the Jumo 004. Although work on converting the aircraft to be powered by the Jumo 004 would continue, the He.280 was dropped significantly down the priority list in a letter dated 15 September 1942 from the Inspector General of the Luftwaffe, effectively ending any hopes that it would enter service as an operational fighter.

From this point onwards, the Luftwaffe were pinning their hopes on the more promising Me.262. A Me.262 flight test report from the Rechlin test Centre dated 1 September 1944 gave the maximum speed as 740 km/h at ground level (sea level) and 810 km/h at 9000 m. This was at a take-off weight of 6100 kg and an engine speed of 8,700 rpm, which was apparently the maximum engine speed permitted at the time. At 2000 m the rate of climb was 14.7 m/sec dropping to 1.3 m/sec at 12000 m.

The aircraft involved in the tests above was used in further tests, fitted with new engines, and a report dated 18 October 1944 gave a ground level speed of 780 km/h, rising to 820 km/h at 9000 m. These performance figures were also quoted in a report from the GL/C-E Technical Office, dated 15 October 1944. The same report calculated performance figures of 760 km/h at ground level and a speed of 850 km/h at altitudes between 6000 and 8000 m. On 12 August 1944, Messerschmitt reported a performance record of 805 km/h at ground level and 878 km/h at 6000 m.

There were a number of trials of captured aircraft post war, although many of these trials were at best unreliable, utilising poor condition aircraft and engines and unreliable test procedures. A US Navy report stated a speed of 840 km/h at 4600 m for a Me.262, which as stated above was in poor condition.

A post war evaluation document, Report No. F-TR-1133-ND by US Air Material Command stated of the Me.262 that "Maximum flight duration at low altitudes is 45 to 50 min; at high altitudes it ranges from 60 to 90 min". This same test series found normal take off speed to be 111 – 124 mph, normal cruising speed to be 465 mph, normal stall 112 – 125 mph and final approach speed to be 155 mph and maximum take-off weight 15,620 lb. This weight was considerably higher than the 12,000 lb or thereabouts of the Meteor III. Max speed at various altitudes was the following:

Pressure altitude feet	True Air Speed
4,900 feet	524
20,200	516

This report found that "Despite a difference in gross weight of nearly 2000 lb, the Me-262 (Me.262) No. T-2-711 was superior to the average Lockheed P-80A in acceleration and speed, and approximately the same in climb performance. This concluded that the Lockheed P-80A, the US's first operational jet powered fighter, was, despite entering service over a year later, inferior to the basic Me.262. It should be noted, however, that developed variants of the Me.262 would have been expected to push the performance margin over the P-80A still further.

Top: **The Me.262 proved to be without a doubt the best of the German Jet fighters to fly during World War II. Like the Meteor, it had two engines, but these were hung under the engines in a similar fashion to that seen on F.9/40 prototype DG204/G.** USAFM

Above: **Me.163B Rocket-Powered interceptor 191095 shows the types extremely small size.** USAFM

Top: The Arado Ar.234 'Blitz' (Lightning) was the only operational jet powered bomber to enter service during World War II. Smithsonian Air and Space Museum

Above: The Heinkel He.162 was a single-engine jet powered fighter, which flew in early December 1944 and began entering operational service in April 1945, only a few weeks before the end of the war in Europe. The primary aim of the He.162 program was to produce a fighter aircraft with almost the same performance as the Me.262, but with only a single engine, thus massively reducing production time, cost and most importantly reducing fuel consumption.

Me.163

The Me. 163 was a small single seat tailless interceptor powered by a single liquid rocket engine. As with the jet powered aircraft, development of the rocket powered Me.163 airframe was ahead of the rocket engine development. Work on the design of the aircraft began in October 1941 and the airframe of the first prototype, V1, was ready by summer 1942, but the rocket engine was not ready, therefore, the aircraft was towed into the air and effectively flight tested as a glider. The HWK 109-509A rocket engine developing a thrust of some 1700 kg was fitted in July 1943. The rocket engine bestowed upon the Me.163 a maximum speed in the order of 940 km/h and a very high rate of climb of 80 m/sec, which simply could not be emulated by any other fighter at the time.

A post war flight test document stated that the Me.163B was "a highly manoeuvrable airplane possessing unusually good stability and control characteristics, especially for a tailless design."

Arado 234

The prototype Arado Ar.234 'Blitz' (Lightning), V1, conducted its maiden flight in summer 1943. This twin engine machine was originally conceived as a twin jet reconnaissance aircraft, but during its development it matured into a twin jet bomber/reconnaissance aircraft. The Arado 234 was a successful aircraft in terms of design and proved to be successful in both reconnaissance and tactical bombing roles, albeit on a very small scale, due to the overwhelming superiority in numbers of the opposing Allied forces.

There were a number of developments, actual and planned, including a night fighter variant and a four engine variant, the Ar.234C.

A US Air Material Command flight test report, AAF No. T2-1010 from 10 October 1946, determined three maximum speed points at 8700 rpm:

Density Altitude	Actual True Airspeed	Air Temp	German Instrument True Airspeed
23,760 feet	474 mph	-27 deg C	720 KM/H
15,840 feet	476 mph	-11 deg C	733 KM/H
5,500 feet	483 mph	+7 deg C	760 KM/H

Note: All quantitative performance data listed above are values obtained on the test day. In order to secure the necessary information to correct these results to standard conditions additional instrumentation and flying would be required.

The actual true airspeeds were obtained from the pacer P-80. It should be noted that the static output of the Jumo 004-B is only 1880 lbs. while the 004-D is 2460 lbs.; therefore, it is entirely possible that in normal development the maximum speed of this bomber would be 40 or 50 miles per hour higher than the values listed above, provided Mach number effects do not become critical.

The conclusions of this report were as follows: "The Arado 234 is a fast, very manoeuvrable light bomber or reconnaissance airplane with many desirable features. As a light bomber the Arado carries an external load of approximately 3300 lbs."

He.162

By early September 1944, it was clear that production of the Me.262 twin-jet fighter would fall "far behind the required number." For the Germans, raw materials were the issue, particularly in regards to fuel. To try and overcome this Heinkel suggested the design and manufacture of a jet fighter, which possess performance levels approaching that of the Me.262, but fitted with only a single engine, thus more or less halving the fuel requirement for the same number of aircraft. On 15 September, Heinkel was instructed to have a mock-up ready by 1 October 1944, fly a prototype by 10 December 1944, commence large-scale production in January 1945, and reach an output level of

1,000 aircraft during April that year, with preparations in place to increase production to 2,000 aircraft at a later date.

The BMW 003 engine was proposed as this would utilise "unused production capabilities" and some parts from existing types were used such as the main undercarriage units taken from the Me.109. Such was the speed at which the program commenced and so austere were the conditions in which the program was conducted, it was impossible to "conduct wind-tunnel tests... before the first flight." Changes were to be introduced on quantity production aircraft. A He.219 twin engine night fighter had flown with a jet engine under the fuselage in summer 1944, as part of the German jet engine development program; this demonstrating the engines flightworthiness before it would fly in a future aircraft program such as the He.162.

The He.162 had "high-manoeuvrability", better than that of the Me.262, with one report stating "The manoeuvrability of the He.162 is far greater than that of the Me.262." The landing characteristics of the aircraft were considered to be better than those of the Me.109, but aircraft was not as fast as the Me.262, with a critical Mach number of 0.75. It was considered that "further reductions of drag on the order of about 8% could be attained according to tunnel tests by the improvement of wing fuselage transition. Because of the difficulties expected by the application of such changes on production airplanes, this improvement was provisionally rejected." One report stated "According to wind tunnel measurements and assuming the same power plant and flight duration, the same performance as the Me.262 should be attained."

The first flight of a He.162 took place on 6 December 1944, four days ahead of the projected timetable first flight. However, mainly through delay of production jigs, quantity production was delayed by 1-2 months, and large-scale deliveries were scheduled for May 1945. "In April 1945, 100 airplanes had been completed and parts for about 800 were ready for assembly. According to the delivery program the He-162 was the only airplane to be manufactured along with the Me-262."

As the war was approaching its climax, 2 He.162's were being prepared for flight powered by the Jumo 004 engine. However, these aircraft were destroyed in a bombing raid at Vienna before their first flight. More He.162's were then allocated to be powered by the Jumo 004, but the war ended before these aircraft were completed.

Many new variants of the He.162 were projected, including a variant powered by the HeS 11 engine, which would have necessitated the fitting of a new wing and "probably" a V-tail, both of which were to feature sweepback. These design changes would have allowed a higher critical speed limit to be attained. Production of this variant, however, was not projected until 1946.

Post war trials at RAE Farnborough on the He.162 showed that this type fell below the published German figures of a top speed of 490 mph at sea level and 523 mph at 20,000 ft. However, this was put down to the poor engine thrust and general condition of the aircraft and engines and it is reasonable to assume that the aircraft attained speeds in that region during German trials.

The following table is taken from RA.E. Tech. Note No. F.A. 235/5

Aero. 1706

Dated October 1945

Aircraft Data

	Me 262	He 162	Ar 234
Wing Area	226 sq.ft.	120 sq.ft.	298 sq.ft.
Aspect Ratio	7.5	4.65	5.8
All up weight of aircraft	14,730 lbs*	592 lbs*	17,700 lbs+
Weight with tanks empty	11,120 lbs	4,610 lbs	11,110 lbs
Wing loading at take-off	65	49	60

* Without ammunition
+ Without bombs

USAAF records show this photograph as a Boeing B-17F four engine heavy bomber falling to Earth after it had its left wing blown off by a Me.262 over Crantenburg, Germany. USAFM

The Me.262 was eventually produced in a number of variants and entered service in summer 1944, with the first contacts between the German jet fighters and allied aircraft occurring in August 1944. Although over 1,000 Me.262's were built before the war ended in May 1945, just over 800 or so of these would enter service with the Luftwaffe. This small number was never capable of stopping the flood of Allied fighters and bombers operating over Europe. At times, mere handfuls of German aircraft would take off to confront aerial armadas of several thousand allied fighters and bombers. These overwhelming odds completely negated any performance superiority of the German jet fighters, which were attacked on the ground, as they were taking off, in the air at all attitudes and when they were landing. Indeed, the majority of German jet casualties occurred through crashes, being destroyed on the ground or intercepted during take-off and landing. That said; the German jets took a heavy toll on Allied bombers and fighters before the war ended.

The first Me.163B's were delivered to the Luftwaffe in May 1944 and a further three were delivered in June followed by 12 in

July. This allowed an operational squadron to be formed at Brandis near Leipzig and the first operational sorties took place on 28 July 1944, one day after the first operational sorties by RAF Gloster Meteor F Mk. I's, which began operating against the jet powered V-1 Flying Bomb on 27 July 1944. The Me.163 suffered from the same problem as its jet powered compatriots – unassailable allied numerical superiority in aircraft, materials, fuel and manpower. Despite this, the small rocket powered fighters took a toll on Allied aircraft, particularly USAAF Boeing B-17 and Consolidated B-24 four engine heavy bombers.

A few Ar.234 prototypes, V5 and V7, were dispatched for reconnaissance operations on the western front a few days before the allied invasion at Normandy, France in early June 1944. However, the lack of infrastructure and equipment precluded operations from being flown until 2 August 1944. As more Arado 234's became available, the aircraft was also produced in a bomber variant and these aircraft flew piecemeal missions against the flood of allied ground forces and airfields on the continent. One of these raid against B.77 airfield near Brussels in early 1945 caused minor damage to one of the No.616 Squadron Gloster Meteor III's, which was operating from this base at the time.

The last of the German jet combat aircraft to see operational service during the war was the He.162, which entered service only days before the end of the war in Europe. The He.162 began to enter service in April 1944, and actually flew a few combat missions before the war ended. A number of aircraft were lost, mainly through accidents and destruction on the ground. However, a few are accepted as having been shot down by RAF Tempest V's and possibly USAAF P-47 Thunderbolts. At least one was confirmed shot down by Tempest V's, but the one often cited as having been shot down by a Thunderbolt is veiled in controversy as it seems that no Thunderbolts were operating in the area that the incident occurred.

There are of course many discrepancies concerning the number of Me.163's delivered, but it thought that a figure of 237 was delivered in 1944, but a much lower total of only 42 were delivered in 1945. Although there are again obvious discrepancies, the number of Me.262's built during World War II was around 1,294, with 809 delivered to the Luftwaffe. Some 364 Me.163's were built, with 225 of these being delivered to the Luftwaffe, 116 He.162's were built, with 40 being delivered to the Luftwaffe and 214 Ar.234's were built, with 196 being delivered to the Luftwaffe.

By contrast, the Meteor F Mk. I and F Mk. III were the only allied jet aircraft to see operational service, and only in very small number compared to their German counterparts. By the time the war in Europe ended Meteors were serving with No.616 and No.504 squadrons and within days of the end of hostilities, No.74 Squadron returned to the UK to commence conversion to the Meteor III. The Meteor I and III were also operated by the Conversion Unit and a number of test and development organisations and by the time the instrument of surrender was signed ending the war against Japan on 3 September 1945, the Meteor III was being flown by No.263 and 245 Squadrons, both of which had taken over the Meteors of No.616 and No.504 Squadrons respectively after these units had been disbanded. In addition No.124 Squadron began conversion to the Meteor III in July 1945 and was declared operational in October that year. In summer 1945, No.222 Squadron commenced conversion to the Meteor III with the Conversion Unit and was flying its own Meteors by October 1945. All told, six squadrons, the Conversion Unit and a number of Test and Development units flew Meteors at one time or another during the Second World War. Four different variants were flown; the Meteor I, Meteor II (prototype only – actually the sixth F.9/40, WG207/G), Meteor III and the Meteor IV, with the latter being the fastest Allied fighter of World War II, albeit not being ready for operational service. Only the Meteor I and III saw operational service. The Vampire F Mk. I was also being prepared for operational service, but the end of the war, with the inevitable drawbacks saw service entry for this type delayed until 1946.

The following two documents dated 21 and 28 July 1944 respectively show the Chiefs of Staff appreciation of the position of German jet and rocket propelled aircraft at the time the Meteor I was entering service with No.616 Squadron at RAF Manston in July 1944:

TOP SECRET.

J.R.D.P. (44) 7. (Final.)

21ST JULY 1944.

WAR CABINET

Joint Committee on Research and Development Priorities.

Jet propelled aircraft which can attain speeds greatly in excess of conventional type aircraft will shortly be brought into operational use by the Germans. Our own development is some way behind the enemy in this class of aircraft. Very great importance, must, therefore, be attached to regaining our lost position and placing ourselves ahead of the Germans in jet propelled aircraft technique.

J.I.C. (44) 316 (0) (REVISED FINAL) (LIMITED CIRCULATION)

28TH JULY, 1944

WAR CABINET
JOINT INTELLIGENCE SUB-COMMITTEE

NEW WEAPONS IN RELATION TO GERMAN STRATEGY

AIR FORCE

19. <u>The Jet or Rocket Propelled Aircraft.</u> Although the G.A.F. is known to have been experimenting with at least five different types of jet or rocket propelled aircraft, it appears that only the Me.163 and the Me.262 are likely to become operational in the near future. The other three types are thought to be still in the prototype stage.

20. The Me.163 is a single-seater fighter using rocket propulsion. Its speed at 30 to 40 thousand feet is believed to be 525-550 m.p.h. The rate of climb is outstanding but the endurance is only sufficient for eight minutes but as the flying technique is thought to be by the use of alternate bursts of power on and power off the endurance can be extended considerably. The indications are that the Me.163 is intended for use as an interceptor fighter for the defence of the Reich but the special requirements, particularly in respect of the long runways and adequate clearance of obstacles in the line of take-off will restrict its employment to a limited number of airfields. Those known to be under development for that purpose are in the Berlin area and extend westwards to the North Sea coast. The Possession of bases in North-Western France would thus not appear to offer any striking advantage in the operation of an aircraft of this type.

21. The Me.262 is a twin-engined single-seater fighter using jet propulsion. Its speed is thought to be about 450-500 m.p.h. and is thus not as high as the Me.163, but it has a greater endurance. The aircraft is designed as a fighter but there are indications that it may be intended for use as a

fighter bomber and possibly also for reconnaissance. The German need for reconnaissance of this country may encourage them to use the Me.262 for this purpose and the possession of bases in N.W. France would give them the advantage of being able to obtain some reconnaissance despite the comparatively limited range of this aircraft.

22.   It is expected that up to 30 Me.163's and a similar number of Me.262's may become operational in the near future. Larger scale employment of these aircraft will probably not occur for some months and is likely to be dependent upon the experience gained through operations in a small number. In any event it is unlikely that more than 90 aircraft of each type will be operational before October.

23.   The main advantage the Germans will gain when these types become operational is a higher speed, faster rate of climb and probably heavier armour than their existing fighter types. It is probable that the manoeuvrability at full speed will be inferior to existing orthodox fighters.

28TH JULY 1944.

Other Nations Jet and Rocket Powered aircraft

The Italians flew the Caproni Campini N.1 experimental aircraft on 27 August 1940 and although there are some doubts over its credibility as a true jet aircraft, it is listed as such here. The aircraft, however, was nothing more than an experimental design with no potential for development as an operational aircraft. Its performance was very limited in comparison to conventional aircraft of the time. Italy, however, did not develop any jet powered combat aircraft during the war years. There were many other Axis jet and rocket aircraft developments, many of which did not get beyond the drawing board or indeed the initial paper idea. Japans fledgling jet and rocket programs led to the Mitsubishi J8M Shusui (Swinging Sword), which was basically a variant of the Me.163 Komet built in Japan with German technical assistance. This aircraft would have had a projected speed of up to 559 mph. The Nakajima Kikki (Orange Blossom) was developed, with German technical assistance, from the Me.262, although it lacked the German fighter's performance.

The Yokosuka MXY7 Ohka (Cherry Blossom) was not a fighter, but designed specifically as a rocket powered high speed manned missile for Kamikaze pilots and was used in small numbers before the war ended. The Kawanishi Baika (Plum Blossom) could be described as a Japanese built manned V-1, from which it was effectively developed, although there were many differences. Like the Cherry Blossom, this aircraft was designed as a kamikaze aircraft, but with jet power instead of the rocket engine used by the Cherry Blossom. The single pulse jet engine was expected to propel this manned missile at speeds up to 460 mph. The Nakijima Ki-201 Karyu (Fire Dragon) was developed from the Me.262, although slightly larger than the German aircraft. This aircraft was under construction when the war against Japan ended in August 1945. Although there were a number of jet and rocket aircraft projects in development, no operational jet or rocket powered fighters entered service with Japans air arms during the war.

With access to British jet technology making a jet powered fighter aircraft for the USAAF a real possibility in the short-term, the pusher propeller concept originally planned for the Bell XP-59 was abandoned in favour of jet turbine power. General Electric in the US took on the job of building the jet engines developed from the British jet engine technology, which had been supplied and Bell Aircraft was selected to build the airframe, which emerged as a mid-set straight wing design, which held little promise of any great leap in capability over existing piston engine fighter programs.

Initially the XP-59 concept featured a twin-boom tail, but this was dropped in favour of a single-vertical tail before production of the prototype commenced. Production P-59's had a shorter vertical tail than the prototypes and the vertical stabiliser and wingtips were squared compared with the rounded stabiliser and wingtips of the X and YP-59's. The YP-59A had nose armament installed allowing them to be easily distinguishable from the XP-59's and XP-59A's. The low thrust ratings of early jet engines dictated that the P-59 would have to be powered by two-engines as were the first production British and German jet fighters; the Gloster Meteor and Messerschmitt Me.262 respectively. The P-59 was to be powered by a pair of General Electric I-16 turbojets based on the British Whittle jet engines, which produced only 1,650-lb's of thrust in the definitive P-59B, which was the main production variant.

Three XP-59A prototypes powered by 2 General Electric I-A turbojet engines, based on the British Whittle design, were ordered, the first of which conducted its maiden flight at Muroc Dry Lake, California, on 1 October 1942, bringing the US into the jet era. Thirteen YP-59A's powered by a pair of I-14 turbojets, which was an improved variant of the I-A and 20 P-59A production aircraft followed the three XP-59A prototypes. The YP-59A's, most of which were delivered during 1944, were used as service test aircraft to gain experience for the introduction of the P-59A and became the first production jet powered aircraft to enter service with the USAAF. The only other variant was the P-59B, which was powered by the further improved I-16 turbojets and was armed with a single 37-mm cannon and a pair of 0.50-in calibre machine guns in the nose.

Performance of the P-59 proved disappointing during evaluation with the USAAF 412th FG (Fighter Group), particularly in comparison to the first jet-powered fighters in Europe. Even the latest piston-engine fighters then in service performed better in practically every respect including maximum speed and range, with the latter being no more than 409 mph achieved on flight tests, well below the hoped for 450+ mph. This resulted in only 66 aircraft being built including prototype and service test aircraft. Although lacking the performance to be a serious candidate for a front line service aircraft, the P-59 provided experience in operation of jet-powered aircraft for the USAAF and the USAF, which succeeded it.

The Lockheed P-80 was the best of the early jet fighters designed for the USAAF during World War II, ultimately becoming the first jet fighter aircraft to enter operational service with the USAAF. Design of the aircraft began in 1943 and like the P-59 before it; the P-80 would be reliant on British jet engine technology, with an early engine and technical data passed over from Britain. The XP-80 was powered by a British de Havilland Halford H-1B turbojet rated at 2,460-lb static thrust. Transfer of this engine to the United States caused some delay to the development program of the British E.6/42, which led to the Vampire F Mk. I.

The airframe of the XP-80 was more or less designed around this engine and at 32-ft long adopted a conventional configuration with straight wings, a single vertical tail and conventional horizontal tail-planes and rudder. Two small air intakes were located on the lower sides of the fuselage to feed the engines, which occupied more or less the entire rear fuselage, which detached for engine maintenance or changes. The cockpit was located behind the solid nose section, which would house the gun armament in production aircraft.

The design team created the basic aircraft in 143 days, which although much lauded and certainly a short period, was hardly remarkable for the time, considering the Germans were churning out jet fighters designs from drawing board to first flight in a matter of weeks or months. Furthermore, the Americans had the nicety of ready-made British turbojets for their new fighter and a manufacturing program free from the inconveniencies of constant air attack and harassment, which the Germans and to a lesser extent the British had to contend with.

The XP-80 conducted its maiden flight on 8 January 1944 and attained a speed of 490-mph. Just over one month later the XP-80 exceeded 500-mph during USAAF tests at Muroc. Although the design was always aimed at fielding an operational jet powered fighter the single XP-80 was merely an aerodynamic test-bed for a larger aircraft, and was followed by three XP-80A's powered by an Allison J-33, which was effectively a licence built variant of the British de-Havilland Goblin.

The first XP-80A conducted its maiden flight at Muroc on 10 June 1944 and these aircraft were followed by 13 YP-80A's used for service evaluation. The first production P-80A was delivered in February 1945, however, production was slow and only handfuls of early production P-80A's entered service with the USAAF before the end of the WW II. Test carried out post war showed that the maximum speed of the P-80A was 526 mph at 12,000 ft and maximum cruising speed was 434 mph at 24,000 ft, although different tests gave different figures dependant on the aircraft used, engine used and aircraft configuration.

Chapter Five

The Battle of the Bombs - The V-1 Campaign

The first Meteor F Mk. I's were delivered to No. 616 Squadron at the height of the First Phase of the V-1 Flying Bomb onslaught against southern Britain. The V-1's, commonly referred to as 'Buzz Bombs' or 'Doodlebugs', where code named 'Divers', a nomenclature that will be used throughout this volume. Although the Meteors were used operationally from 27 July 1944, only four days after the first operational aircraft were delivered to the squadron at RAF Manston, the First Phase of the V-1 campaign was in its closing stages and the air and ground defences had been completely re-organised and re-distributed into three (four counting the Balloon defences) zones.

In brief, the Fieseler Fi.013 V-1 'Flying Bomb' was a pilotless missile about the size of a small aircraft. It was designed to achieve high-speeds, in excess of 400 mph at low altitudes, courtesy of its single Argus pulse jet engine mounted above the fuselage, which housed the fuel and the roughly one ton warhead. The aircraft had a rudimentary guidance system, whereby a rotor in the nose turned a certain number of times indicating that it should be in the general region of its intended target, which would be area targets such as cities or ports. Once it had reached this point the bomb then went into a steep dive onto its target; hence the reason the codename 'Diver' was applied.

Argus began ground testing the pulse-jet in January 1941, followed by flight tests on a Gotha 145 from April that year. In February 1942, the first crude drawings were laid down of what would emerge as the V-1 Flying Bomb. Initially known as the Fieseler P35, the air vehicle was later designated Fi.103, the first of which had been built by the end of August 1942, followed soon after by the commencement of flight trials, which were plagued with problems, many of which were eventually overcome allowing the un-piloted variant of the Fi-103 to eventually attain operational status in summer 1944.

V-1 Main Characteristics

Length	25 ft 4.5 in
Width (wing span)	17 ft 6 in
Missile weight	1,685 lb
Fuel weight	1,185 lb
Warhead weight	1,988 lb
Total weight	4,858 lb
Range	125 – 200 miles
Altitude (minimum)	3,000 ft (note: many V-1's operated at and were intercepted at altitudes lower than this)
Altitude (maximum)	8,000 ft
Speed	300 – 420 mph (speeds in excess of 420 mph were reported by some pilots attempting to intercept the bombs.)
Time of flight	20 – 25 minutes
Accuracy	50% within a circle of an 8 mile radius
Crater effect:	
Depth of crater	2–5 ft
Width of crater	10-20 ft
Launch rate	Maximum rate of launchings per site per day 15
Detect-ability	Could be detected by sound, visually and radar

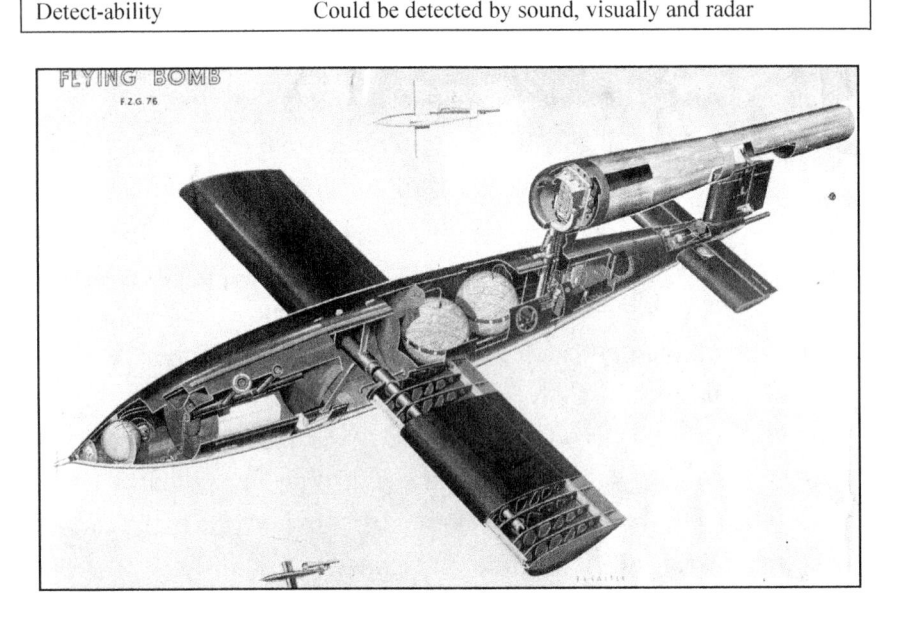

Part cutaway of a German V-1 Flying Bomb showing the fuel cells, warhead and various other equipment, such as the rudimentary guidance system in the nose. USAFM

On 1 December 1943, a directive designated the German LXV Armee Korps, z.b.v. (under proper translation this unit was known as LXV Infantry Corp for Special Employment, with the z.b.v. part an acronym for 'zur besondern Verwendung.') as the headquarters that would be responsible for directing operations of all long range weapons to be employed against the United Kingdom. Under this order the Commander in Chief West would assume command over the Commanding General of LXV Corp, which would command all long range weapon operations from both the Luftwaffe and Army, therefore, a joint Army-Air Force headquarters was set up. The V-1 was to be fielded by the Luftwaffe and the V-2 and Railroad Artillery by the Army. Under the command structure arrangement, the Corp commander would be drawn from the Army, while the Chief of Staff came from the Luftwaffe. The Corp Commander was Lt. General Erich Keinemann, an Artilleryman, whom had previously been commander of the German Artillery School. Luftwaffe Colonel Niemeyer assumed the position of Chief of Staff. The units assigned to LXV Corp were the 155th Flak Regiment, "all V-2 units already in the West under Senior Artillery Commander 292, and a long-range artillery unit under Artillery Commander 141."

In brief the chronology of events leading to the commencement and conduct of the V-1 campaign was as follows:

July 1941: Development and Preliminary Training of Field Units under Air Force Technical Service.
22 Nov 1943: Commencement of launch site construction and training of field units under command of LXV Corp.
20 May 1944: LXV Corp reported it was ready for operations.
12-13 June 1944: Commencement of campaign
September: Continuation of campaign following reorganisation and move into Holland.
19 October 1944: Campaign continued under command of XXX Corp
28 January 1945: Campaign came under the command of Corp z.V.
30 March 1945: End of the German V-Weapon campaign (V-1 and V-2).

The Field Command for V-Weapon Operations until 1 September 1944, by which time the first phase of the attacks, a period known as the 'Battle of the Bombs' was coming to an end, was the following: Overall command of LXV Corp (commanded by General Heinmann); V-1 operations were conducted by 155

Flak Regiment. V-2 Operations of LXV Corp was commanded by Senior Artillery Commander 191 (General Wetz). The Headquarters of 155 Flak Regiment controlled V-1 operations from France until 4 September 1944, when it moved to Deventer, Holland, by which time the firing units had withdrawn to Holland.

This aerial reconnaissance photograph shows a heavily bomb cratered area identified as a V-1 storage site at Beauvoir, France, which was attacked 12 times by USAAF 9th Air Force bombers. USAFM

The anti-V-1 campaign was conducted under the command of Air Chief Marshal Sir Roderic Hill, RAF as Air Marshal Commanding ADGB (Air Defence of Great Britain), who was appointed on 15 November 1943, until ADGB was dissolved on 15 October 1944, when he assumed the position of Air Officer Commanding-in-Chief, Fighter Command, RAF, serving in this post until the cessation of the war in Europe in May 1945. On 17 November 1943, Air Marshal Hill effectively outlined the responsibility of his headquarters which included the following verbatim:-

    (a) To be responsible for the air defence of Great Britain and Northern Ireland.
    (b) To command Nos. 9, 10, 11, 12, 13, 60 and 70 Groups and exercise operational control of fighters in Northern Ireland.
    (c) To control operationally the activities of A.A. Command, the Royal Observer Corp, Balloon Command, "and other static elements of air defence formerly controlled operationally by Fighter Command".
    (d) To conduct "defensive and offensive operations which involve the use of squadrons of both A.D.G.B. and T.A.F. as heretofore under instructions issued to both headquarters until fresh instructions are issued".
    (e) To develop interception methods and apparatus for eventual use in A.D.G.B. and other theatres.

"The A.D.G.B. had an establishment of ten day fighter squadrons and 11 night fighters' squadrons. To this was added six additional night fighter squadrons, which were 'earmarked for allotment to No. 85 Group – a group formed for the purpose of defending the overseas base after the land forces should have advanced beyond the lodgement area (following the landings in France)'. While night fighters of 85 Group were under A.D.G.B. Command, the latter would be 'responsible for the night fighter defence of the lodgement area as well as the United Kingdom and the waters between. Similarly, six day fighter squadrons intended ultimately for No. 85 Group were to be put at my disposal to enable me to keep German reconnaissance aircraft at bay, and perform a number of other tasks arising directly out of the situation created by the coming assault. Finally, another fifteen day-fighter squadrons were to remain nominally in A.D.G.B., but be lent to the Second Tactical Air Force for the duration of the assault phase. Only in an emergency would these squadrons revert to my operational control before the end of that phase. It was agreed, however, that if a serious situation should arise, the Air Officer Commanding, No.11 Group, would be justified in using any part of his uncommitted resources (other than American Units) for the daylight defence of his Group area. A few aircraft of the Royal Navy would also operate under my control."

"Thus, the maximum number of Royal Air Force, Dominion and Allied squadrons on which I was expected to call – including the fifteen squadrons lent to the Second Tactical Air Force – would be 48: rather less than half the number that had been considered necessary for the defence of the United Kingdom at the end of 1941, when the main theatre was Russia."

During winter 1943/44, preparations were made by A.D.G.B. for any major German air attacks that might be expected to try and interfere with the preparations for the landing in France, against the landings themselves or against British area targets such as cities. The German night bomber force was known by intensive intelligence operations to have been severely depleted in the west and capable only of operations on a much smaller scale than was the case a few years previously. It was expected that perhaps 50 to 150 sorties per night could be maintained for small periods, with higher sortie numbers available with periods of "inactivity" between. In spring 1944, the Germans launched a bomber offensive against the United Kingdom, subsequently dubbed 'The Baby Blitz'. This campaign, achieved little of real military significance for the German Air Force, which lost a substantial portion of its night bomber force to the various systems of the A.D.G.B.

While the British High Command had been confident of its defence system to combat conventional bombing by the small German Night bomber force, it was the increasing intelligence evidence of German developments of long-range rockets and "Pilotless missiles" in 1943 and the first half of 1944 that was causing real concern and a bombing campaign against sites thought to be associated with these new weapons was initiated.

A V-1 gets its wings attached to the fuselage during the assembly process prior to launch from a site in France. RAF

As the bombing campaign against known and suspected sites thought to be associated with the development, production and employment of the V-1 was ramped up, the estimated date that an attack by these weapons against the UK could begin was continually put back. By January 1944, it was estimated that an attack would not be likely before March, and then this estimate was further put back to a point where it was thought possible that it could coincide with the assault phase of the planned landings in France by the Allied Armies massing in Britain. This possibility required a new plan of possible counters to the Flying Bombs to be drawn up, this time utilising only those "resources not directly required for the European Operations". This modified plan was known as the "Concurrent Air Defence Plan for 'Overlord' and 'Diver'", shortened to the "Overlord/Diver Plan", which was submitted at the end of February 1944, and approved, allowing it to be distributed to the various commands in early March. With a few "minor amendments", it was this plan that was put into effect when the Flying Bomb assault commenced in June 1944.

In the 'Overlord / Diver' Plan the first line of defence against the Flying Bombs was to be the fighter element of ADGB. The best piston engine fighters available were the Hawker Tempest V, North American North American Mustang III and the Supermarine Spitfire XIV. This Spitfire XIV was destroyed in a landing accident in October 1944. RAF

As with the earliest plans to counter the 'Diver' threat, confidence remained high of the "ability of our existing radar chain stations to detect pilotless aircraft in the same way as they could detect ordinary aircraft". Furthermore, it was considered that the radar chains would "be able to tell pilotless from piloted aircraft by 'track behaviour' – that is to say the characteristics of their flight as interpreted by their radar responses". It was also assumed that the Royal Observer Corp would be capable of differentiating pilotless aircraft from piloted aircraft "by their appearance and the noise they made".

While in theory the plan was for defence of all areas threatened, "the principal object... was the defence of London, which was the target threatened by the vast majority of the 'Ski Sites'" (this was the common description given to V-1 launch sites, due to the layout, which was thought to resemble a ski). The secondary object was the defence of Bristol "which was threatened by a smaller number of Ski sites near Cherbourg". A tertiary consideration was the "possibility that, as a counter-measure to our preparations for the European operations, pilotless aircraft might be used against assembly areas on the south coast, and particularly round the Solent".

The first line of defence was always considered to be fighter aircraft. "For the defence of London the arrangement envisaged in both plans was that whenever an attack in daylight seemed imminent, fighters of No.11 Group would patrol at 12,000 feet on three patrol lines, 20 miles off the coast between Beachy Head and Dover, over the coastline between Newhaven and Dover and between Hayward's Heath and Ashford respectively. Once an attack had begun, additional aircraft would patrol these lines at 6,000 feet. At night, fighters would patrol under the control of G.C.I., Type 16 and C.H.L. radar stations, and would be reinforced, if necessary, by further aircraft under sector control". The increased warning time and lighter scale of attack that was anticipated in the Bristol area led to the decision not to mount standing fighter aircraft patrols in the Bristol and Solent areas, although fighters would be held on alert to intercept reported 'Divers'.

The second line of defence depicted in the 'Overlord/Diver' plan was the guns serving with ADGB such as this RAF Regiment 40 mm Bofors emplacement, which formed part of the 'Diver' 'gun belt' in the Surrey/Kent area of South East England in summer 1944. As the campaign progressed and the guns were redeployed they gradually overtook the fighters as the primary means of destroying the V-1's. RAF

Both the original and the revised plan called for the positioning of heavy A.A. guns in folds and hallows on the southern slopes of the North Downs, where their radar equipment would be liable to minimum interference from "jamming" by the enemy. In addition, some 346 light AA guns were to be deployed "largely on searchlight sites" for the defence of London, but after the flying bomb attacks commenced this was altered and the light

AA guns were removed from the searchlight sites and positioned in front of the heavy AA gun belt. Four light AA guns would be linked to a heavy gun predictor and G.L. radar set, allowing the light AA guns to be used against "unseen as well as 'visual' targets".

Under the revised plan submitted in February 1944, the numbers of AA guns were significantly reduced due to the demands on the Overlord invasion plans. Under the original plan, large numbers of the AA guns, particularly light AA guns were to be drawn from 21 Army Group, but as the invasion date neared, this was no longer a practicable proposition, resulting in the new plan with reduced gun numbers. The heavy guns defending London were practically halved with each of the sites being reduced from eight to four guns, a reduction of 208 heavy AA guns. The proposal in the new plan also called for the number of light AA guns defending London to be reduced from 346 in the original plan to 246. The number of heavy AA guns defending Bristol remained at 96 in both plans, although the 216 light AA guns of the original plan was reduced to 36 in the revised plan, as many of the guns were required for 21 Army Group. The revised plan also proposed that Bristol "do without searchlights… other than those provided by the normal layout". The Solent was already well defended against air attack as the build up to the Overlord invasion increased, therefore, no additional AA defences, save a few searchlights were allocated to this area.

A balloon barrage would form the third line of defence for London. It was "originally proposed to put a permanent barrage of 480 balloons immediately behind the guns on the high ground between Cobham (Kent) in the east and Limpsfield in the west". At the time, Air Chief Marshal Hill was "already seeking authority from the Chiefs of Staff to reduce the balloon defences of the country by 500 balloons: by appropriating this saving to defence against pilotless aircraft the problem of providing the 'Diver' barrage could be solved". These surplus balloons were not required for Overlord; therefore, in the revised plan they were retained as an anti-'Diver' barrage.

A Barrage Balloon is raised to form part of the barrage at RAF Biggin Hill Kent. Balloons such as these formed the third line of defence under the Overlord/Diver plan. Once the guns had been re-deployed in mid-July, necessitating splitting the fighter zones, the Balloons then formed the fourth line of defence, although for operational reasons this was always referred to as the third line of defence. RAF

As A.D.G.B. awaited the commencement of the anticipated 'Diver' assault, it was clear that there were many causes for concern. One such concern was that if the 'Divers' flew "between 2,000 and 3,000 feet instead of at the greater altitude expected by the Air Ministry, the guns would have a very awkward task, for between those heights the targets would be too high for the light anti-aircraft guns and too low for the mobile heavy guns which at that time could not be traversed smoothly enough to engage such speedy missiles". As the campaign progressed some of the mobile heavy AA guns would be converted into fixed guns allowing them to more successfully engage fast targets at the lower altitudes.

Once the Flying Bomb campaign against southern Britain began in earnest, it was quickly realised that the 282 heavy and 282 light AA guns required in the revised plan and even the 528 heavy and 804 light AA guns required for the original defence plan would be woefully inadequate to meet the scale of attack. By the middle of August, when the campaign was at its height, no less than 800 heavy A.A. and 1,100 x 40-mm light/medium AA guns were employed, along with more than 700 rocket barrels and 600 light AA guns (mostly 20-mm calibre). The A.A.

weapons were manned by the Royal Air Force Regiment and the Royal Armoured Corp.

As well as organising the more conventional gun, balloon, fighter aircraft and radar defences against the 'Diver' threat, many other ideas were considered. For instance; it was considered "theoretically" possible that the V-1 Flying Bombs could be countered by "diverting them by means of an electro-magnetic field". Studies into its practicality found, however, that such a defensive system would have required "so much copper and electric power that it was quite impracticable", therefore, this idea was dropped. For the coming onslaught, ADGB would have to rely on the conventional defences used against manned aircraft. What would change, however, was the tactics that would be employed as the campaign progressed.

LXV Corp reported that the V-1 was ready to be deployed on operations on 20 May 1944, and this resulted in orders being issued from the Armed Forces Operations Staff to commence operations on 12 June. A report signed by General Heinmann on 14 June 1944, disclosed the authorised and actual strength of V-1 units on the eve of the commencement of the campaign on 12 June 1944, as the following:

	Authorised allowance	Actually on hand
V-1		
1st Battalion	192	240
2nd Battalion	192	240
3rd Battalion	192	192
4th Battalion	192	201

As can be seen from the above table, far from being depleted by air attacks, the firing units were actually 105 V-1's over the authorised establishment.

The German assault on southern Britain commenced just after midnight on the night of 12/13 June 1944. Ironically, it was not the new 'V' weapon that commenced this attack, but the long-range coastal guns. Although there was nothing new about these coastal guns opening fire on the British coast, this was the first and the only time during the war that they had shelled a town, which lay inland several miles from the coast. During this bombardment eight shells landed on Maidstone, a single shell landed at Otham (2 and a half miles south east of Maidstone) and twenty four landed at Folkestone. A Me.410, probably on a reconnaissance flight over London, was shot down near Barking during this initial phase of the renewed German assault on southern Britain.

The bombardment by German coastal guns continued until 04.00 hours and a few minutes later an aircraft, which made a "swishing sound", with a "bright glow from the rear", was reported by a ROC (Royal Observer Corp) post in Kent. Having been briefed on the Flying Bomb threat, the ROC post issued the report "Diver", and so commenced the Flying Bomb assault. This particular bomb flew on over the North Downs before going into its dive, hitting the ground and exploding at Swanscombe, near Gravesend at 04.18 hours on the morning of 13 June 1944.

A V-1 Flying Bomb dives on its target, London, after its flight from France. This bomb is falling on the Piccadilly District of London USAFM

Over the course of the next hour another 3 V-1's landed at Cuckfield, Bethnal Green and Platt (near Sevenoaks). Casualties were light, with nine people killed and nine injured at Bethnal. The most serious material damage was a railway bridge demolished.

Following this small scale attack in the early hours of 13 June, the V-1 attacks ceased until 22.30 hours on the night of 15 June, when a much heavier scale of attack commenced, with more than 200 Flying Bombs launched over the next 24 hours, 144 of which crossed the coasts of Kent and Sussex, with 73 of these reaching the Greater London area. A.D.G.B. claimed 33 Flying Bombs shot down, although eleven of these subsequently fell in the "built up area of Greater London". Of V-1's claimed shot down, 7 were claimed by fighters, 11 by guns and 1 by fighters and guns combined, outside the London area and 11 were claimed by guns inside the London area. It is possible that some of those brought down inside the London area were actually at the end of their flights and simply went into the terminal phase of their flights and struck the ground as planned.

On 16 June, orders were issued defining the areas for the fighter to patrol as "the Channel and the land between the coast and the southern limit of the gun-belt except when actually pursuing a flying bomb". It quickly became clear that in good weather conditions the fighters had a much higher rate of success than the static fixed ground defences. This was due to a number of factors, not least of which was the "fact that the flying bombs did not fly at the height of 6,000 or 7,000 feet previously estimated by the Air Ministry, but at the very height of 2,000 to 3,000 feet which we had always realised would make the gunners task more difficult". On the flip side, it was found that in poorer inclement weather conditions the guns would prove to be a more effective counter than fighter aircraft. This led to an order issued on 19 June "that in very good weather the guns would abstain from firing in order to give the fighters complete freedom of action. Conversely, when the weather was bad, the guns would have freedom of action and no fighters would be used. In middling weather fighters would operate in front of the gun belt and enter it only when pursuing a flying bomb. When a fighter entered the gun belt for this purpose the guns would of course withhold their fire; otherwise the guns inside the belt would be free to fire up to 8,000 feet. Outside the gun belt firing was prohibited in these circumstances, except that light A.A. gunners linked to the communications network might open fire on targets they could see, provided no fighters were about". This new set of 'Rules of Engagement' was issued to the various commands and units on 26 June 1944. The plan was to prevent "mutual interference between guns and fighters", although in this respect it did not have the planned effect.

In the immediate aftermath of the commencement of the flying-bomb attacks, the authorities deliberated for a period before ordering attacks on the modified launch sites. Although several sites were classified as having been put out of action, Air Marshall Hill made it clear that "the number remaining was always sufficient to have launched a scale of attack several times greater than that which we experienced". This indicated that the rate of launches was being dictated by another reason; most likely it was thought was the "rate at which the flying-bombs could be supplied to the sites". In the Air Marshalls words "It was therefore arguable that the attacks on the 'modified sites' amounted to locking the stable door after the horse had been stolen, and were a waste of effort". However, despite this, the authorities ordered the attacks to be continued, if for no other reason than to "harass the launching crews and thereby reduce their efficiency". Air Marshall Hill continued "I cannot say how far that object was achieved... The Germans have told us since the armistice, however, that the bombing of the 'modified sites' made little difference to them".

The scale of attack during the first two weeks was around 100 flying-bombs per day, with this scale being maintained until "the end of the first week in July, when the effort fell for about ten days to an average of less than 70 a day". After the first week of July when the scale of attack fell temporarily, it was thought that a "successful' attack on one of the flying-bomb main storage sites on 7 July was responsible, however, it was also acknowledged that this may well have been due to "good weather" as the German tactic was to save "their biggest efforts for days when the weather was likely to hamper the defences".

The improved weather in the second week of July favoured the fighter defences. However, roughly half the bombs that crossed the coast were still reaching the Greater London area.

In summary, for the five weeks up to 15 July it was calculated that "just fewer than 3,000 flying bombs came within the compass of the defensive system". Of this, the fighter defences had "shot down" slightly more than a tenth of the flying bombs over the sea, with a small number brought down by AA guns over the sea. This left around 2,500 flying bombs which went on to cross the coast. The combined defensive system of fighters, guns and balloons claimed roughly half of these "destroyed or brought down". Again, the fighter defences proved most successful, claiming ten bombs brought down for every four by the guns and every one claimed by the balloon defences.

Although the defences were increasing their effectiveness against the bombs, between 13 June and 15 July 1944, averages of 40 bombs a day were still getting through to their targets. During this period, around 3,000 people had been killed and 10,000 "seriously injured" and some 13,000 houses had been "irreparably damaged" as well as many public buildings. On the grand scheme of things, the scale of attack was small, much smaller than that experienced by conventional aircraft bombing in 1940/41, but for a public expecting victory within months the "intermittent drizzle of malignant robots seemed harder to bear than the storm and thunder of the "Blitz".

Although the defences had improved since the beginning of the campaign, by the middle of July it was noted that the "limit of improvement with our existing methods had been reached". The time had come for a sea change in the defensive tactics. By this stage of the campaign, it had been realised that the flying-bombs were faster than intelligence estimates had previously indicated. "Most of the bombs seem to have left the launching sites at about

200 m.p.h. Their speed increased throughout their flight, reaching 340 m.p.h. at the English coast and 400 m.p.h. or thereabouts over London". This presented problems for the fighters trying to intercept them as many lacked the speed to overhaul the bombs in level flight. During this period, known as first phase, the fastest fighters available to A.D.G.B. were a Wing of Supermarine Spitfire XIV's, and a wing of Hawker Tempest V's. To increase the numbers of fighters with high speeds at low altitudes, Air Marshal Hill obtained the loan of a flight (later increased to a wing) of North American Mustang III fighters from the Second Tactical Air Force operating in support of ground forces on the continent; these contributing to the effectiveness of the fighter defences "after the first week in July".

By 15 July, thirteen single engine fighter and nine twin-engine Mosquito squadrons were being employed against the Flying Bombs. Of this total, six of the Mosquito squadrons were also tasked with operations over the lodgement area in France in support of the Allied Armies embroiled in the Normandy operations. Four of them alternated between this work and anti-'Diver' patrols, while two of the Mosquito squadrons alternated between these two tasks and the additional task of bomber support.

The faster than anticipated speed of the flying-bombs was one of the most serious problems to overcome for intercepting them. An order was passed through that aircraft that were to be used "exclusively against flying bombs should be stripped of their armour and all unnecessary external fittings and that their paint should be removed and their outer surfaces polished. The engines were modified to use 150-octane fuel and accept a higher boost than usual. In this way we managed to increase the speed of some of the single-engine fighters by as much as 30 m.p.h."

The Tempest V powered by the Sabre 2A piston engine was capable of 372 mph at the flying bomb operating altitudes. To increase the speed, Boost was increased from +9 to +11 on 3 aircraft with 150 grade fuel. This resulted in speed being increased to 386 mph, an increase of 14 mph over unmodified aircraft. This led to the decision to modify one Flight in each of the Tempest squadrons employed on anti-'Diver' operations, with plans to modify all remaining aircraft if the tests proved successful. The Spitfire IX powered by the Merlin 66 piston engine was capable of a speed of 335 mph at the flying bomb operating altitude. To increase speed, Boost was increased from +18 to +25 with 150 grade fuel, resulting in speed being increased to 358 mph, an increase of 23 mph. The Spitfire XIV powered by the Griffon 65 was capable of 360 mph. Initially no modifications were introduced to this type as the engine was "cleared for operation at +21 boost with 150 grade fuel giving small increases in speed". The Spitfire XIV was to be modified later.

Although these modifications gave a modest, but welcome increase in speed, this only allowed a very small speed margin over the flying bombs and that had to be achieved by diving onto the target from a height advantage of several thousand feet. The Germans had been reasonably confident of the inability of the main fighter defences to intercept the flying bombs because of a reported demonstration of a captured Spitfire, which showed that the Spitfire could not catch the flying bomb. However, this demonstration was against earlier variants of the Spitfire and not against the variants that formed part of the ADGB. It was certainly true that a Spitfire V had no chance of intercepting a flying bomb at full speed and even the Spitfire IX was pushed to the very limit to catch the flying bombs, and interception was possible only by diving onto the target. However, the higher speeds of the Spitfire XIV, the Tempest V and the Mustang III allowed these aircraft to be successfully flown against the new weapons, albeit with only a small speed margin over their quarry, again by diving onto the target.

The radar chain normally gave around six minutes warning before a flying bomb crossed the coast, but the time delays for squadrons to be notified usually meant that this was reduced further. The problem of standing patrols was further complicated as it was undesirable to "risk our modified aircraft on the far side of the Channel where they might be surprised by German fighters". This time problem was eased slightly very late, almost at the end of the first phase of the campaign, when the Royal Navy introduced a "chain of small craft which operated at three mile intervals seven miles from the French coast, carrying observers who warned our pilots by means of signal rockets and star-shells that flying bombs were on their way".

Although the flying bombs were unable to "hit back deliberately", the operations against them were far from risk free. In the six weeks after the commencement of the campaign on 13 June 1944, eighteen fighter aircraft were seriously damaged, and five pilots and 1 navigator/radio operator killed by flying bombs exploding while being engaged by the aircraft.

Near the end of June, the AA defence was augmented by the delivery from the United States of S.C.R. 584 radar sets, which had been ordered many months before. These, along with improved predictors, enhanced the effectiveness of the gun defences, although the effects would take a while as personnel had to be trained in their use, a factor, hindered by the requirement for personnel to be released from operations for the training program. The Balloon barrage was slightly "re-distributed", mainly as a counter to bombs penetrating to the northern edge of the barrage "being brought down in built-up areas".

There were many conflicts between the gun defences and the fighter defences, with each claiming the other was hindering them and infringing the rules designed, in theory at least, to separate them. The high speed of the engagements between the flying bombs and fighters caused difficulties for some pilots who would fail to realise that they were fast approaching the gun belt, with the result that infringements were frequent. On the ground, the gunners had their own unique problems. Gunners busy engaging a flying bomb, sometimes were unaware that a fighter was "legitimately entering the belt in pursuit of this or another missile and would go on firing to the peril of the pilot…" The many infringements by both fighters and guns led to accusation and counter accusation and no small measure of animosity between commands.

A hazy image of a V-1 Flying Bomb taken from the gun camera of an RAF fighter seconds before the bomb was shot down. The haze is caused by the extreme heat from the exhaust flame of the V-1's pulse-jet engine. RAF

To try and reduce the friction between commands, Air Marshal Hill prohibited "fighters from entering the gun belt, whatever the circumstances", after 17 July. This order was passed on 10 July. A conference was held to discuss this and other possible changes. General pile proposed that all the guns should be in the "one place" inside the gun belt, which would then give the guns and fighters "clearly-defined spheres of operation". Air Marshal Hill agreed the logic of this proposal and that it should be examined further, with the exception that a few guns would remain at the coast acting as "marker". Having their own sphere of action would allow the guns complete freedom of action and allow training to be conducted in periods of no flying bomb activity, something which had not been possible while fighters were using the same operating areas as they. The negative in this plan was that there was a reduction in the "field of action open to the fighters".

After the redeployment of the guns along the coast the fighter zone was divided into two separate sections. The first fighter zone was a belt over the sea, which started just off the French coast and extended to the boundary of the gun belt, some 7 miles off the English coast. The second fighter zone covered the area behind the coastal gun belt reaching to the balloon barrage.

The new system was adopted and implemented and was completely operational by dawn on the 17th. Over the next six days, 473 flying bombs reached the defensive system, of which 204 got through to the Greater London area. Naturally this caused some concern as the number of bombs getting through to their targets in relation to the number of bombs reaching the defences was higher than it was during the last week that the old system had been in operation. The rate of flying bomb destruction by the guns had certainly improved as had the balloon barrage, which was now a denser concentration than under the old system. These were more than offset by the decreased rate of destruction by the fighters. However, Air Marshal Hill stated that the decline in shoot downs by fighters was "no more than I had expected". As an example of the increased performance of ground based defences over the fighters under this new system, 60 flying bombs were brought down "between sunset on the 20th and sunset on the 21st July". Of this number, the guns alone brought down 23 flying bombs, the balloon barrage brought down 17, the fighters brought down 19, whilst the fighters and guns brought down 1 shared. From this can been seen that the guns were bringing down more bombs than the fighters; with the latter only slightly ahead of the balloon barrage.

The justification for the gun-belt re-deployment came in the second week following the move. In this week, the combined defences brought down more flying bombs that reached the defensive zone than in any of the previous weeks since the commencement of the campaign. Of the bombs that reached the "compass" of the defences, slightly more than a quarter went on to their target, London. The performance of the fighters was much poorer the following week due to bad weather conditions. The gun-belt defences, however, continued to up their performance and for the first time since the campaign began, the guns "maintained a higher rate of destruction than the fighters over a full week".

In rough terms, a fighter trying to shoot down a V-1 travelling at roughly six miles a minute had to fly at roughly the same speed or higher, particularly in the case of the Meteors when they would be deployed, while operating at the same general height "across a narrow belt of undulating country bounded by balloons and guns". It should not be underestimated how difficult a target the flying bombs were for both fighters and guns. Despite flying straight and level, their high speed and operating altitude made it extremely difficult, particularly for the fighters who were in real peril if they entered the gun belt or did not break off in time to avoid the balloon barrage. Many flying bombs escaped destruction because of fighters having to break off as they neared the balloon barrage. Flying dead astern of the bomb, which all too often was the only way to engage a target flying at 400 plus miles per hour meant that the sighting view was often obscured by the haze from the V-1's pulse-jet engine. This distortion required several short bursts to allow for range aim corrections.

When the inland gun belt was abolished, the searchlights stayed, allowing them to assist night fighters operating against the 'Divers'.

As the campaign was developing in late July, the Germans varied tactics, sometimes salvo firing the bombs, along with launches from a new direction, the Low Countries. This led to Sir Charles Portal, at a meeting of the War Cabinet Chiefs of Staff Committee (C.O.S. (44) 247th Meeting (0) on 25 July 1944, stating that it was "desirable that an increased number of fighter squadrons should be allocated to flying bomb operations." If the Air Marshal Commanding ADGB required additional resources such as additional fighter squadrons, he first made his "representation" to the A.O.C.-in C. A.E.A.F., Air Chief Marshal Leigh Mallory, as it was here that the allocation of squadrons between A.D.G.B and Second Tactical Air Force operating over Normandy was decided. In the event that Leigh Mallory required "guidance" he could then "apply for a ruling to the Chiefs of Staff." Air Marshal Hill had previously stated that he had sufficient fighter resources, and with the infrastructure in place he "could not satisfactorily handle a larger number", which was pointed out by Sir Charles Portal.

The opinion of Mr Duncan Sandy's was that "defence against flying bombs would be improved by more fighters". He pointed to a "recent night when a number of bombs had been fired up the Thames Estuary, A.D.G.B. had only been able to keep a section of two aircraft in the air at any one time to deal with these bombs – a number which was insufficient to cover the area."

There was much debate about the lower numbers of bombs being shot down by fighters, which it was pointed out was in part attributable to poor weather conditions. However, it was also pointed out that the potential need for more fighters was not merely based on the fact that few bombs had been brought down in recent days, but more due to the fact that a larger area now had to be covered.

The preserved detachable wingtip of Meteor F Mk. I, EE216, which was the aircraft flown by Flying Officer Dean on 4 August 1944, when he destroyed a V-1 by tipping it over with his wingtip, sending the aptly named 'Diver' into the ground. The inscription on the wingtip reads 'On 4th August 1944, over S.E Kent, Flying Officer Dean of 616 Squadron, in Gloster Meteor I aircraft EE 216. destroyed a Flying Bomb by directing it into the ground with this wingtip.' Gloster Aircraft Company

As this argument was playing itself out, the Meteor Flight of No. 616 Squadron was busying itself to become operational, having received two non-operational Meteors for training on 12 July. The squadron then received a further five operational Meteor I's, which were delivered to RAF Manston, Kent on 23 July. Air Marshal Hill, fully aware of the Meteors high speed at low altitudes, was hopeful that this new weapon would further increase the effectiveness of the combined defences. He was, however, under no illusions, fully aware that the scale of contribution would be very small indeed due to a number of factors; the small number of Meteors available and the limited endurance by no means being the least of the problems. With the Meteor on the threshold of service, Air Marshal Hill stated later "I decided to match jet against jet by trying it out against the flying bomb. At first only a few of these aircraft were available, and various problems, including that of limited endurance, had to be overcome before we could get the full benefit out of the Meteors great speed".

The Meteors would be employed in the Inland operating area between the gun-belt and the balloon barrage. This negated the chance of their straying over enemy territory on the other side of Channel. The limited endurance of the Meteor meant that it was far better suited to operations over the Inland area as the fighters were much closer to landing grounds in case these were required in an emergency. As it was a new type just entering service, a certain amount of teething problems would naturally have been expected. The first claim for a V-1 brought down by Meteors was recorded on 4 August, when F/O Dean used his wingtip to tip the V-1 over; sending it diving to the ground after his cannon had jammed.

Under the new system, it was estimated around mid-August that regardless of weather conditions the defences would be capable of shooting down between half to three quarters of all flying bombs that entered the defensive system. In the last three weeks of the first phase of the flying bomb campaign when many of the launch areas had been captured by 21st Army Group on the continent, only a single bomb out of every seven launched actually reached their target area, London. By the end of August, "only an occasional bomb eluded the defences and got through to its target". The last flying bomb launched from a site in France came over on 31 August 1944, following which there was a lull.

Just before this lull there had been a flurry of activity and on 28 August, the combined defences had one of the most successful days of operations against the flying bombs. Ninety seven bombs approached the coast, of which 90 were claimed destroyed by the defences, with only four of the remaining seven reaching London. The statistics for bombs destroyed on this date were: 13 shot down by fighters over the sea; 10 shot down by fighters over land; 46 shot down by guns over the sea; 19 shot down by guns over land and only 2 brought down by balloons, as very few bombs were actually making it as far as the balloon barrage. The days figure for bombs shot down over land included one flying bomb shot down by two No. 616 squadron Meteor I's, each claiming half a kill.

Of the 28 August operations, Air Marshal Hill wrote in his Despatch, "Flying towards the south coast on 28 August, I could see over Romney Marsh a wall of black smoke marking the position of the 'Diver' barrage. From time to time a fresh salvo would be added to repair the slow erosion of the wind. On the far side of the barrage fighters were shooting down flying bombs into the Channel; on the nearer side more fighters waited on its fringe to pounce on the occasional bomb that got so far. The whole was as fine a spectacle of co-operation as any commander could wish to see".

Attacks from flying bombs air launched from converted Luftwaffe Heinkel He.III twin-engine bombers operating from bases in Holland had been identified as early as 9 July 1944. These bombs, which came in from the East necessitated a further re-organisation of the gun defences with a "gun box" situated in the "quadrilateral Rochester-Whitstable-Clacton-Chelmsford", area. This consisted of 208 heavy, 178 40 mm, 404 20 mm guns and 108 rocket barrels being redeployed by mid-August. The balloon barrage was also extended to Gravesend and standing air patrols over the mouth of the Thames were instigated. From 9 July until the end of August, 120 air launched flying bombs were recorded as approaching the defences from the East. Following the lull from the 31st August to the early hours of 5 September, a further nine bombs were recorded as approaching the coast from the East. This effectively marked the end of the first phase of the flying bomb campaign against Britain.

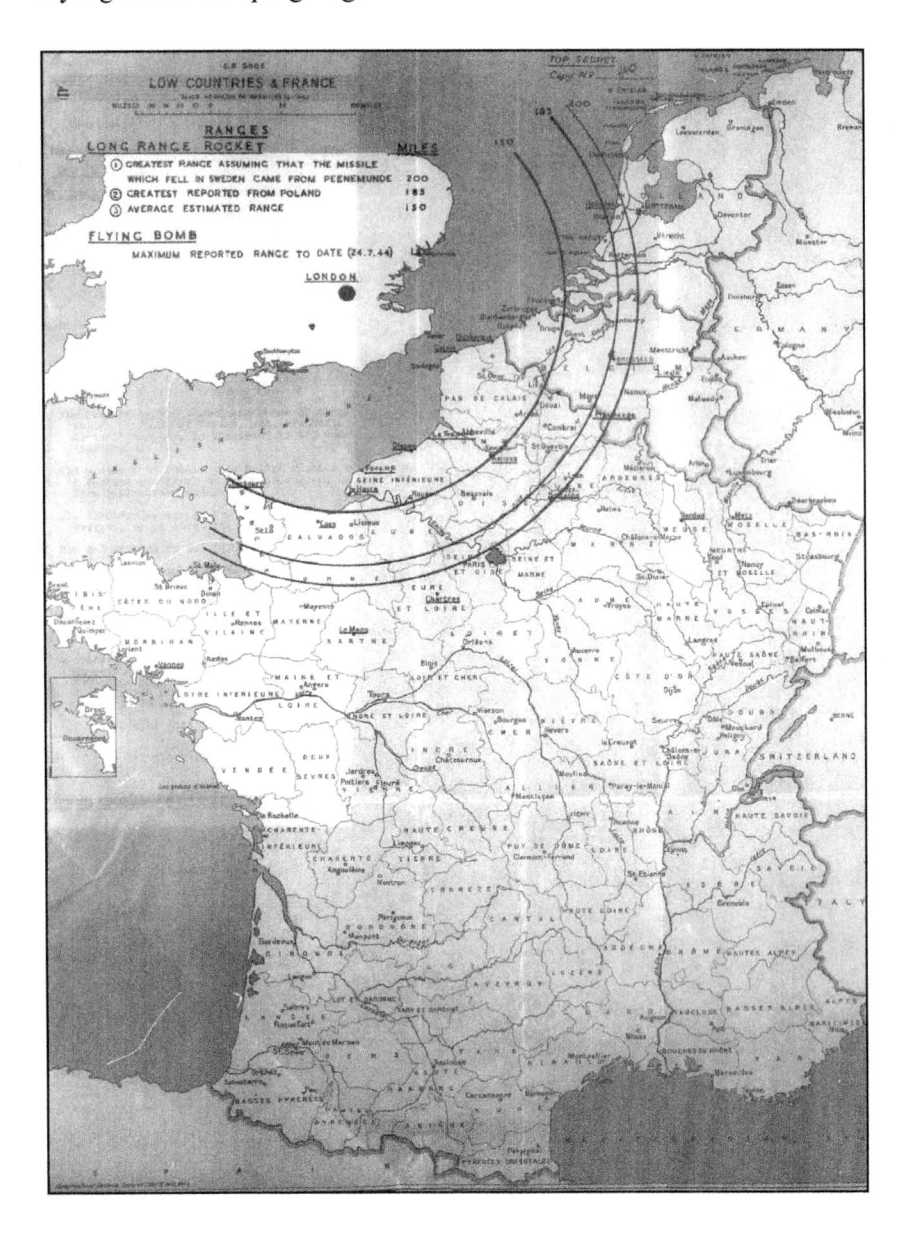

Operational map showing the estimated operational ranges of V-1 Flying Bombs and the anticipated Long Range Rocket (the V-2 ballistic missile, which commenced operations against Britain in September 1944) and their respective estimated operational radius in France and the Low Countries from their main target, London. This appreciation of the situation is dated 24th July 1944.

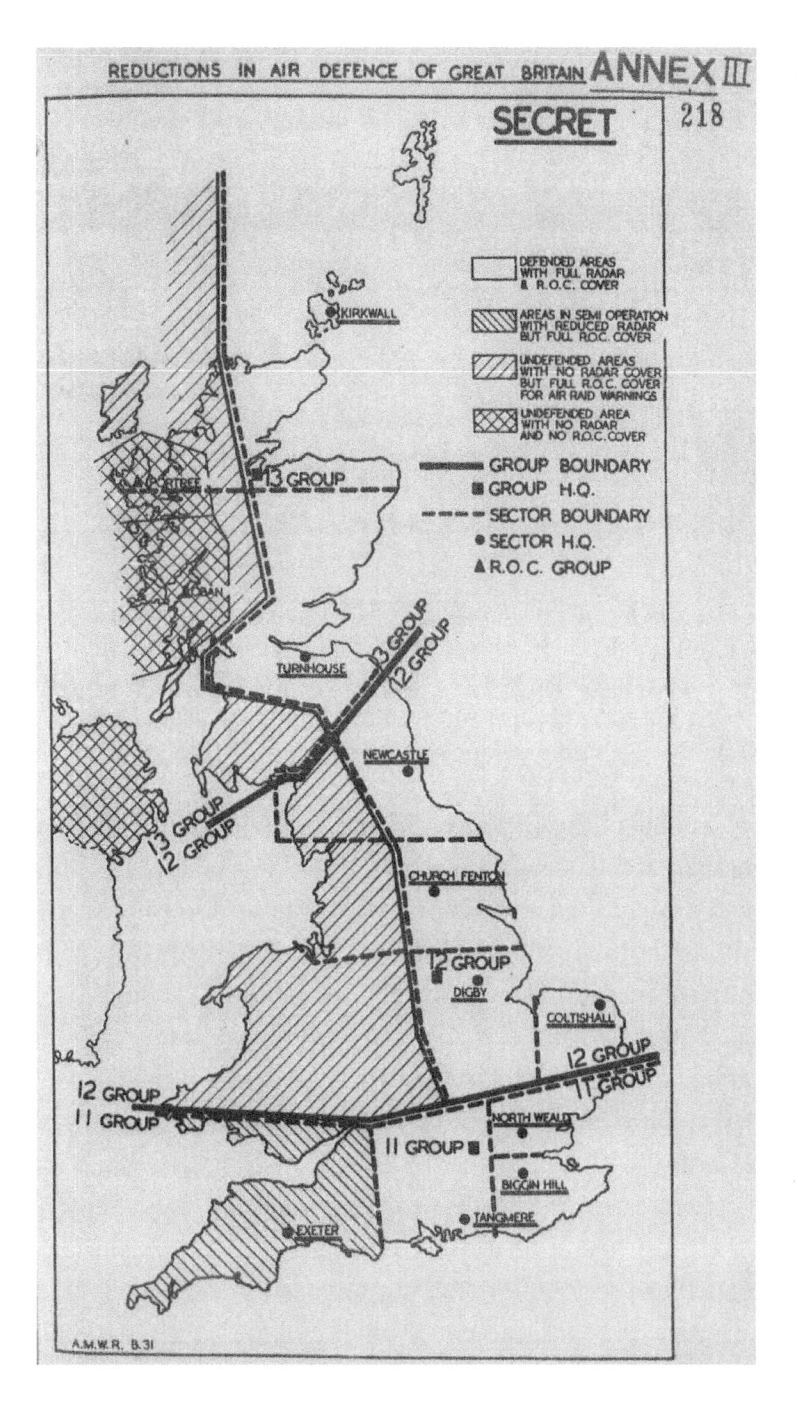

This map shows the planned reductions in the Air Defence of Great Britain following the end of the First Phase of the V-1 campaign in September 1944. The map also shows the boundaries of the various Groups, with 11 Group, which included the Meteors of No. 616 Squadron outlined in the bottom right of the map.

The Luftwaffe began air launching V-1's from converted He.III bombers from 9 July 1944. These launches were mainly confined to the hours of darkness, therefore, the Meteors of 616 Squadron were not tasked with countering this threat, which was on a much reduced scale compared with that from the V-1's ground launched from France. USAFM

The second phase of the campaign, which commenced on 16 September and lasted until 14 January 1945, was on a much reduced scale compared with the first phase, due to the fact that the flying bombs now had to be air launched from aircraft operating from Germany, with night launchings proving to be the safest option for the Luftwaffe crews tasked with these operations. The first attack from this new phase commenced in the early hours of 16 September 1944, with the first bomb falling in Essex at 05.49 hours. No.616 Squadron with their Meteors had been released from 'Anti-Diver' operations in early September, with their last operational 'Anti-Diver' sorties of this phase being conducted on the 3rd of the month.

The Third Phase commenced on 3 March 1945, with Flying Bombs launched from ramps in Holland. The Germans built a few launch sites in South-West Holland. Two sites were identified, one at Ypenburg near the Hague and one at Vlaardingen, 6 miles to the west of Rotterdam. A third site was also built near the Delftsche Canal, but initial reconnaissance failed to spot this site, whose existence was not known until later.

To counter this new threat, the gun defences between the Isle of Sheppey and Orfordness were to be augmented by the addition of 96 heavy AA guns and a number of batteries that were still undergoing training were to be allocated to the northerly part of the "strip" from where the 96 heavy AA guns were to be taken from. The new dispositions were ordered on 27 February 1945, with nine of the twelve batteries in position by 6 March. Only one more battery was actually deployed due to the low scale of the attack that actually materialised.

The fighter defences allocated to counter the new threat consisted of six Mustang III squadrons, one Tempest squadron and 2 Mosquito squadrons for night defence and No.616 squadron with its Meteor III's. Air Marshal Hill had to arrange for No.616 squadron with its Meteors to be borrowed from Second Tactical Air Force for which they had been allocated and were about to depart for the continent. Indeed, the ground elements had already embarked and reached Ostend before being returned to RAF Andrews Field in southern England, the base from which No.616 squadron was to operate against the flying bombs.

For day fighter defence the Meteors of 616 Squadron along with three Mustang squadrons were to patrol the area between the guns and London, while the other three Mustang squadrons would patrol forward of the guns. At night, the two Mosquito squadrons were to be used for patrols over the sea, while the Tempest squadron would patrol behind the guns. To increase the chance of bombs being detected in time to be intercepted a direct link was set up between the home defences and the radar stations of the Second Tactical Air Force in Belgium, in order to increase the warning time of bombs approaching the defences from the direction of the Scheldt.

This new phase of the flying bombs attacks on Britain commenced in the early hours of the morning of 3 March 1945, and the first of the bombs that got through the defences impacted at Bermondsey at 03.01 hours. The six continuing bombs later that morning were all destroyed by the gun defences with five of the six exploding in the air while the sixth fell into the sea.

Following a lull of some nine hours the attacks began again that afternoon and continued "intermittently" with ten bombs through the day and up to noon on the 4th. Of these ten bombs, four were destroyed by the gun defences and only two reached their target, London. Another lull followed, ending in the late morning of the 5th. From then until the attacks ceased on 29 March, there were a number of periods of bomb activity, which would be followed by periods of no activity. The success of the defences in this particular phase belonged first and foremost to the guns. Of the 125 bombs which approached the area of the defences during this phase, 87 were shot down by the guns, one of which was shot down by the shore based guns and the Royal Navy jointly. The fighter defences claimed only four flying bombs during this phase, none of which were claimed by the Meteors of No.616 squadron. Only thirteen bombs actually reached their targets during this last phase of the flying bomb campaign against southern Britain.

The success of the gun defences, combined with the light scale of attack, allowed Air Marshal Hill to relinquish five of the six Mustang squadrons and 616 Squadron with its Meteor III's, allowing the latter to prepare for its imminent deployment to the continent where it would join the Second Tactical Air Force.

The V-1 launch site at Vlaardingen was attacked by Typhoons of the Second Tactical Air Force on 23 March 1945, while the launch site at Ypenburg was attacked by Spitfire fighter-bombers from Fighter Command on 20 and 23 March 1945.

The end phase of the flying bomb campaign against Britain came with a series of intermittent launches between 21.30 on 28 March and 'lunch-time' on 29 March, during which 21 bombs approached the defences, with 20 of these being shot down and the remaining bomb landing at Datchworth, a village located around seven miles from London Bridge. This bomb being distinctive in that it was the last V-1 to land in Britain during World War II.

Attempts have been made to compare the performance, in regards to numbers of V-1's claimed shot down, of the Meteor I with those of the Spitfire, Tempest V and Mustang III. However, such a comparison is simply not capable of providing an objective outcome. The Spitfire and Tempest were operating from the beginning of the offensive in mid-June right through until the end of the first phase in early September, while the Mustang's were operating against the bombs in numbers from early July, continuing operations right through until the end of the first phase. Of the Tempest V squadrons, No. 3 Squadron alone is credited with 288 V-1's destroyed during the first phase of the campaign. The Meteor I did not fly its first operational patrol until 27 July, and was, therefore, flying operational sorties for less than half the period of the piston engine fighters. Furthermore, the Spitfire, Tempest V and Mustang III were operating in Wing Strength, while the Meteors were operating at little more than Flight Strength by the beginning of September. Although it had relinquished its Spitfire VII's on 13 August, there were not enough Meteor I's available to operate at Squadron strength. Lastly, but by no means least is the fact that the Meteors operated only over the inland fighter zone between the gun belt on the coast and the balloon barrage. This meant that there was only small numbers of potential targets getting through to their operating area, which was shared by the piston engine fighters. Most of the ADGB fighter claims against flying bombs during the period the Meteors were operational were claimed by piston engine fighters over the English Channel fighter zone ahead of the gun belt. While the Meteors flew 260 operational sorties, the sortie numbers for all piston engine fighters were numbered in the several thousands.

What is clear is the fact that Meteors were able to overhaul and shoot down V-1's after Tempest V and Mustang III's were forced to break off through lack of speed. This fact alone shows that the Meteor was more capable of intercepting a V-1 under operational conditions, than were its piston engine counterparts.

There were three distinct phases of the V-1 campaign, although Phase I is divided into Phase I (a) and Phase I (b). The total number of flying bombs reported for all four phases between 12.6.44 and 29.3.45 was 7,488 of which 2,420 got through to the target area.

The table below "summarises the progress of the campaign and its results achieved by the defences in its various phases".

	Phase 1 (a) 12/6–15/7/44	*Phase 1* (b) 16/7–5/9/44	*Phase 2* 16/9/44–14/1/45	*Phase 3* 3/3–29/3/45	*Total* 12/6/44–29/3/45
(i) No. of bombs reported	2,934	3,791	638	125	7,488
(ii) No. of bombs in target area ...	1,270	1,070	67	13	2,420
(iii) Percentage of (ii) to (i)	43·3	28·5	10·5	10·4	32·3
(iv) No. of bombs brought down					
(*a*) by fighters	924 1/3*	847	71 1/2	4	1,846 5/6
(*b*) by guns	261 1/3	1,198 1/2	331 1/2	87	1,878 1/3
(*c*) by balloons	55 1/3	176 1/2	—	—	231 5/6
(*d*) by all arms	1,241	2,222	403	91	3,957
(v) Percentage of (iv) (*d*) to (i)	42·3	58·6	63·2	72·8	52·8

* The fractions relate to claims shared between different arms of the defence.

The tables below are taken from various War Cabinet 'Crossbow Committee Meeting' documents such as C.B.C. (44) 22, 15TH JULY. 1944, from which the first table is taken.

War cabinet
"CROSSBOW COMMITTEE"
"CROSSBOW"

ANNEX A

24 hr. period ending 0600 hours.	Estimated number of bombs launched	Brought down by Fighters	Brought down by Guns	Brought down by Balloons	Total brought down.	Incidents in London.
		(Figures in brackets show percentage of number launched).				
July 9th	81	38 (47%)	7 (9%)	1 (1%)	46 (57%)	22 (27%)
July 10th	89	38 (43%)	5 (6%)	2 (2%)	45 (51%)	31 (35%)
July 11th *	83 (27)	18 (22%)	7 (8%)	2 (2%)	27 (33%)	19 (34%)
July 12th *	116 (24)	27 (23%)	13 (11%)	6 (5%)	46 (40%)	31 (34%)
July 13th	137	58 (42%)	17 (12%)	7 (5%)	82 (60%)	44 (32%)
July 14th *	73 (22)	19 (26%)	6 (8%)	2 (3%)	27 (37%)	17 (33%)
July 15th *	59 (18)	23 (39%)	3 (5%)	1 (2%)	27 (46%)	12 (29%)
Daily average for 6 days ending -						
June 24th	107	38 (36%)	8 (8%)	5 (5%)	52 (48%)	41 (38%)
Daily average for week-ending						
July 1st	121	36 (30%)	18 (15%)	1 (1%)	55 (46%)	43 (36%)
July 8th	128	45 (35%)	11 (9%)	4 (3%)	60 (47%)	52 (41%)
July 15th	91 (13)	32 (35%)	8 (9%)	3 (3%)	43 (47%)	25 (32%)

* On these dates FLY were launched against the PORTSMOUTH - SOUTHAMPTON area. The numbers so launched are given in brackets, and the percentage incidents in LONDON have been based on the estimated number aimed at LONDON.

ANNEX A

24 hour period ending 0600 hours	Estimated No. of bombs launched	Persons killed #	Bombs brought down by Defences + Fighters	Guns	Balloons	Total	Incidents in London+	Approximate tonnage of bombs dropped France and Belgium Fly targets	Rocket targets	Targets in Germany	Total on all targets
July 16th ∅	65	29	12 (18)	7 (11)	3 (5)	22 (34)	23 (35)	1,200	0	0	1,200
July 17th ∅	63	53	20 (32)	1 (2)	1 (2)	22 (35)	25 (40)	100	0	0	100
July 18th	37	21	9 (26)	7 (19)	3 (8)	19 (51)	10 (43)	950	150	0	1,000
July 19th	85	56	22 (26)	5 (6)	6 (7)	33 (39)	30 (42)	200	0	950	1,150
July 20th	136	49	53 (40)	18 (13)	3 (2)	74 (55)	41 (31)	700	0	250	950
July 21st	90	50	21 (23)	11 (12)	4 (5)	36 (40)	39 (45)	950	600	0	1,550
July 22nd	207	80	10 (5)	31 (15)	13 (6)	54 (26)	66 (32)	0	0	0	0

Daily Average for week ending:

June 24th	107	130	38 (36)	8 (8)	5 (5)	52 (48)	41 (38)	1,100	100	0	1,200
July 1st	121	119	36 (30)	12 (15)	1 (1)	55 (46)	43 (36)	1,300	350	0	1,650
July 8th	128	136	45 (35)	11 (9)	4 (3)	60 (47)	52 (41)	1,450	250	0	1,700
July 15th ✱	91 (13)	76	32 (35)	8 (9)	3 (3)	43 (47)	25 (32)	750	0	0	750
July 22nd	97	62	21 (22)	11 (12)	5 (5)	37 (38)	35 (36)	600	100	150	850

NOTES:
+ The figures in brackets in Columns (4) - (8) show percentage of number launched
# Up to date about 95% of the fatal casualties have occurred in London
∅ During these days the guns were in course of re-deployment
✱ During this week a number of flying bombs were launched against the PORTSMOUTH-SOUTHAMPTON area. The numbers so launched are given in brackets, and the percentage incidents in LONDON have been based on the estimated number aimed at LONDON.

ANNEX

24 hour period ending 0600 hours	Estimated No. of Bombs Launched	Persons Killed #	Bombs brought down by Defences + Fighters	Guns	Balloons	Total	Incidents in London+	Approximate tonnage of bombs dropped France and Belgium Fly Targets	Rocket Targets	Targets in Germany	Total on all Targets
July 23rd	156	30	48 (31)	28 (18)	8 (5)	84 (54)	36 (23)	150	0	0	150
July 24th	93	59	36 (41)	13 (14)	2 (2)	53 (57)	21 (23)	550	0	0	550
July 25th	62	61	13 (21)	7 (11)	3 (5)	23 (37)	23 (37)	300	0	0	300
July 26th	46	4	17 (37)	8 (17)	3 (7)	28 (61)	8 (20)	700	100	0	800
July 27th	107	25	54 (50)	23 (25)	6 (6)	83 (77)	18 (17)	0	0	0	0
July 28th	151	79	40 (26)	23 (15)	3 (2)	66 (43)	56 (37)	200	0	0	200
July 29th	119	91	32 (27)	35 (29)	3 (2)	70 (58)	37 (31)	1,000	0	0	1,000

Daily Average for Period 12th-25th June: 105 | 110 | 22 (21) | 11 (10) | 3 (3) | 36 (34) | 36 (34) | 1,100 | 100 | 0 | 1,200

Daily Average for week ending 0600 hours:

July 1st	121	120	36 (30)	14 (11)	1 (1)	51 (42)	43 (36)	1,300	350	0	1,650
July 8th	128	136	45 (34)	8 (6)	4 (3)	55 (43)	52 (41)	1,450	250	0	1,700
July 15th ✱	91 (13)	75	31 (34)	7 (8)	3 (3)	41 (45)	25 (32)	750	0	0	750
July 22nd	97	62	21 (23)	12 (12)	5 (5)	39 (40)	35 (36)	600	100	0	650
July 29th	105	60	35 (33)	20 (19)	4 (4)	59 (56)	29 (28)	300	100	(10)	350

Total since start of Attack: 4,995 | 4,441 | 1,414 (27) | 544 (12) | 149 (3) | 2,132 (43) | 1,716 (34) | 42,000 | 7,000 | 1,000 | 50,000

NOTES:
+ Figures in brackets show percentage of number launched.
✱ Figures in brackets show number aimed at PORTSMOUTH and SOUTHAMPTON. The percentage in LONDON is based on estimated number aimed at LONDON.
Up to date about 95 per cent of fatal casualties have occurred in London.

---

24 Hour Period Ending 0600 Hours	Estimated Number of Bombs Launched	Persons Killed#	Bombs brought down by Defences+ Fighters	Guns	Balloons	Total	Incidents in London+	Launching Sites & Airborne Launching Bases	Supply	Production	Total on all Crossbow Targets
Sat. Aug 19th	35	2	8 (23)	21 (60)	1 (3)	30 (86)	3 (9)	200	850	0	1,050
Sun. " 20th	78	2	23 (29)	40 (51)	2 (3)	65 (83)	7 (9)	0	0	0	0
Mon. " 21st	118	24	15 (13)	39 (33)	1 (1)	55 (47)	26 (22)	0	0	0	0
Tue. " 22nd	128	61	1 (1)	20 (39)	10 (8)	61 (48)	24 (19)	0	0	0	0
Wed. " 23rd	70	29	9 (0)	25 (36)	2 (3)	27 (39)	13 (21)	0	0	0	0
Thu. " 24th	59	33	14 (14)	38 (57)	0 (0)	70 (71)	15 (15)	0	0	0	0
Fri. " 25th	136	33	11 (8)	65 (48)	0 (0)	76 (56)	27 (20)	0	0	250	250

Daily Average for week ending:

June 30th	117	145	36 (31)	15 (13)	2 (1)	53 (45)	42 (36)	1,200	450	0	2,000
July 7th	134	154	31 (30)	7 (5)	5 (3)	52 (39)	57 (42)	500	1,100	0	1,850
July 14th	101	79	36 (36)	7 (7)	3 (3)	46 (46)	29 (29)	400	450	150	850
July 21st	76	52	22 (29)	8 (10)	3 (4)	33 (43)	27 (36)	400	250	0	900
July 28th	117	64	29 (25)	19 (16)	5 (4)	53 (45)	33 (28)	300	0	0	300
Aug 4th	126	93	20 (16)	26 (21)	6 (5)	52 (42)	42 (33)	300	1,250	100	1,250
Aug 11th	87	30	21 (25)	20 (23)	5 (6)	58 (54)	17 (19)	250	900	150	1,250
Aug 18th	91	31	17 (19)	38 (42)	3 (3)	50 (54)	13 (14)	250	0	50	750
Aug 25th	95	37	10 (11)	42 (44)	2 (2)	54 (57)	17 (18)	50	100	0	200

Since Start of Attack:

Daily Average: 104 | 77 | 25 (24) | 19 (18) | 4 (4) | 47 (45) | 31 (30) | 430 | 500 | 50 | 1,000
Total: 7,664 | 5,688 | 1,840 | 1,382 | 269 | 3,491 | 2,314 | 30,000 | 36,700 | 3,350 | 75,200

Notes:
+ Figures in brackets show percentage of number launched.
∅ During these weeks a number of bombs were aimed at PORTSMOUTH. These reduced the incidents in LONDON.
Up to date about 92 per cent of fatal casualties have occurred in LONDON. The weekly casualty figures are based upon the latest revised information and do not therefore tally with the daily returns.

C.B.C. (44) 31 (0)

24TH JULY, 1944

WAR CABINET
CROSSBOW COMMITTEE

Scale of Attack

2.   The average number of bombs dropped each day on London during the last 5 weeks has been as follows:-

Week ending	No. of bombs
24th June	45
1st July	43
8th July	52
15th July	25
22nd July	35

3.   The number of bombs launched during the early part of the week has been very small. However, during the last three days the scale of attack was stepped up sharply. During the 24 hour period ending 0600 hours on 22nd July over 200 bombs were launched. Of these 66 reached London. This is the second heaviest attack we have sustained since the start of the bombardment.

4.   There have been further attacks on Portsmouth and Southampton.

5.   There are indications from intelligence sources that the enemy's policy is to take advantage of periods of bad weather, during which the operation of our defences is restricted, in order to intensify the weight of his attack.

6.   During the past week 387 persons have been killed and 1,300 seriously injured. Total casualties since the start of the bombardment have been approximately as follows:-

Killed	4,000
Seriously injured	14,000
Houses irreparably damaged	15,000

7.   Of the fatal casualties about 95 per cent have occurred in the London area.

<u>C.B.C. (44) 69</u>

28TH AUGUST, 1944

WAR CABINET
CROSSBOW COMMITTEE
FIFTEENTH REPORT BY THE CHAIRMAN
FLYING BOMB

This report refers to the seven days period ending 6.a.m. on 25th August.

Scale of Bombardment

The attached table shows in broad outline the scale of recent bomb attacks on London and the degree of success achieved by our defences.

The daily average number of bombs which has fallen in the London Region during each of the last nine weeks has been as follows:-

Week ending:		
	30th June	42
	7th July	57
	14th "	29
	21st "	27
	28th "	33
	4th August	42
	11th "	17
	18th "	13
	25th "	17
Since start of bombardment:		31

The rate of launchings is slightly above the level of the previous week. However, in spite of cloudy weather which interfered seriously with the operation of fighters and balloons, the percentage of incidents in London remained comparatively low. This was in the main due to a still further improvement in the performance of the anti-aircraft guns, which destroyed some 42 flying bombs per day.

Casualties

During the week under review some 260 persons have been killed and 940 seriously injured. This compares with a weekly average of 550 and 1,600 respectively since the start of the bombardment. The total casualties up to date have been approximately as follows:-

Killed	5,700
Seriously injured	16,600
Slightly injured	22,200
Houses irreparably damaged	23,500

Launchings from the East

Airborne launchings from the East have started again on a light scale. On the night of 21st/22nd August, when the weather over our bases prevented the operation of intruders and night fighters, a small number of flying bombs was launched from the Ostend area. One bomb was shot down by the guns. Of the remainder, three landed in London.

Defences

During the week 384 flying bombs were brought down by the combined defences. This is 57 per cent of those launched and compares with 64 per cent in the previous week. In view of the unfavourable weather conditions with which the defences had to contend, this small fall in the percentage destroyed is not unsatisfactory.

The anti-aircraft guns accounted for 296 flying bombs, which is about three quarters of the total destroyed. This is the highest result yet attained and shows that, even under conditions of low cloud which necessitates unseen fire, the guns can be relied upon to maintain the highest standard of performance previously achieved.

The table below shows the number of flying bombs entering each of the successive defence belts and the proportion brought down by the various arms:

	Bombs entering the respective Defence belt	Brought down	
Fighters over sea	538	25	(5%)
Guns in coastal belt	513	296	(58%)
Fighters over land	217	47	(22%)
Balloon barrage	155	16	(10%)

Changes in Deployment

The advance of our armies up to the Seine has forced the enemy progressively to reduce the scale of attack from the sites south of the Somme, and there now seems little likelihood that flying bombs will any longer be launched from this area.

It has, therefore, been decided to withdraw the defences from the western ends of the coastal gun belt and of the balloon barrage. The guns and balloons thus released are being used to extend the defence system further to the east and to increase the density throughout.

(Signed)   DUNCAN SANDYS

Offices of the War Cabinet, S.W.1.

28TH AUGUST 1944

C.O.S. (44) 795 (0)
2ND SEPTEMBER, 1944

WAR CABINET
CHIEFS OF STAFF COMMITTEE
CROSSBOW

Twenty-first Report by Assistant Chief of Air Staff (Intelligence)

FLYING BOMBS

Launching Sites

12   In view of the quickly changing military situation it is impossible at present to give an exact picture of the launching site position, although it is clear that the enemy has abandoned all sites South of the Bresle and probably also those between the Bresle and the Somme. North of the Somme it is believed that there are at present 20 launching sites in an operational condition and recently accumulated evidence has tended to confirm that previous estimates of availability of sites has been extremely accurate.

Scale of Effort

13   The total of flying bombs launched since the attacks began is now approximately 7,800 according to Radar evidence. An accumulation of Ground and P/W. reports, however, strongly suggest that a considerable proportion of the bombs launched are either misfires or so erratic that they may never appear as Radar tracks. There is now firm evidence that actual launchings are about 10% in excess of those recorded by Radar.

14. During the fortnight ending at 0600 hours on 30.8.44 there was a further decline in the average daily scale of effort as compared with the two previous fortnightly periods. The average for the period under review amounted to 90 launchings per day.

15. There are two noticeable features in the activity during the fortnight. In the first place there was a marked tendency to concentrate attack during the daylight period and over 80 percent of the launchings were made during the daylight hours (0600 to 2100). Secondly, activity was more sporadic than in previous weeks. There were several periods of inactivity of which one extended for as long as 40 hours and another for approximately 30 hours. The policy of launchings in salvoes is still being pursued and as many as 32 flying bombs were recorded in a half hour period.

Offices of the War Cabinet
        S.W.1.,
2ND SEPTEMBER.1944

Extract from:

C.O.S. (44) 298th Meeting (0).
WAR CABINET
CHIEFS OF STAFF COMMITTEE.
5TH SEPTEMBER, 1944, at 10.30 am.

C.O.S. (44) 795 (0) AND 806 (0)
(Previous Reference: C.O.S. (44) 297th Meeting (0), Minute (5)

The only threat which would remain after the next few days was that of flying bombs launched by aircraft. It was therefore doubtful if we were justified in retaining the number of fighter squadrons now employed in the "CROSSBOW" defences or the effort involved in maintaining radar watches for the rocket.

C.O.S. (44) 809 (0)

5TH SEPTEMBER, 1944

WAR CABINET
CHIEFS OF STAFF COMMITTEE
FLYING BOMB

Draft Statement to the Press by the Joint Parliamentary Secretary, Ministry of Supply

FIGHTER ZONES

39.　During the first few weeks of the flying bomb attacks, the fighters operated in a single zone stretching over sea and land from off the French coast right up to the gun belt. During this period the fighters shot down over 1,000 flying bombs. This represents nearly 30 per cent of the number launched.

40.　When the guns were redeployed along the coast, the fighter zone was divided into two parts. There was a sea belt extending from off the French coast as far as the forward boundary of the gun belt about 7 miles out from the English coast. Behind the gun belt there was a second fighter zone stretching as far as the balloon barrage.

41.　This redeployment gave the guns much greater scope and led to an improvement in the overall results of the combined defences. On the other hand, it restricted the opportunities of the fighters. So many bombs were shot down by the guns on the coast that the number of targets presented to the fighters inland was much reduced. This is the main reason for the falling off in fighter results since the redeployment in the middle of July.

PROBLEM OF HIGH SPEED INTERCEPTION

42. In the battle against the flying bomb, our fighters were faced with a number of difficulties. The first was the speed of the bombs. Only our fastest fighters possess the high speed needed to overtake the bomb in level flight. The other types, in order to obtain an interception, had to dive onto the bomb from several thousand feet above. The problem of exactly hitting off the correct angle of dive was a very difficult one and could only be mastered with experience.

43. Fighter defence against ordinary bomber aircraft has usually relied upon scrambling the aircraft off the ground on receipt of the warning. However, the flying bomb travelled too fast for this to be possible. In consequence, it was necessary to maintain constant standing patrols by day and by night, over land and sea, in readiness for any bombs that might come over.

44. In times of intense activity, between 30 and 40 aircraft had to be continuously in the air. This off course placed a great strain on both pilots and machines.

SPOTTING THE BOMB

45. Another awkward problem was that of seeing the bomb at all. Pilots on patrol had the greatest difficulty in spotting this very small, fast moving object several thousand feet below. Over land, help could be given to the pilots by means of a running commentary over the radio telephone telling them where the bomb was in relation to various landmarks.

46. So far as the fighters over land were concerned, any remaining difficulties of this kind disappeared when the guns were redeployed along the coast. The bursts of ant-aircraft fire over the gun belt showed the pilots clearly where the bombs were and enabled them to dive on to those which had not been shot down.

FIGHTER RESULTS

51.   In the last 2½ months it has been unusually wet and cloudy for the time of year. This has made the work of the fighters more difficult. Nevertheless, since the start of the bombardment our fighter aircraft have brought down over 1,900 flying bombs. This is a very fine achievement, of which Air Marshal Sir Roderic Hill and Fighter Command have good reason to be proud.

52.   Hitler will be painfully disillusioned, if he is still capable of disillusionment, when he hears how well our fighters have done. Some time ago a special trial was arranged for him in the Baltic. A German fighter ace flying a captured Spitfire demonstrated to the satisfaction of the Fuhrer that British fighters did not possess the necessary speed to intercept the flying bomb. They reckoned without the increased efficiency of our latest types and overlooked the superior skill and resource of our pilots.

RESULTS OF COMBINED DEFENCES

57.   During the 80 days of the bombardment the enemy has launched over 8,000 bombs, that is to say about 100 a day. Of these, some 2,300 (29 per cent) got through into the London Region.

58.   These figures do not include the many bombs which came to grief in France. Even of the bombs launched some 25 per cent were inaccurate or erratic. Many dived into the sea of their own accord. Others have strayed as far as Northampton.

59. The remaining 46 per cent were brought down by the combined efforts of guns, fighters and balloons.

61. In the first week about 33 per cent were brought down whilst 35 per cent reached London. By the end of the period there was a very different story to tell. Some 70 per cent of the bombs launched were being brought down by the defences and only 9 per cent were reaching London.

62. The record day was 28th August when over 100 bombs were launched; 97 were brought down by the defences and only 4 got through to London.

Offices of the War Cabinet,
           S.W.1.

5TH SEPTEMBER, 1944.

The following information comes from Marshall of the Royal Air Force, Sir Charles F.A. Portal, Chief of the Air Staff's reports to the War Cabinet, Chiefs of Staff Committee on various dates during July, August and September 1944. It should be noted that the number of launches listed refers to those bombs identified by plots and not the actual number of launches, which was higher as some bombs failed on launch:

During the 24 Hours ending at 6 am 19 July, 85 Divers had been detected, 37 had reached the London area, while 33 had been brought down; 22 by fighters, 5 by guns and 6 by balloons.

During the 24 hours ending at 6 am on 20 July, 134 Divers had been detected, 37 reached the London area, while 74 were brought down; 53 by fighters, 18 by guns and 3 by balloons.

During the 24 hours ending at 6 am on 21 July, 90 flying bombs had been launched, 39 of which reached the London area, with 39 brought down; 25 by fighters, 10 by guns and 4 by balloons.

During the 24 hour period ending at 6 am on 22 July, 207 flying bombs had been launched, 69 of which reached the London area and 52 had been destroyed; 10 by fighters, 29 by guns and 13 by balloons.

During the 24 hour period ending at 6 am on Sunday 23 July, 156 flying bombs had been launched, 43 penetrating to the London area, while 80 were destroyed; 48 by fighters, 24 by guns and 8 by balloons.

During the 24 hour period ending at 6 am on 24 July, 93 flying bombs were launched, 22 of which penetrated to the London area, whilst 42 were destroyed.

During the 24 hour period ending at 6 am on 26 July, 46 flying bombs were launched and 16 reached the London area. 15 were destroyed by aircraft, 13 by guns and 3 by balloons.

During the 24 hour period ending at 6 am on 27 July, 105 flying bombs were launched, 25 of which reached the London area. 83 flying bombs were destroyed; 54 by fighters, 25 by guns and 4 by balloons.

During the 24 hour period ending at 6 am on 28 July, 151 flying bombs were launched, 57 reaching the London area. 66 were destroyed; 40 by aircraft, 23 by guns and 3 by balloons.

During the 24 hour period ending at 6 am on 29 July, 119 flying bombs were launched, 40 of which reached the London area. 70 were destroyed; 32 by aircraft, 35 by guns and 3 by balloons. Of this total, 28 were brought down at night.

During the 24 hour period ending at 6 am on 30 July, 134 flying bombs had been launched, 42 of which reached the London area. 64 were destroyed; 22 by aircraft, 41 by guns and one by balloons.

During the 24 hour period ending at 6 am on 31 July, 95 flying bombs were launched, 29 of which penetrated to the London area. 30 were destroyed; 20 by aircraft, 8 by guns and 2 by balloons.

During the 24 hour period ending at 6 am on 1 August, 34 flying bombs had been launched, 17 of which penetrated to the London area. 14 were destroyed; 7 by aircraft, 5 by guns and 2 by balloons.

During the 24 hour period ending at 6 am on 2 August, 81 flying bombs were launched, 32 going on to reach the London area. 22 were destroyed; one by aircraft, 17 by guns and 4 by balloons.

During the 24 hour period ending at 6 am on 3 August, 219 flying bombs were launched, 92 going on to reach the London area. 58 were destroyed; 7 by aircraft, 33 by guns and 18 by balloons.

During the 24 hour period ending at 6 am on 4 August, 193 flying bombs were launched, with 40 (21%) penetrating to the London area. 124 (64%) destroyed; 57 by fighters, 58 by guns and 9 by balloons.

During the 24 hour period ending at 6 am on 8 August, 94 flying bombs were launched, 16 of which penetrated to the London area. 52 were destroyed by the combined defences; 25 by aircraft, 25 by guns and 2 by balloons.

During the 24 hour period ending at 6 am on 9 August, 37 flying bombs were launched, 12 of which penetrated to the London area. 14 were destroyed; 6 by aircraft, 4 by guns and 4 by balloons.

During the 24 hour period ending at 6 am on 10 August, 52 flying bombs were launched, 10 reaching the London area. 32 (61%) were destroyed by the combined defences.

During the 24 hour period ending at 6 am on 11 August, 34 flying bombs were launched, 3 of these reaching the London area. 25 flying bombs were destroyed by the combined defences.

During the 24 hour period ending at 6 am on 24 August, 99 flying bombs had been launched, 22 of which reached the London area. 70 flying bombs were destroyed; 14 by fighters and 56 by guns.

During the 24 hour period ending at 6 am on 25 August, 136 flying bombs had been launched, 30 penetrating to the London area. 76 were destroyed; 11 by fighters and 65 by guns.

During the 24 hour period ending at 6 am on 26 August, 17 flying bombs had been launched, none of which reached the London area. 7 were destroyed; one by fighters and 6 by guns.

During the 24 hour period ending at 6 am on 27 August, 4 flying bombs were plotted, with none reaching the London area and 2 were destroyed by fighters.

During the 24 hour period ending at 6 am on 28 August, 33 flying bombs were plotted, 6 penetrating to the London area. 25 were destroyed; 13 by fighters, 11 by guns and 1 by balloons. (This period of launches was confined to a short period during the morning of 27 August).

During the 24 hour period ending at 6 am on 29 August, 105 flying bombs were plotted, 4 of these reaching the London area.

98 flying bombs were destroyed by the combined defences; 24 by fighters, 72 by guns and 2 by balloons.

During the 24 hour period ending at 6 am on 30 August, 154 flying bombs were launched, 21 of which reached the London area. 112 were destroyed by the combined defences; 19 by fighters, 89 by guns and 4 by balloons.

During the 24 hour period ending at 6 am on 31 August, 44 flying bombs were launched, with 2 reaching the London area. 21 were destroyed by the combined defences. Of the total launchings detected during this period, 17 were air launched from Heinkel He.111 bombers. However, none of the air launched flying bombs reached the London area.

During the 24 hour period ending at 6 am on 5 September, "14 flying bombs were launched by aircraft from the direction of the Hook of Holland." None of these penetrated to the London area and two were destroyed by fighters.
C.A.S.

The LXV Corp z.v. Report dated April 1945 detailed the scale of V-1 and V-2 attack. The V-1 part is detailed below:

V-1 LAUNCHINGS			
Launching Area	Target	No. Launched	No. Crashed
France	London	8,564	1,006
France	Southampton	53	9
Holland	London	275	37
Holland & Germany	Antwerp	8,696	1009
Holland & Germany	Brussels	151	18
Holland & Germany	Liege	3,141	366
Total for Ground Launchings		20,880	2,445
Air Launchings	England	875	
Total successful launchings		21,755	2,445 (?)

Chapter Six

Chronology of 616 Squadron Meteor Operations during the Flying-Bomb Campaign – 12 July - 3 September 1944

There was no special selection of the first squadron designated to convert from single-engine piston engine fighters to the twin jet Meteor. No. 616 Squadron was selected as it was scheduled to re-equip with more modern aircraft from its existing Supermarine Spitfire VII, with which it operated with No.10 Group in early summer 1944. To this end, the pilots themselves were not specially selected for any specific reason, as it was planned to convert a standard squadron with standard pilots, which would represent an average cross section of RAF fighter pilots. This was decided upon as this was not merely a conversion to a new higher performing conventional piston engine fighter, but a switch to a complete revolutionary new type of propulsion unit and the powers that be needed to know if the average pilot would be able to make the switch for piston to jet, without undue difficulties.

Before the pilots would fly Meteors they began their conversion to twin engine aircraft by flying Airspeed Oxford twin-engine training aircraft in order to learn the technique of operating multi-engine aircraft. Once they had flown solo on the Oxfords, a further six hours or so Oxford flying was conducted before they pilots were judged ready to move onto the Meteor. For this, the pilots travelled to RAE Farnborough in small batches and in secret where they got they first look at the new jet fighters, which were fresh off the factory assembly lines. Before they would fly the new jet fighters, the pilots received a few hours of ground instruction from the F.9/40 and Meteor test pilots and or experimental pilots who had flown the type. Following this, they would fly their first flights in the Meteor. Over the next few days the pilots would fly several hours on the Meteor, before they would return to their squadron base, at first

Culmhead and later Manston, with the Meteors guarded day and night by special security Police.

The following is a chronology of No. 616 Squadron Meteor I operations from 12 July 1944 until 3 September 1944, the last day of Meteor I operations against the V-1 Flying Bomb.

July 1944 - RAF Culmhead/Manston

12.7.44: In the afternoon 2 non-operational Meteors I's, EE213/G and EE214/G were delivered from RAE Farnborough, Hampshire to RAF Culmhead, Somerset for No. 616 Squadron type familiarisation. The aircraft were closely guarded while at Culmhead. No.616 Squadron was at the time operating Supermarine Spitfire VII's from Culmhead under 10 Group, A.D.G.B.

21.7.44: The first Meteor I's arrived at RAF Manston, Kent on this date and not 20 July as is sometimes stated. The aircraft, EE213/G and EE214/G, which flew into Manston from Culmhead, were both non operational at the time, not being brought to operational standard until sometime later. After arrival the aircraft were quickly placed under cover inside a hanger with a Security Police guard. It was from this date that the Squadron Flight Record Sheets began recording Meteor training and other non operational flights, recording the 2 delivery flights and 1.30 flying hours.

This date also saw the operational echelon of No.616 Squadron arrive at Manston from Culmhead with their Spitfire VII's. Operational control of No.616 passed from 10 Group to 11 Group on this date.

22.7.44: There was a visit to Manston from the Parliamentary Under Secretary for Air, Captain Harold Balfour M.C., M.P. For this occasion W/Cdr (Wing Commander) McDowall took off in a Meteor I and flew some demonstration manoeuvres. This flight, which lasted 15 minutes, was the only Meteor flight by the squadron on this date.

23.7.44: The first operational Meteors I's arrived at Manston when the five aircraft were flown in from Farnborough. The Meteor Flight of 616 Squadron (which it should be remembered was still an operational Spitfire VII squadron) was completed on this day. It consisted of W/Cdr McDowall, W/Cdr Wilson, S/Ldr (Squadron Leader) Watts, F/O (Flying Officer) Rodger, F/O McKenzie (RCAF), P/O (Pilot Officer) Clere (France), F/O Dean and W/O (Warrant Officer) Wilkes. There were ten Meteor sorties on this date.

24.7.44: Ground crew were busy working on the Meteors as they prepared to become operational. There was some local flying and cannon testing.

25.7.44: As the Meteor Flight worked tirelessly to attain an operational standard, flying training continued with 18 sorties, local flying with 6.30 flying hours.

26.7.44: The Meteor Flight was alerted that it would fly anti-'Diver' operations against the V-1 Flying Bomb attacks and several aircraft were placed at readiness. A few V-1's were reported over Manston at night, flying in a South Easterly direction. Flying training continued with 7 sorties in 4.00 flying hours.

27.7.44: This was the date that operational flights with the Gloster Meteor commenced against Flying Bombs in what was known as 'Anti-Diver' operations. Meteor I 'Anti-Diver' patrols commenced at 14.30 hours when Red 1 (F/O McKenzie) took off in Meteor I EE219 at 14.30 hours to patrol an area between Ashford and Robertsbridge, which "covered the main in roads of the Flying Bombs".

Red 2 (S/Ldr Watts) took off at 15.00 hours. Red 1 landed back at 15.15 hours after an uneventful patrol followed by Red 2 landing back at 15.25. A 'Diver'/Flying Bomb was sighted by Red 2 near Ashford. The Meteor was positioned to shoot the Flying Bomb down, but unfortunately the 20 mm Hispano cannons jammed.

Yellow 1 (W/Cdr Wilson) took off on an 'Anti-Diver' patrol at 16.00, landing back at 16.55 hours after an uneventful patrol.

Yellow 2 (F/O Rodger) took off at 16.40, landing back at 17.25 after an uneventful patrol.

White 1 (W.Cdr McDowall) took off at 15.30, landing back at 16.25 after an uneventful patrol.

White 2 (F/O Dean) took off at 17.25. White 2 sighted a 'Diver' and "followed it line astern at 405 mph... closed in to 1,000 yards on bomb estimated flying at 390 mph, when he was turned back by control owing to the proximity of the balloons (balloon barrage)."

Hugo 32 (W/O Wilkes) took off at 18.00 hours, landing back at 18.30 hours after an uneventful patrol.

Hugo 12 (W/Cdr McDowall) took off at 18.25 hours, landing back at 19.10.

During the day a total of 8 'Anti-Diver' sorties were flown with two 'Divers' sighted. The Meteor Flight continued flying training with 3 non operational sorties flown.

28.7.45: Hugo 25 (W/O Clere) took off on an uneventful 'Anti-Diver' patrol at 08.00 hours, landing at 08.45.

Hugo 15 (F/Lt Graves) took off at 08.30, landing at 09.15.

Hugo 19 (F/O McKenzie took off at 09.00, landing at 09.50.

Hugo 14 (S/Ldr Watts) took off at 09.25, landing at 10.15.

Hugo 18 (F/O Rodger) took off at 10.00, landing at 10.45.

Hugo 12 (W/Cdr McDowall) took off at 10.40, landing at 11.25.

Hugo 24 (F/O Dean) took off at 11.10, landing at 12.00.

Hugo 32 (W/O Wilkes) took off at 11.40, landing at 12.35.

The Squadron Form 541 lists only the eight operational sorties detailed above, however, the squadron report to the H.Q.A.E.A.F. and 11 Group for the 28th states that 15 Anti-Diver patrols were flown. The Squadron 'Record Sheet A' also states quite clearly that 15 sorties were flown.

Two more Meteor I's joined 616 squadron, arriving at Manston in the evening, flown in by F/O McKenzie and W/O Wilkes. There were two training flights conducted in 1.80 flying hours during which 320 rounds of 20 mm cannon ammunition was expended.

29.7.44: From 10.25 to 21.10 hours four Meteor I's were scrambled and W/Cdr Wilson flew a Meteor on an engine test flight, which turned into an anti-Diver patrol. During the flight he saw a Diver, which was flying at "3,000 ft near Rye, flying at an estimated speed of 360 mph on course 320°." Wilson positioned his aircraft and "opened fire, but was out of range and finally the flying bomb was lost in cloud." P/O Clere (France) "sighted 3 Divers at heights between 2000 and 4000 ft. Speed 400 mph. He was unable to engage one near Rye owing to a Mustang aircraft firing at extreme range. The course of Divers was again 320°.' Five operational sorties flown.

30.7.44: From 13.55 to 16.50 there were two scrambles. A Diver was sighted by F/O Dean, who gave chase and opened fire with unobserved results as the 'Diver' entered clouds. Two operational sorties flown.

The Meteor Flight was visited by Air Marshall Sir Roderick Hill, Commander in Chief, A.D.G.B. Training flights continued with 7 sorties in 4.45 flying hours, during which 165 rounds of 20 mm was expended.

31.7.44: Low cloud and poor visibility. No operational flying by the Meteors. Local flying and cannon testing with 8 sorties in 3.45 flying hours, during which 1,789 x 20 mm rounds were expended.

August 1944 - RAF Manston

1.8.44: Weather poor. No operational flying by the Meteor Flight, but some local flying with 3 training flights totalling 0.45 hours flying.

2.8.44: There was limited operational flying. Between 14.45 and 17.09 there were four uneventful patrols flown by S/Ldr Watts, F/O Dean, F/O McKenzie and F/O Clere between Ashford and Robertsbridge, each patrol lasting around 45 minutes. The Squadron operational records list the four operational Meteor sorties above. However, the squadron OPREP report to A.E.A.F. and 11 Group states only three Meteor sorties were flown, making no mention of the sortie claimed to have been flown by F/O Clere in the Squadron Operation Record Book. W/O George made a 45 minute local flight in a Meteor. This was the only non-operational Meteor flight by the squadron on this date.

The strength of the No.616 Squadron Meteor flight was now 6 operational and 2 non-operational aircraft. There were many official visitors to the Flight including Group Captain Fleming, A.D.G.B.

3.8.44: Better weather conditions allowed an increase in operational flying. There were 10 'Anti-Diver' patrols flown in the Ashford/Robertsbridge area commencing at 09.30 hours. During one patrol, F/Lt Graves sighted a Diver' in the area between Ashford and Tenterden at an altitude of 2,000 ft, flying in a North Westerly heading. Graves gave chase, having "no difficulty in overtaking the Diver and was able to fire a 2 sec burst at 400/500 yards – results not observed". Graves was clear that he was impeded by a Mustang, which was also attacking and if unimpaired he could have recorded the squadrons first 'Diver' kill. At night, V-1 Flying Bombs were observed flying over Manston. Ten operational sorties flown.

4.8.44: Conditions in the morning were hazy, with reduced visibility, but clearer conditions prevailed in the afternoon. From after midday until dusk, seven Meteors were scrambled, five of which were uneventful, but two resulted in successful interceptions and destruction of Flying Bombs. "F/O Dean took off in Meteor I, EE216 from Manston at 15.45 to patrol inland under Kingsley II (Biggen Hill) control. At 16.16 hours a Diver was sighted at 1,000 ft near Tonbridge on a course of 330° at speed of 365 I.A.S. Dean dived down from 4,500 ft at speed of 450 mph, and attacked from dead astern: his 4 x 20 mm cannons failed to fire owing to a technical trouble… so flying level alongside the bomb, Dean manoeuvred his wing tips up a few inches under the wing of the Flying Bomb and by pulling upwards sharply he sent the bomb diving to earth four miles south of Tonbridge". After this first successful interception of a Flying Bomb by a Jet powered fighter, Dean Landed back at Manston at 16.35. This was a historic occasion for a number of reasons, not least of which was the fact that it was the first successful interception of an enemy aircraft by the RAF's new jet fighters and it was also the first time a jet powered fighter had successfully engaged and caused the destruction of another jet powered aircraft, albeit unmanned.

F/O Rodger took off from Manston at 16.30 hours and "sighted a Diver at 16.40 near Tenterden on course 318° at 3,000 ft, speed 340 mph. Attacking from astern, Rodger fired 2 bursts each of 2 seconds and saw the Diver crash and explode 5 miles N.W. of Tenterden". Rodger landed at Manston at 16.55.

SECRET

CONSOLIDATED DIVER REPORT
No.616 SQN.
R.A.F. STATION MANSTON

F/O J.K. RODGER

Under "Kingsley II Control" I was "scrambled" and vectored to patrol in vicinity of Ashford/Tenderton. Divers were reported to be coming in at 3,000 feet between Tenderton and coast.

At 16.40 hours I sighted a Diver near Tenderton flying on a course 318° at 3,000 feet, estimated speed 340 m.p.h.

I immediately attacked from dead astern and fired a 2 seconds burst at range 300 yards. I observed hits and saw petrol and/or oil streaming out of Diver which continued to fly straight and level. I fired another 2 seconds burst from my 4 cannon still from 300 yards. Both Meteor and Diver were flying at 340 m.p.h.

The Diver then went down and I saw it explode on ground about 5 miles North West of Tenterton.

Claim 1 Diver Destroyed

Date	4.8.44.
Squadron	616
Aircraft	Meteor Mark I
Pilot	F/O J.K. RODGER
Callsign	Hugo 18
Time up	16.30 hours. Time down 16.55 hours
Weather	3/10 cloud at 5,000 feet. Visibility excellent.

5.8.44: Between 16.25 and 19.20 there were five scrambles and two 'Anti Diver' patrols, all uneventful. 7 operational sorties flown.

Another 2 Meteor I's were delivered to No.616 squadron at Manston, bringing the number of operational Meteors to 10, with two non-operational aircraft.

6.8.44: Low cloud and mist in the morning, but clearer conditions in the afternoon. Between 13.20 and 18.15 hours there were four scrambles, two in the afternoon and another two in the early evening, all uneventful. 4 operational sorties flown.

7.8.44: Between 05.55 (first up) and 13.45 (last down) hours there were six aircraft scrambled by Maidstone Control, with an average time for each scramble of 2 minutes. One diver was shot down near Horsham at 06.20 hours. "F/O Dean intercepted the Diver 4 miles east of Robertsbridge at 1,000 ft flying on a course of 330° at 390 mph. Dean came in to attack at 400 mph, and opened fire in line astern from 700 yards to 500 yards; after firing all his cannon Dean broke away and saw the Diver go down in a shallow dive. It was later confirmed by R.O.C. (Royal Observer Corp) that the Diver had crashed at 06.25 hours".

At 13.00 hours, the squadron was visited by the Secretary of State for Air, Rt. Hon Sir Archibald Sinclair MP. F/O Rodger and F/O McKenzie were scrambled during his visit. Six operational sorties flown.

8.8.44: No operational flying. W/Cdr Wilson and F/Sgt Epps conducted local flying and air firing test.

9.8.44: Between 06.30 (first up) and 22.00 (last down) hours there were eight Meteors scrambled and three aircraft on 'Anti-Diver' patrols. All scrambles and patrols were uneventful.

In the afternoon the squadron C/O flew to High Malden to assess its possibility of being used as a forward base for Meteors on 'Anti-Diver' patrols. Use of this forward strip would allow the Meteors to reach the inland patrol area much quicker than was possible from Manston.

There are conflicting records for this date. The Squadron records state that there were eight scrambles and 3 patrols launched for a total of 11 operational sorties mentioned above.

However, the Squadron report to H.Q.A.E.A.F. and 11 Group, OPREP. A. 19/M, states in its 'A' section that there were eight scrambles and four Anti-Diver patrols for a total of 12 operational sorties. The OPREP goes on to state in its 'B' section "(i) 12 Meteor Mk.I. (ii) 12 Meteor Mk.I." It is possible, however, that the OPREP has included the C/O's flight to High Malden as an operational flight.

With the increasing numbers of Meteors and pilots for the Meteor operations and the imminent end to Spitfire VII operations, No.616 Squadron was organised into two Meteor Flights, 'A' and 'B'

Officer Commanding: Wing Commander McDowall

'A' Flight	'B' Flight
S/Ldr Watts	S/Ldr Barry
F/Lt Graves	F/Lt Gosling
F/O Dean	F/Lt Clegg
F/O Rodger	F/O Mullander (Belgian)
F/O Clere (France)	F/O Kilstruck
F/Lt Jennings	F/O Ritch
F/O Cooper	F/O Hobson
F/O Moon	F/O McKay
F/O Stodhart	P/O Ridley
F/O Miller	P/O Wilson
W/O Wilkes	W/O Kelly
F/O McKenzie (RCAF)	W/O George
F/Sgt Cartmel	W/O Woodacre
F/Sgt Packer	F/Sgt Gregg
F/Sgt Easy	F/Sgt Epps
F/Sgt Watts	F/Sgt Amor

10.8.44: There was an increase in the tempo of operations. From Dawn until late in the evening there were six Anti-Diver patrols and 12 Meteors scrambled on 'Diver' alerts under Kinglsey II control "Inland areas were patrolled in vicinity of South East Kent".

F/O Dean got a third V-1 Flying Bomb "when he shot down a Diver near Ashford with two short bursts of his cannon. F/O Moon who was with F/O Dean saw the Diver sent spinning to Earth". Dean had taken off at 20.55 and landed back at 21.40 hours.

There are conflicting reports as to how many sorties were flown on this date. The Squadron Form 540 states 6 patrols and 12 scrambles, which assuming each patrol and scramble is counted as a single sortie, amounts to 18 sorties. However, the squadron OPREP to H.Q.A.E.A.F. and 11 Group states there were 19 Meteor sorties. The number of scrambles is assumed to be accurate as the Operation Record Book (ORB) states 12 pilots were scrambled; however, it is possible that one of the routine patrols is counted as two aircraft.

11.8.44: There was a reduction in the tempo of operations with only four Meteors scrambled between 14.00 and 18.45, all returning after uneventful patrols. Four operational sorties flown.

12.8.44: No operational Meteor flying. Some aircraft were flown on local non-operational flights. There was a visit to the squadron by Air Marshall Sir Roderick Hill Commander of A.D.G.B.

13.8.44: At 17.55 W/Cdr Wilson took off in a Meteor I on an air test, which doubled as an Anti-Diver patrol, landing back at 18.40 after an uneventful patrol. There were no other operational flights, but three aircraft were flown on local non-operational flights. According to the Squadron Record Sheet 'C' for August 1944, there were four non operational flights on this date and not the 3 stated in the ORB. It is, however, possible that the air test by W/Cdr Wilson, which doubled as an operational patrol is included in the Record Sheet C non operational flight numbers. One operational sortie.

14.8.44: Between 06.50 and 22.00 hours four Meteor I's were scrambled from Manston and two were scrambled from the forward operating base, High Halden, and two routine Anti-Diver patrols were also flown from High Halden. All patrols proved to be uneventful. Forward basing Meteors at High Halden was designed to allow the Meteors to reach the "Inland Patrol-Line" in the minimum time possible.

With the ending of No.616 Squadron Spitfire operations from Manston the previous day, The Squadron Record Book shows that No.504 Squadron arrived at Manston with Hawker Tempest V's to take on the weather reconnaissance role previously carried out by No.616 Squadron Spitfire VII's. However, other records show that 504 Squadron was equipped with Spitfire IX's at this time.

15.8.44: At 06.15 two Meteor's took off on an 'Anti-Diver' patrol from Manston. Four aircraft were launched on 'Anti-Diver' patrols from High Halden and two others were scrambled from High Halden, all patrols and scrambles taking place between 06.15 and 09.50 hours and proving to be uneventful. Meteors were kept at readiness at High Malden throughout the rest of the day.

The squadron had its first fatal accident with a Meteor on this date. F/Sgt Gregg had taken off from Manston in EE224 to fly to High Halden to take up readiness duties. Unfortunately Gregg was apparently unable to locate High Halden and instead attempted a landing at Great Chart airfield, near Ashford, but crashed on his approach. Eight operational sorties flown.

16.8.44: The tempo of Meteor operations markedly increased on this date with 23 "uneventful patrols and scrambles" between 06.15 and 21.50 hours. Two sorties proved successful and two more 'Divers' were shot down. In the morning F/O McKenenzie (RCAF) intercepted a 'Diver' and shot it down by "shooting the wing off..." the Diver then "... crashed 8 miles South East of Maidstone." The second kill of the day was by F/O Mullanders (Belgian) in the evening.

In the evening W/Cdr McDowall "intercepted two Divers North West of Tenterden flying at speed estimated 430 mph. Attack was made from astern and closing to 300 yards the C.O. fired and saw strikes. Diver slowed up, but, W/Cdr McDowall had to break away owing to balloon barrage thus being unable to observe the end of Divers flight. The second was attacked near Tenterden and again after recording strikes, W/Cdr McDowall was forced to break away on reaching balloon barrage without observing results."

There are conflicting reports as to how many operational sorties were flown on this date. The Form 540 states 23 'uneventful patrols and scrambles.' It also states that two Divers were destroyed by separate pilots. Adding these, it could then be assumed to bring the number of sorties to 25. W/C McDowall intercepted two Divers, hitting both, but unable to observe results. If this sortie is added them this could take the number to 26. However, the squadron OPREP to HQAEAF and 11 Group states that "30 uneventful patrols were made…"

17.8.44: There were nine "uneventful" Meteor patrols in the inland area. Other sorties aren't listed in squadron Form 540, but it states that three Divers were shot down. It could, therefore, be assumed that these were additional sorties as the nine reported above were recorded as uneventful. The three claims consisted of one each by F/O Ritch, W/O Woodacre and F/Sgt Easy. All sorties were flown between 06.15 and 18.15.

Assuming the practise of classifying a single sortie as a patrol, has generally with very few exceptions been the case in the squadrons records for July and August 1944, then there are again conflicting records regarding the number of operational Meteor sorties on this date. It is possible that some of the "patrols" were conducted by more than one aircraft, but the discrepancies within the records for this date are very large, with the squadrons OPREP to H.Q.A.E.A.F. and 11 Group stating that 21 Meteors sorties were flown on this date. The Squadrons Record Sheet 'A' for the month also states 21 operational Meteor sorties on this date.

CONSOLIDATED DIVER REPORT	SECRET.
616 SQUADRON, MANSTON	**ADGB**
(Handwritten)	
F/O RITCH (R.C.A.F.)	17th August 1944.

At 0615 hours F/O. Ritch was on patrol (inland area) from Manston (under Biggin Control).

2. One Diver was seen flying at 2,000 ft. from direction of Hastings to Maidstone.

3. F/O. Ritch intercepted the Diver at 2,000 ft. in vicinity of Tenderton at 0654 hours.

4. Two Tempests were seen flying approximately 300 yards behind the Diver. One Tempest was seen to fire but no strikes were observed by F/O Ritch who was then flying alongside the leading Tempest. The Tempests then broke away and the Diver continued on its course straight and level.

5. F/O. Ritch then went in to attack and fired one long burst from line astern at range of 150 to 100 yards. Strikes were seen and the Diver rolled over and fell to explode on the ground 4 miles South East of Maidstone at 0657 hours.

6. No other aircraft were seen at time Diver crashed. The Tempests did not follow after they had broke away some 4 miles away.

7. Royal Observer Corps confirm Diver crashed at 0657 hours at Chart Sutton.

<u>CLAIM</u>: 1 Diver destroyed by F/O. J. Ritch (R.C.A.F.)

<u>SQUADRON</u>: 616 Squadron <u>AIRCRAFT</u>: Meteor Mk. I.

<u>CALL SIGN</u>: Hugo 22. <u>TIME UP</u>: 0615 hours. <u>DOWN</u>: 0705 hours.

<u>WEATHER</u>: 10/10 cloud at 3,000 ft. Visibility good.

CONSOLIDATED DIVER REPORT.   **SECRET**
616 SQUADRON, MANSTON.
F/SGT R. EASY.   17th August 1944.

F/Sgt. Easy was orbiting High Haldon being scrambled by Biggin Control (Kingsley II).

2. Control then reported 3 Divers approaching Ashford at 1-3000 ft. Immediately F/Sgt. Easy was vectored to Ashford and intercepted one Diver 1 miles N.W. of Ashford at 1000 ft. flying on course 320 degrees at 370/380 mph.

3. F/Sgt. Easy opened his attack from line astern with one burst of 1 second at 400 yards. Observing a few strikes on starboard wing root, the Meteor closed in and fired from slightly below and astern at range of 250 to 200 yards. Three more 2 second bursts were fired and strikes were observed all over the Diver. The Diver then appeared to waggle its wings sharply and climb slightly to port. More strikes were seen when F/Sgt. Easy fired another burst of 2 seconds.

4. Diver then fell away to starboard and was seen to explode in a field close to Canterbury/Maidstone Railway Line – map reference R.2973 at 1355 hours.

CLAIM: 1 Diver destroyed by F/Sgt. R Easy.
SQUADRON: 616 Squadron, Manston. **CALL SIGN:** Hugo 38.
AIRCRAFT: Meteor Mk. I .   **TIME UP:** 1320 hours.
WEATHER: Cloud base 1600 ft. **TIME DOWN:** 1405 hours
              Visibility below cloud good

CONSOLIDATED DIVER REPORT.
616 SQUADRON, MANSTON. **SECRET**
W/O Woodacre T.S. Date:- 17th August 1944.

While on 'Anti-Diver' Patrol under Biggin Control W/O Woodacre saw a 'DIVER' coming in from direction-of north of Dover.
2. 'DIVER' was intercepted by Meteor I 3 miles south of Canterbury and estimated flying at 400 m.p.h. at height of 1500 feet.
3. One 'Mustang' aircraft was seen 700/1000 yards astern of the 'DIVER' but did not fire.
4. W/O Woodacre had no difficulty in overtaking both Mustang and Diver then attacked and fired three short bursts at range of 200 yards. Strikes were seen on the root of starboard wing of 'DIVER' which rolled over and went down and was seen to explode on ground 4 miles south of Faversham at 07.08 hours.
CLAIM: 1 Diver destroyed by W/O Woodacre T.S.
SQUADRON: 616 Squadron **AIRCRAFT:** Meteor Mk. I.
CALL SIGN: Hugo 33 **WEATHER:** 10/10ths
TIME UP: 06.45 hours **DOWN:** 07.30. cloud 3000 ft. visibility good.

18.8.44: Between 06.10 and 11.30 hours 'A' Flight flew 8 anti-Diver patrols and two Meteors were scrambled. Between 10.55 and 22.00 hours 'B' Flight flew 5 'Anti-Diver patrols. All of the day's patrols and scrambles were uneventful. 15 operational sorties flown.

19.8.44: From 06.25 to 21.40 hours, 616 Squadron flew a number of 'Anti-Diver' patrols with several Divers claimed shot down. In the morning F/O Hobson claimed one 'Diver' destroyed and another shared destroyed with another fighter. F/Sgt Watts claimed one 'Diver' destroyed. The Flying Bombs were shot down "in the vicinity of inland patrol line (Canterbury / Chilham / Ashford / High Halden / Tenderton / Nottsbridge). During an afternoon patrol F/Sgt Cartmel intercepted a 'Diver' near Chilham and engaged it, observing strikes before having to break off due to the gun sight bulb failing. Cartmel was not able to observe the end of the 'Divers' flight, therefore, no claim was submitted. In the afternoon a Flying Bomb flew over Manston at an altitude of 2,000 ft. The other notable event of this day was a visit by Air Marshal Linnel C.B. O.B.E. in the morning. Squadron records show a Meteor damaged on this date, although this was not on operational flying.

20.8.44: Reduced 'Diver' activity saw a reduction in the tempo of operations. Between 07.45 and 16.15 hours there were five scrambles, all proving to be uneventful. 5 operational sorties flown.

21.8.44: Rain, low cloud and mist reduced visibility resulting in no flying on this date.

22.8.44: Poor weather. No flying.

23.8.44: From 14.10 to 21.30 hours 'A' Flight conducted sixteen 'Anti-Diver' patrols and one scramble, all proving to be uneventful. 17 Operational sorties flown.

24.8.44: From 08.05 to 18.20 hours ten Meteors conducted 'Anti-Diver' patrols and there was one scramble, all proving to be uneventful. 11 operational sorties flown.

25.8.44: From 06.30 to 15.30 hours thirteen Meteors were launched on 'Anti-Diver' patrols and another two were scrambled, all proving to be uneventful. 15 operational sorties flown

26.8.44: From 10.30 to 11.20 hours two Meteors conducted uneventful patrols in the inland area (Canterbury – Robertsbridge). There was some non-operational local flying in the afternoon. The squadron records note that no "'Diver' activity reported for 36 hours." 2 operational sorties flown.

27.8.44: Beginning at 07.20 hours and ending at 14.15 hours there were two routine 'Anti-Diver' patrols and four scrambles, all uneventful. Only a few Divers were actually reported on this day. 6 operational sorties flown.

28.8.44: The reduced tempo of operations of recent days was broken by a busy operational day. From 06.40 to 21.15 hours there were twelve routine 'Anti-Diver' patrols and ten scrambles. One 'Diver' was shot down, F/O Hobson and F/Sgt Epps claiming half a kill each of the Flying Bomb, which was shot down near Ashford. Up to this date 616 squadron had claimed 12 ½ 'Diver' destroyed. The half kill was shared with a Hawker Tempest.

There are conflicting reports on the number of operational sorties for this date. The Form 540 suggests 22 sorties were flown, while the OPREP to H.Q.A.E.A.F. and 11 Group, states that 23 sorties were flown. Furthermore, the Form 540 states 12 patrols and 10 scrambles, while the OPREP states 10 patrols and 13 scrambles. 23 operational sorties (Form 540 suggests 22).

No. 616 Squadron pilots confer around Meteor I EE227 (YQ-Y) at RAF Manston, Kent in 1944. The pilots are Squadron Leader Dennis Barry in the cockpit and from left to right; P/O Wilson, W/O Packer, W/O Woodacre and F/O Moon. RAF

CONSOLIDATED DIVER REPORT.

SECRET   616 SQUADRON, MANSTON.

F/O Hobson   28.8.44.

At 16.25 hours F/O Hobson was "scrambled" with F/Sgt Epps (Maidstone Control) and vectored to orbit at Tenterden.

2. One "Diver" was seen coming in 2000 feet over Rye on a course of approximately 320 Derees (should read Degrees) speed estimated at 380 m.p.h.

3. F/O Hobson intercepted the "Diver" approximately 2 miles north of Tenterden at 1657 hours. Three Tempests were seen 2000 yards behind and on same course of "Diver". The Tempests appeared to be losing ground and gradually fell behind.

4. Diving down in a shallow dive from 4000 feet, F/O Hobson passed over the Tempests and fired 2 x 3 seconds bursts at range of 300 yards from behind and slightly above "Diver". Strikes were seen on the Diver which dipped on its starboard wing and continued on its course. Continuing to close in F/O Hobson fired 1 x 5 second burst from 100 yards, the Diver immediately spun to earth to explode on ground R2759 16.58 hours.

5. F/O Hobson transmitted for a fix at the time the Diver crashed.

6. No other aircraft were seen at the time of the attack but as F/O Hobson broke away to starboard after seeing the Diver spin down he saw a Meteor break away to his portside.

CLAIM:	1 Diver destroyed shared with F/Sgt Epps 616 Sqdn
SQUADRON:	616 Squadron
AIRCRAFT:	Meteor Mk. I.
CALL SIGN:	Hugo 29
TIME UP:	1625 hours.
TIME DOWN:	17.26 hours.
WEATHER:	7/10 cloud at 3000 feet. Visibility very good.

CONSOLIDATED DIVER REPORT.
SECRET
616 SQUADRON, MANSTON.

F/SGT. EPPS   28.8.44.

F/SGT Epps was vectored with F/O Hobson to orbit Tenterden (Maidstone Control) when one Diver was seen approximately 10 miles north of Rye on a course approximately 320 degrees height of 2,000 feet.

2. The Diver was intercepted by F/S Epps a few miles north of Tenterden. One Tempest was seen to break away from approximately one mile behind the Diver.

3. F/Sgt Epps attacked level behind and opened fire at 600 yards with one short burst, strikes were seen and the Diver dipped on its starboard wing. Continuing to fire a few more short bursts F/Sgt Epps saw the Diver spin and explode on the ground R.2759 at 16.58 hours.

4. Pilot then broke away to port and saw another Meteor break away on his right.

CLAIM:	1 Diver destroyed and shared with F/O Hobson (616 Sqdn)
SQUADRON:	616 Squadron
AIRCRAFT:	Meteor MK. I.
CALL SIGN:	Hugo 41
TIME UP:	16.25 hours.
TIME DOWN:	17.20 hours.
WEATHER:	7/10 cloud at 3000 feet. Visibility very good.

29.8.44: From 06.35 to 18.50 hours seven 'Anti-Diver' patrols were flown as well as 8 scrambles. Another Diver was claimed destroyed by the squadron from one of the Meteors scrambled. F/O Miller "was scrambled at 13.45 hrs and intercepted a Diver near Ashford. Two attacks were made and the Flying Bomb crashed South West of Sittingbourne".

At 12.30 hours W/Cdr McDowall "took off… on an Anti-Diver patrol. When returning to base he was forced to crash land 3 miles south of Manston". The Meteor I was very badly damaged, but McDowall escaped with only slight superficial injuries. This was the second Meteor lost to accidents on 'Anti-Diver' operations.

30.8.44: From 09.30 to 21.20 hours five Anti-Diver patrols and one scramble were flown, all uneventful.

There are conflicting reports for the number of operational sorties flown on this date. The squadron Form 540 suggests 6, while the squadron OPREP states 7. The discrepancy is in the number of scrambles with the Form 540 stating one and the OPREP stating two. Operational sorties: 6 (Squadron ORB) or 7 (OPREP to H.Q.A.E.A.F. and 11 Group).

31.8.4: From 06.20 to 13.15 hours there were 14 uneventful 'Anti-Diver' patrols and scrambles flown. There was no report of 'Flying Bombs' on this date. 14 operational sorties flown.

September 1944 - RAF Manston

1.9.44: From 13.05 to 20.00 ten uneventful 'Anti-Diver' patrols were flown according to the Form 540. However, this conflicts with the OPREP, which states that there were "21 uneventful Anti-Diver patrols". It goes on to state in the 'B' section (i) 21 Meteor Mk.I. (ii) 21 Meteor Mk.I. Operational sorties: 10 (Form 540) or 21 OPREP to H.Q.A.E.A.F. and 11 Group.

2.9.44: From 09.45 to 11.45 four Meteors conducted uneventful 'Anti-Diver' patrols. There was no 'Diver' activity reported on this date. 4 operational sorties flown.

3.9.44: From 08.05 to 10.50 hours there were three uneventful 'Anti-Diver' patrols. No diver activity was reported on this date. The significant drop off in reported 'Diver' activity was brought about by the continued advance of 21st Army Group in the Pas de Calais area, which was one of the main launch areas for the Flying Bombs. The reduced 'Diver' activity meant this was the last day operational 'Anti-Diver' sorties were flown by the

Meteor I as the Squadron was released from 'Anti-Diver' operations.. 3 operational sorties flown.

No.616 Squadron **OPREP Reports**

TO: H.Q.A.E.A.F. (Att. Ops. Records) 2 Copies 11 Group.
FROM: 616 Squadron, Manston.
Ref: 616S/14/Air.   SECRET.

OPREP. A.   6/M for 24 hrs. ending sunset 27.7.44.

A.   **Anti-Diver Patrols.** 8 Meteor aircraft made uneventful patrols between Ashford and Robertsbridge. Duration of each patrol approximately 40 minutes each. S/Ldr. Watts was first to sight a Diver flying N.W. direction near Ashford, but experienced bad luck as his guns jammed when about to open fire. F/O. Dean sighted one flying bomb and closed in to 1000 yards, but was recalled by control owing to proximity of balloons.
First up – 0930. Last down: 2205.

B.   (i) 8 Meteor Mk.1.   (ii) 8 Meteor Mk.1.
C.   Nil.   D (i) 5.40   (ii) Nil.
E.   1200 x 20 mm. in each aircraft.   (ii) 81 SAPI. 77 H.E.I. 20 mm.
F -   H. Nil. J – K. Nil   L (i) 3 (ii) Nil.
M (i) 2.05 (ii) Nil.   N – O. Nil.

for Wing Commander Commanding, 616 Squadron.

TO: H.Q.A.E.A.F. (Att. Ops. Records) 2 Copies 11 Group.
FROM: 616 Squadron, Manston.
Ref: 616S/14/Air.   SECRET.

OPREP. A.   7/M for 24 hrs. ending sunset 28.7.44.

A.   Anti-Diver patrols continued today, 15 patrols being made between Ashford and Robertsbridge. Duration of each patrol approximately 45 minutes.
First up – 0800. Last down: 1745.
B.   (i) 15 Meteor. (ii) 15 Meteor.

for Wing Commander Commanding, 616 Squadron.

TO: A.E.A.F. (Att. Ops. Records) 2 Copies 11 Group.
FROM: 616 Squadron, Manston.
Ref: 616S/14/Air.   **SECRET.**

OPREP. A.   6/M for 24 hrs. ending sunset 2.8.44.

A.   3 patrols were made by S/Ldr Watts, F/O Dean and F/O McKenzie between Ashford and Tenderton. No Divers seen – nothing to report.
First up – 1445. Last down: 1709.
B.   (i) 3 Meteor Mk.I.   (ii) 3 Meteor Mk.I.

for Wing Commander Commanding, 616 Squadron.

TO: H.Q.A.E.A.F. (Att. Ops. Records) 2 Copies 11 Group.
FROM: 616 Squadron, Manston.
Ref: 616S/14/Air.   SECRET.

OPREP. A. 13/M for 24 hrs. ending sunset 3.8.44.

A.	10 Anti-Diver patrols in Ashford Area. F/Lt. Graves fired a 2 sec burst at one Diver near Tenderton – results not observed. F/Lt. Graves was impeded at the time owing to Mustangs attacking at the same time.
First up – 0930. Last down: 2205.
B.	10 Meteor Mk.I.	(ii) 7 Meteor Mk.1.
C.	Nil.	D (i)	6.45	(ii) Nil.
E.	1200 x 20 mm. in each aircraft.	(ii) 42 SAPI. 38 HEI. 20 mm.
F - H. Nil. J – K. Nil	L (i) 1 (ii) Nil. M (i) 45 mins. M (ii) Nil. N – O. Nil.

for Wing Commander Commanding, 616 Squadron.

TO: H.Q.A.E.A.F. (Att. Ops. Records) 2 Copies 11 Group.
FROM: 616 Squadron, Manston.
Ref: 616S/14/Air.	SECRET.

OPREP. A-14/M for 24 hrs. ending sunset 4.8.44.

A.	7 Anti-Diver patrols of approximately 45 mins. each duration in Ashford area. Two were successful, F/O Dean making history by recording the first flying bomb destroyed by a jet propelled aircraft. F/O Dean sighted Diver near Tonbridge at 1000 ft. and dived down from 4500 ft. at 470 m.p.h. and attacked from astern. F/O Deans guns failed to fire, so he flew alongside and level with flying bomb and by manoeuvring his wing tip a few inches under flying bomb, sent it diving to earth near Tonbridge.

F/O. Rodger sighted a Diver near Tenderton at 3000 ft. 340 m.p.h. and attacked, firing two bursts of 2 seconds. The Diver crashed and exploded 5 miles N.W. of Tenderton. Up: 1545. Down: 1935.

B. (i) 7 Meteor Mk.I. (ii) 7 Meteor Mk.1.
C. Nil. D (i) 3.45 (ii) Nil.
E. 1200 x 20 mm. in each aircraft. (ii) 52 SAPI. 48 HEI.
F - G. Nil. H (i) 2 Divers destroyed. J - K Nil.
L (1) 4.M (i) S.15. N. Nil O. 240 x 20 Ball.

<u>for Wing Commander Commanding, 616 Squadron.</u>

TO: H.Q.A.E.A.F. (Att. Ops. Records) 2 Copies 11 Group.
FROM: 616 Squadron, Manston.
Ref: 616S/14/Air. SECRET.

<u>OPREP. A. 20/M for 24 hrs. ending sunset 10.8.44.</u>

A. 19 Anti-Diver patrols from 0605 to 2140 hours. F/O. Dean completed his Diver hat trick when he shot down a Diver near Ashford. F/O. Dean intercepted the Diver at 5000 ft. and with two short bursts from his four cannon sent the Diver spinning to earth. F/O. Moon was flying with F/O. Dean at the time but was too far behind to take part in the "kill".
F/O. Dean up: 2055. Down: 2140.
B. (i) 19 Meteor Mk.I. (ii) 19 Meteor Mk.1.
C. Nil. D (i) 13.00 (E) (i) 1200 x 20 mm. each aircraft.
E. (ii) 123 S.A.P.I. 111 H.E.I. x 20mm.
F - G. Nil. H (i) 1 Diver destroyed.
J - K Nil.
L (i) M (i) 1.25. N – O Nil.

<u>for Wing Commander Commanding, 616 Squadron.</u>

TO: H.Q.A.E.A.F. (Att. Ops. Records) 2 Copies 11 Group.
FROM: 616 Squadron, Manston.
Ref: 616S/14/Air.   SECRET.

OPREP. A. 26/M for 24 hrs. ending sunset 16.8.44.

A.   30 uneventful anti-Diver patrols were made in the inland area. First up 06.25 hrs. Last down 2150 hrs. F/O. McKenzie (R.C.A.F.) claimed one Diver attacked and shot down 8 miles east of Maidstone, while F/O. M. Mullanders (Belgium) claimed another which crashed near Ashford. W/Cdr. McDowall attacked and saw many strikes on two Divers intercepted near Tenderton but was unlucky to be forced to break away owing to balloon barrage, thus being unable to observe the end of the Divers. Weather fine and warm, but slight ground haze.
F/O. McKenzie – Up 0910 hrs. Down 0950.
F/O. Mullanders Up 1825 hrs. Down 1910.
B.   (i) 30 Meteor Mk.I.   (ii)   30 Meteor Mk.I.
C.   Nil.   D   (i)   21.45 hrs.   (ii)   11.
E.   1200 x 20 mm. in each a/c.   (ii)   962 x 20mm.
F   -   G. Nil. J – K Nil. L (i) 5 M (i) 1.10 hrs
N. Nil. O. 120 x 20 mm.   H. (i) 2 Divers destroyed.

             for Wing Commander Commanding, 616 Squadron.

TO: H.Q.A.E.A.F. (Att. Ops. Records) 2 Copies 11 Group.
FROM: 616 Squadron, Manston.
Ref: 616S/14/Air.   SECRET.

OPREP. A. 27/M for 24 hrs. ending sunset 17.8.44.

A.   21 Meteor aircraft were engaged on Anti-Diver Patrols. Eighteen patrols proved uneventful. Claims were made:

F/O Ritch (R.C.A.F.) 1 Diver destroyed near Maidstone.
W/O T.P. Woodacre. 1 Diver destroyed near Faversham.
F/Sgt R. Easy. 1 Diver destroyed near Maidstone.

Uneventful.   First up: 0715.   Last down: 1815.
F/O Ritch.   Up: 0615.   Down: 0705.
W/O Woodacre.   Up: 0645.   Down: 0730.
F/Sgt. Easy   Up: 1320.   Down: 1405.
B.   (i) 21 Meteor Mk.I.   (ii)   21 Meteor Mk.I.
C.   Nil.   D   (i)   15.25 hrs.   E. 1200 x 20 mm.
in each a/c.   (ii)   1356 x 20mm.   F -   G. Nil.
H (i) 3 Divers des. J – K Nil. L (i) Nil. M – N. Nil. O. 44 x 20 mm. by inadvertent firing.

             for Wing Commander Commanding, 616 Squadron.

TO: H.Q.A.E.A.F. (Att. Ops. Records) 2 Copies 11 Group.
FROM: 616 Squadron, Manston.
Ref: 616S/14/Air.   SECRET.

OPREP. A. 29/M for 24 hrs. ending sunset 19.8.44.
A.   17 patrols and 4 scrambles against Divers were made during the day. Claims were made by:

F/O. G. Hobson (1 destroyed and 1 shared with Tempest)

F/Sgt. P. Watts. (1 destroyed).

B.   (i) 21 Meteor Mk.I.   (ii)   21 Meteor Mk.I.
C.   Nil.   D   (i)   11.50   E. (i) 1200 x 20 mm. each aircraft.   E (ii) 1208 x 20 mm. F - G. Nil. H (i) 2 Divers destroyed and 1 Diver destroyed (shared).
J – K. Nil. L (i) 2 M (i) 1.05. N. Nil. O. Nil.

             for Wing Commander Commanding, 616 Squadron.

TO: H.Q.A.E.A.F. (Att. Ops. Records) 2 Copies 11 Group.
FROM: 616 Squadron, Manston.
Ref: 616S/14/Air.   SECRET.

OPREP. A. 38/M for 24 hrs. ending sunset 28.8.44.
A.   10 anti-Diver patrols and 13 scrambles between first and last light. F/O. Hobson and F/Sgt. Epps took off at 1625 hrs. and were successful in shooting down one Diver near Ashford. Both pilots returned to base at 1720 hrs. First up: 0640. Down: 2115. Weather: 7/10 to 10/10 cloud at 3000 ft. Visibility good.
B.   (i) 23 Meteor Mk.I.   (ii)   23 Meteor Mk.I.   C. Nil. D (i)   17.40 hrs.   E. (i) 1200 x 20 mm. (ii) 875 H.E.I. 462 S.A.P.I.   F - G. Nil.   H (i) 1 Diver destroyed (F/O. Hobson F/Sgt. Epps ½ each) J – K. Nil. L (i) 5 M (i) 2.55. N. Nil. O. 150 rds. Ball.

                    for Wing Commander Commanding, 616
        Squadron.
TO: H.Q.A.E.A.F. (Att. Ops. Records) 1 Copy to H.Q. 11 Group.
FROM: 616 Squadron, R.A.F. Manston.
Date: Period ending sunset 29th August 1944.
Ref: 616S/14/Air.   SECRET.

OPREP NO. 19/M.

A.   **ANTI-DIVER**   A total of 7 patrols and 8 scrambles during the day. F/O Miller was successful in shooting down one Diver near Sittingbourne.
First up: 0635 hrs. Last Down: 1850 hrs..
Weather: 10/10 cloud at 3000 ft. Vis. good.
B.   (i) 15 Meteor Mk.I.   (ii)   15 Meteor Mk.I.   (vii) 1 Meteor Cat. H. crash landed.
C. Nil. D (i)   10.05 hours. E. (i) 1200 x 20 mm. each aircraft (ii) 336 H.E.I.   318 S.A.P.I..   F. Nil. G. One pilot slightly

injured. H. (i) 1 Diver destroyed. J – K Nil. L (i) 3 M. (i) 1.45 hrs. N – O Nil.

<u>for Wing Commander Commanding, 616 Squadron.</u>

TO: H.Q.A.E.A.F. (Att. Ops. Records) 1 Copy to H.Q. 11 Group.
FROM: 616 Squadron, R.A.F. Manston.
Date: Period ending sunset 29th August 1944.
Ref: 616S/14/Air.   <u>SECRET.</u>

<u>Oprep. 44/m FOR 24 HRS. ENDING SUNSET 3.9.44.</u>

    A.   No Diver activity. 3 patrols flown between 08.05 and 10.50 hours.

    B. (i) 3 Meteor Mk.I.   (ii)   3 Meteor Mk.I.
C. Nil.   D (i)   2.25 hrs.
E. (i) 1200 x 20 mm. each aircraft (ii) Nil.
F. – H. Nil.
J. – K. Nil.
L. (i) 1. M. (i) 40 mins.
N. Nil. O. 840 rounds Ball.

<u>for Wing Commander Commanding, 616 Squadron.</u>

A 616 Squadron Meteor F Mk.I over South East England in the area between Haugham and Dover. The Meteor is operating out of RAF Manston, Kent, the base from which the squadron would fly it's the first operational jet powered fighter sorties of the war. RAF

A 616 Squadron Meteor I lands back at RAF Manston after a sortie in 1944. The Squadron operated Meteors from Manston and High Halden airfield during the V-1 Campaign, flying its last operational sorties of the first phase of the campaign on 3 September 1944. RAF

Meteor F Mk. I EE227 (YG-Y) of No.616 Squadron is inspected on the ground at RAF Manston, Kent in summer 1944. RAF

No.616 Squadron Spitfire VII Operations 27 July – 16 August 1944

27.7.44: The Spitfire VII element of 616 Squadron flew four sorties on weather recces (reconnaissance) "to a position 5 miles S.W. of Brussels…"

28.7.44: Two Spitfire VII's from 616 Squadron were scrambled to conduct an uneventful weather recce of the Lille area at an altitude of 25,000 ft.

29.7.44: Four Spitfire VII's conducted uneventful weather recces of the Brussels area.

30.7.44: No. 616 Squadron launched two sections of two Spitfires each, on uneventful weather recces in support of the operations on the continent. One section covered the Abbeville area, while the other covered the Lille area.

31.7.44: No. 616 Squadron flew six Spitfire VII sorties on weather recces in three 2 aircraft sections. The uneventful recces covered the Paris and Abbeville areas.

1.8.44: There were four Spitfire VII sorties, 2 sections being flown on uneventful weather recces "over Amiens/Paris and Cherbourg areas respectively". The adverse weather conditions resulted in the section that had flown over the Cherbourg area having to land at Exeter.

5.8.44: Between 10.10 and 13.10 hours No.616 flew two sections of 2 Spitfire VII's each on uneventful weather recce sorties in support of Allied operations on the continent. The first section covering areas 50 miles North of Ostend, "then to Dunkirk to 30 miles South of St Omar at 15,000 ft". The other section flew a weather recce to Dieppe/Cherbourg at 15,000 ft.

6.8.44: Between 11.13 and 12.20 hours four Spitfire sorties were flown on uneventful weather recces, one section of which covered the Dutch coast and the other the Channel areas.

7.8.44: From 06.15 to 08.20 hours 2 sections, each of 2 Spitfires were flown on uneventful weather recces, one section covering Rotterdam/Cambrai and the other Le Havre. Another section of 2 Spitfires conducted a shipping recce, taking off at 11.25 hours to orbit an "area approx. 8-10 miles South East of South Foreland", before they returned to base, landing at 11.50 hours.

8.8.44: Although the Meteors flew no operations on this day, four Spitfire sorties were flown on weather recce when two sections, each of two aircraft took off at 12.00 hours. One section covered Yarmouth/Flushing before returning to Manston, while the other covered the Cherbourg area before landing at Exeter owing to a fuel shortage. The last aircraft landed at 13.10 hours.

9.8.44: Between 06.15 and 07.50 (last down) hours, four Spitfires were flown on weather recces, one section of two aircraft covering Boulogne/Amiens and Dieppe, while the other section covered Ostend/Valenciennes.

10.8.44: The Spitfire element of 616 Squadron continued operations, launching 2 sections, each of two aircraft each at 0600 hours. These aircraft flew weather recces with one section covering Ostend/Valenciennes and the other covering Boulogne/Amiens/Dieppe. Another section of two Spitfires took off from Manston at 10.10 hours and flew a weather recce of the Le Havre/ Beauval and Ostend areas. All of these sorties proved uneventful and the Spitfires returned to base with the last aircraft landing at 1225 hours.

11.8.44: Two sections of 2 Spitfires each conducted weather recces over 'Le Havre, Beauval and Boulogne, Ostend, Valenciennes respectively'. The first section took off at 0835 and landed at 1015, while the second section took off at 0930 and landed at 1030.

12.8.44: Although the Meteors flew no operations on this day, the Spitfire element remained operational; flying a section of 2 Spitfire VII's on a weather recce covering Ostend, Valenciennes and Boulogne between 0930 and 1040 hours.

13.8.44: The last operational sorties by 616 Squadron Spitfires were flown today when two sections of 2 aircraft each conducted weather recces. One section "flew to Le Treport then followed the coast west to Fecamp, then straight to Cherbourg and base. The other section covered Dunkirk and Valenciennes at 25,000 ft." The first aircraft took off at 11.20, the last landing at 13.30.

Chapter Seven

No. 616 Squadron Chronology of Operations
4 September 1944 – 31 January 1945

September 1944
RAF Manston

4.9.44: No operational flying. Training flying continued with air firing and formation flying practice.
5.9.44: No operational flying. Training flying continued with air and Cine firing and practice formations flights.
6.9.44: There was no 'Diver' activity reported over South East England. No operational flying. Local and formation flying.
7.9.44: No operational flying.
8.9.44: No operational flying. Air to sea firing practice and formation flying.
9.9.44: No operational flying. Formation flying practice.
10.9.44: No operational flying. Local flying and air to sea firing practice.
11.9.44: No operational flying. Formation flying and air to sea firing practice.
12-13.9.44: Nothing reported. No operational flying
14.9.44: No operational flying.
15.9.44: No operational flying. Local and formation flying.
16.9.44: No operational flying. Flight formation flying and firing practise.
17.9.44: No operational flying. In the afternoon six Meteor I's "flew in formation over town square, Margate, during the Battle of Britain Parade".
19.9.44: No operational flying. Practice flying in the afternoon.
20-22.9.44: No flying on these dates. Adverse weather.
23.9.44: No operational flying. Six Sections flew in formation between 10.00 and 18.00 hours.
24.9.44: No operational flying.
25.9.44: No operational flying. Formation flying.

26.9.44: Three Meteors from 'A' Flight flew formation and battle formation practice flying at altitudes up to 14,000 ft.

27.9.44: No operational flying. Practise formation flying during the morning and the afternoon.

28.9.44: No operational flying. Meteors flew air to sea firing practice near Bradwell Bay. F/O Kilstruck and P/O Wilson conducted test flights in a Spitfire, with both reaching 40,000 ft altitude.

29.9.44: No operational flying. Formation flying practice.

30.9.44: No operational flying. Four Meteors were flown in formation. The press now revealed that "jet propelled aircraft were employed with success against the flying bomb and that most valuable experience had been gained".

October 1944
RAF Manston

1.10.44: Some aircraft conducted local flying in the morning with formation flying practice in the afternoon.

2.10.44: Five aircraft were airborne flying in "formation".

3.10.44: Fair weather allowed Blue and Red Sections to conduct formation flying at 10,000 ft during the morning.

4.10.44: Local flying and formation practice.

5.10.44: Local flying was conducted and Green section conducted a training "beat up" of the gun positions at Sheppey Island, just off the northern coast of Kent.

6.10.44: Seven Meteors conducted formation flying training at 10,000 ft. W/Cdr McDowell flew to the USAAF base at RAF Debden for a "conference". This was to pave the way for the use of Meteor training in attacking USAAF bomber formations to allow the latter to try and develop tactics aimed at combating German Me.262 jet and Me.163 Rocket powered fighters.

7.10.44: Local flying was conducted during the morning.

8.10.44: There was no flying conducted due to heavy cloud and rain.

9.10.44: Fair weather allowed some local flying.

10.10.44: Five Meteors flown by W/Cdr McDowell, S/Ldr Barry, F/Lt Gosling, F/O Stodhart and F/O Doughton were flown to the USAAF base, RAF Debden to participate in a series of tactical trials against USAAF bombers heavily defended by conventional piston engine fighters. This was to evaluate "offensive and defensive" tactics that the USAAF could employ against the German Me.262 twin jet fighter. The large scale exercises would also "indoctrinate as many flying personnel as possible to actual flying missions involving jets". Four Meteors were temporarily based at Debden, requiring not only pilots, but ground crew to be transported to the station.

11.10.44: There was nothing reported for the squadron on this day.

12.10.44: On this date, the Meteor detachment at Debden participated in the first of a series of exercises with the USAAF. Opposing the Meteors were 140 Consolidated B-24 Liberator four engine heavy bombers from the 2nd Bombardment Division, escorted by 40 Republic P-47 Thunderbolt and North American P-51 Mustang single engine fighters. The B-24's were flown on a route from Peterborough to Colchester and were intercepted and attacked in the general vicinity of Colchester by four Meteors I's, which had taken off from Debden.

13.10.44: There was no exercise involving Meteors at Debden, but local flying was conducted by Meteors at Manston and two pilots, F/O Doughton and F/O Ridle flew from Manston to Debden.

14.10.44: The Meteor detachment at Debden participated in another large-scale exercise, flying against over one hundred USAAF Heavy Bombers escorted by P-47 and P-51 fighters. During this exercise the Meteors intercepted and conducted a series of attacks on the bomber formations to allow the escorting P-47 and P-51's to try out various tactics to try and counter the jet powered Meteors. Another two pilots F/O Ellis and F/Lt Watts joined the detachment at Debden. Some local flying was conducted at Manston.

15.10.44: At Debden, a practise "dogfight" was conducted between three Meteors and in excess of twenty USAAF fighters.

The results were mulled over in a critique at the US Wing Intelligence Office to glean as much useful data on the performance of all aircraft. As well as allowing the US pilots to practise tactics for flying against jet powered fighters, the exercise was valuable to Meteor pilots as it allowed then to practise fighting conventional piston engine fighters, which were far more likely to be encountered than German jet powered fighters in the event that Meteors moved to the continent.

16.10.44: F/O Miller flew from Manston to join the detachment at Debden. During the afternoon, three Meteors participated in a "dog fight" exercise against USAAF P-51 Mustangs. At the conclusion of these "dog fights" over the previous few days, the No.616 Squadron detachment stated that the "pilots and ground crews alike of the P-51's were left in no doubt as to the jets capabilities."

17.10.44: The Meteor detachment departed Debden for Manston.

18.10.44: Formation flying was conducted from Manston and Meteors conducted a practice "beat up" of gun posts at Sheppey Island, just off the northern coast of Kent.

19.10.44: There was local flying from Manston and another practice gun position "beat up". The Arms Liaison Officer later telephoned the squadron to "congratulate the pilots on their cooperation and excellent 'beat up'."

20.10.44: Poor weather resulted in no Meteor flying other than two aircraft, which conducted a practice "beat up" of gun posts.

21.10.44: Three sections of Meteors conducted formation practice flying in generally dull weather.

22.10.44: Battle formation flying was conducted by four Meteors of Red Section and local flying was conducted.

23.10.44: In the morning S/Ldr Watts, DFC, and F/O Rodger took off from Manston on an affiliation exercise with a pair of de Havilland Mosquito's from No.605 Squadron, which operated in the intruder role. Results were considered poor due to low cloud, which reduced visibility.

24.10.44: Three sections conducted formation flying.

25.10.44: An improvement in the weather allowed seven Meteors to conduct practice formation flying, while other Meteors conducted gun practice with Cine Cameras and the affiliation exercise with 605 Squadron Mosquito's was completed.

26.10.44: No flying.

27.10.44: One Section of Meteors conducted formation and Battle flying.

28.10.44: Poor weather limited flying to one section on formation flying.

29.10.44: Local flying and some formation flying conducted during the afternoon.

30.10.44: Improved weather allowed local flying to be conducted during the afternoon.

31.10.44: No flying.

November 1944
RAF Manston

1.11.44: Fairer weather allowed an increase in flying training with four sections conducting formation flying.

2.11.44: Red and Yellow Section of 'A' Flight and "two sections of 'B' Flight flew on practice interception under sandwich control." There was some local flying training throughout the day.

3.11.44: No Flying.

4.11.44: Two sections of 'A' Flight and two of 'B' Flight conducted formation flying and some air to air firing was conducted in this days training program.

5.11.44: Fair weather allowed formation flying practice and local flying.

6.11.44: Nothing reported in the squadron ORB for this date, but Record Sheet 'C' states that 16 sorties were flown in 9.15 flying hours.

7.11.44: This day saw a resumption of affiliation exercises with the USAAF, this time with the Meteors flying from their home base, Manston. In excess of 60 B-24 Liberators escorted by 20 P-51 Mustangs from Eighth Air Force Command participated. The

Liberators, which were grouped in three boxes, flew from "Peterborough to Beachy Head via Manston, while the Mustangs acted as close escort". The B-24's were operating at 10,000-ft, with the P-51 escort flying at 15,000-ft. Ten Meteors took part, flying in five sections of two aircraft each, with each section taking off at half hour intervals before attacking the bombers over Manston. Following this exercise S/Ldr Watts flew in a Spitfire to Debden for a critique with P-51 Mustang pilots.

8.11.44: During the morning two sections of Meteors flew Battle formation practice while five aircraft piloted by S/Ldr Barry, F/O Hobson, F/Lt Clegg, W/O George, F/Sgt Amor and W/O Woodacre conducted a cross country flight at altitudes between 10,000 and 15,000 ft "to test new type of electrical compass".

9.11.44: The Squadron ORB sates Nothing reported due to unfavourable weather, but the Record Sheet 'C' for the month states that there were nine training or non-operational sorties on this date.

10.11.44: Formation flying was conducted by three Sections each of 3 aircraft.

11.11.44: Practice formation and local flying conducted.

12.11.44: Formation flying was conducted by one section in the morning and two sections in the afternoon.

13.11.44: Local flying only was conducted.

14.11.44: Three aircraft from 'A' Flight flew formation flying practice and F/Lt Mullanders "flew a Meteor on IFF test.."

15.11.44: Local flying only was conducted.

16.11.44: Formation flying was practised during the course of the morning. During the afternoon two Meteors flown by F/Lt Mullanders and F/O Hobson took off and flew to Sheerness to conduct a "practice 'beat up' of Army Gun Sights." During this day Crown Prince Olar of Norway visited the squadron at Manston.

17.11.44: Formation and local flying was conducted.

18.11.44: Local flying.

19.11.44: Nothing reported for this day.

20.11.44: Meteors conducted a practice "Beat up" of gun positions at Sheppey during the morning and local flying and cannon testing were conducted during the afternoon. On this day a Mr Nathan visited the squadron to take Cine film of the squadron's aircraft and pilots for the (Ministry of Aircraft Production). A Meteor flown by F/O Ridle conducted a "beat up" of the airfield over the squadron dispersal in order that the aircraft could be photographed.

21.11.44: Six aircraft from 'B' Flight led by S/Ldr Barry flew formation flying practice during the afternoon.

22.11.44: 'B' Flight flew formation flying while the days training also included Cine Gun firing and local flying.

23.11.44: Poor weather reduced the program to local flying only.

24.11.44: Poor weather with nothing reported in the ORB, but the squadron Record Sheet 'C' shows that 8 non-operational sorties were flown.

25.11.44: 'Blue' Section of 'B' Flight flew formation practise flying.

26.11.44: An affiliation exercise was flown against 35-40 RAF Lancaster four engine heavy bombers escorted by three squadrons of Spitfires. The Lancaster's flew a route from "Newmarket to Gravesend/Manston/Redhill/Beachy Head and return via Manston." Eight Meteors participated, flying in two aircraft sections at intervals, with the first section flown by W/Cdr McDowall and F/O Ridle. The other sections were piloted by S/Ldr Barry, S/Ldr Watts, F/O Hobson, F/Lt Gosling, F/O Ritch (RCAF) and F/O Menzie (RCAF). The Meteors intercepted and conducted their attacks against the Lancaster's somewhere between Manston/Gravesend/Beachy Head. It was noted that the Lancaster's proved to be "easy targets in their straggling formation for Meteors while Spitfire escort offered no serious opposition". The Meteors were flying between 14.50 and 16.20 hours.

The OPREP for the affiliation exercise is reproduced below:

> TO: H.Q.A.E.A.F. (Att. Ops. Records) 2 Copies 11 Group.
> FROM: 616 Squadron, Manston.
> Ref: 616S/14/Air.   SECRET.
>
> OPREP. A. 128/M for 24 hrs. ending sunset 25.11.44.
> Operation Exercise "Bemould One"
>
> 8 Meteors took part in affiliation with 35/40 Lancaster Bombers. Bombers were escorted by 3 Squadrons of Spitfires. Meteors took off in Sections of 2 in intervals of approx. 15 minutes.
>   Bombers flew from Newmarket to Gravesend / Manston / Beachy Head / Redhill / Manston / Newmarket.
>   Meteors under FIRST NIGHT? (Partly illegible) Control intercepted and attacked bombers in area between Manston/Gravesend/Beachy Head. Bombers flew at 5000 feet in straggling formation of threes and proved easy targets for Meteors. Spitfires offered little opposition were easily led away from Bomber formation.
>   Weather 8/10 cloud, base at 5000 feet. Vis. 4/5 miles.
>   First up 1450 hours Last down 1620 hours.
> B.   (i) 8 Meteor Mk.I.   B (ii)   8 Meteors.
> - H nil.   J – K Nil.   L (i) 24
> M (i) 11.00 hours. N. Nil   O. 840 Rounds Ball

27.11.44: Two Meteors flown by F/O Cooper and F/O Moon flew an AA (Anti-Aircraft) co-Operation flight at 5,000-ft over the Isle of Sheppey. Other training included local flying during the afternoon.

28.11.44: A busy training day included aerobatics, local flying, Cine gun firing and GC (Ground Controlled) interception flying practice.

29.11.44: Limited flying included air to air Cine gun firing at a target banner towed behind a Miles Martinet off Margate. Once film was processed the results were assessed as having some "good shots".

30.11.44: Cine gun camera practice was again flown as well as local flying. No.616 Squadron received an Airspeed Oxford for squadron communications.

December 1944
RAF Manston

1.12.44: Two Meteors flown by F/O McKenzie (RCAF) and F/Sgt Watts participated in an AA co-operation exercise over the Isle of Sheppey in the afternoon. F/Sgt Watts encountered engine trouble with one of the aircraft's engines during the flight, although the aircraft was able to be landed safely. A Meteor flown by F/O Moon conducted air to ground firing practice on the Graveney firing range near Whitstable, Kent. Two sections of Meteors flew on Cine camera gun firing practice.

2.12.44: Another AA co-operation affiliation flight was conducted over the Isle of Sheppey by two Meteors flown by F/O Kistruck and P/O Wilson. In the afternoon, S/Ldr Barry flew a Meteor from Manston to "Kistree and back at 15,000-ft on practise I.A.Z. run". Five Meteors flown by F/O Stodhart, F/O Miller, S/Ldr Watts, F/O McKenzie (RCAF) and F/Lt Jennings conducted air to ground firing at Graveney.

3.12.44: Cine gun exercises were conducted by two Sections of 'A' Flight during the afternoon.

4.12.44: One Section of Meteors conducted a GCI run over the Isle of Sheppey. During the morning six Meteors were flown on air to air firing practice. A Meteor was flown on a 30 minute air test by W/Cdr McDowall.

5.12.44: Local flying.

6.12.44: Local flying was conducted as well as an I.A.Z. co-operation flight over London and air to air firing practice.

7.12.44: Local flying was conducted by 'B' Flight and two Meteors piloted by F/Lt Cooper and W/O Wilkes conducted Cine gun firing.

8.12.44: Cine gun firing practice was carried out by four Sections of 'A' Flight.

9.12.44: Cine gun and formation flying practice conducted on this day.

10.12.44: Battle formation flying practice and Cine gun practice conducted by 'A' Flight.

11.12.44: Flight formation practice by four Sections of 'B' Flight during the morning and flight formation flying by 'A' Flight in the afternoon.

12.12.44: There was no Meteor flying on this date other than a single flight by F/O Moon on a weather test flight lasting some 15 minutes.

13.12.44: No flying.

14.12.44: Improved weather allowed formation flying to be flown by five Sections of 'B' Flight.

15.12.44: The improved weather with increased visibility allowed Cine gun practice to be flown by eight Meteors of 'A' Flight. While the ORB states 8 sorties, the Squadron Record Sheet 'C' states only 7 sorties were flown on this date, with 4.30 flying hours recorded.

16.12.44: Both 'A' and 'B' Flights flew Cine gun exercises. A Colonel Clark arrived from the USAAF HQ in London for a few days with No.616 squadron. After permission was granted by the AOC (Air Officer Commanding) Fighter Command, Col Clark was allowed to take off for a local flight in a Meteor. (J of 'A' Flight).

17.12.44: Cloud and fog prevailed and there was no flying on this date.

18.12.44: An AA co-operation exercise was flown over the Isle of Sheppey by four Meteors flown by S/Ldr Barry, F/O McKay, F/O Kistruck and P/O Wilson. 'A' Flight conducted Battle formation and Cine gun practise. USAAF Col Clark conducted another local flight in a Meteor.

The squadron received its first Meteor III on this date when W/Cdr McDowall and F/Sgt Easy flew to Moreton Valence, Haresfield to take delivery of the aircraft. Sometime around

16.00 hours W/Cdr McDowall landed the Meteor III, EE231, at Manston with a turn out by the squadron to inspect the new improved variant.

19.12.44: The Squadron ORB states that two Meteors were flown on local flights with no other fling on this date due to cloud and fog. However, the Squadron Record Sheet 'C' states that there were 7 non-operational Meteor sorties, accumulating 4 flying hours on this date.

20.12.44: Fog prevailed resulting in no flying by the squadron on this date.

21.12.44: No flying by the squadron due to fog.

22.12.44: No flying due to bad weather.

23.12.44: A slight improvement in the weather allowed two Meteors to be flown on local flights. While the ORB states the two flights mentioned above, the Squadron Record Sheet 'C' states that 7 non-operational sorties were flown. Further confusing this is the fact that the Record Sheet 'C' states that 8.15 flying hours were accumulated, something that would be unlikely for 7 Meteor sorties owing to the very short endurance of the Meteor I/III, which had a typical endurance of 45 minutes. That said; one of the operational flights conducted during the V-1 Campaign was listed as lasting 55 minutes.

24.12.44: The squadron received another 3 Meteor III's when four pilots flew to Moreton Valence in the squadron's communication Airspeed Oxford. Three of the pilots then flew the new aircraft back to Manston. One Section of Meteors flew formation flying and Cine gun firing practice and another Section flew air to sea firing practice off Margate, while a further Section flew local flying.

25.12.44: No flying.

26.12.44: There was no Meteor flying today other than a single gun test flight off Margate, flown by W/Cmdr McDowall.

27.12.44: No flying.

28.12.44: Improved weather allowed an increase in flying with three Meteors participating in an AA co-operation flight over the Isle of Sheppey. Other flying included local flying and Cine gun firing practice. The Squadron Record Sheet 'B' shows another three Meteor III's were delivered to the squadron on this date.

29.12.44: Eight Meteors flew on air to sea gunnery firing at the range off Margate. S/Ldr Barry led a formation practice flight by 'B' Section at 15.20 hours.

30.12.44: Fog. No flying.

31.12.44: Cine Gun firing and formation flying were practised in the morning and S/Ldr Watts led 'A' Flight for formation practice flying later in the day.

January 1945
RAF Manston and RAF Colerne

1-8.1.45: Fair weather allowed training flights to be conducted.

9-10.1.45: Adverse weather. No Meteor flying on these dates.

11.1.45: Fair weather saw a resumption of training flights.

12.1.45: Adverse weather. No Meteor flying on this date.

13.1.45: Improved weather. Training flights conducted.

14.1.45: Increased training flights.

15.1.45: Adverse weather. Only two Meteor flights were conducted.

16.1.45: The Squadron packed up house in preparation for a move to RAF Colerne, Wiltshire the following day.

17.1.45: No.616 Squadrons Meteors were flown from Manston to Colerne where the squadron was being transferred.

18.1.45: Training flights flown from Colerne.

19.1.45: Training flights flown. The Squadrons Record Sheet, sheet number 2 for January 1945 states that it was transferred to Second Tactical Air Force on the this date. However, the Squadron Record Sheet 'B', sheet number 2 states that it was transferred to Second TAC on 21 January. It seems that the transfer order was for the 19th, but transfer took effect from the 21st. The Record Sheet 'B', sheet number two has the squadron under command of Fighter Command, 11 Group, while the sheet number one has the squadron under command of Second TAC, 84 Group. Confusing the situation even more, the Record Sheet

'C', sheet number 1 and 2 has the squadron under Fighter Command, 11 Group control up until the 19th, and states the squadron was transferred to Second TAC on the 20th. However, as the squadron was under command control of two separate commands during the month, there were multiple Record Sheets issued. The second issue of Record Sheet 'C' has the squadron transferred from Fighter Command on the 19th and under Second TAC, 84 Group control from the 20th.

20.1.45: Training flights. On this date No.616 Squadron was transferred from ADGB to 84 Group 2nd TAF (Second Tactical Air Force) and received a "provisional order to move 4 aircraft and 8 pilots and sufficient ground personnel to Brussels".

21.1.45: Training flights continued. The Squadron was completely transferred to control of the Second Tactical Air Force on this date.

22.1.45: Snow and a mist. No Meteor flights on this date.

23.1.45: No entry in Squadron records for this date.

24-26.1.45: Snow and fog. No Meteor flying on these dates.

27.1.45: Mist remained until midday, thereafter, three training flights were flown.

28.1.45: A number of Dakota Transports arrived at Colerne for the air lift of equipment and personnel to the European Continent to support the planned move of four aircraft to the Brussels area, Belgium.

29.1.45: Snow remaining on the aerodrome combined with mist led to no flying on this date.

30-31.1.45: Poor weather meant there was no flying on these dates.

A No. 616 Squadron Meteor F Mk. I is inspected prior to a training flight at RAF Manston, Kent on 4 January 1945. RAF

A line-up of No. 616 Squadron Meteor F Mk. I and F Mk. III's are refuelled at RAF Manston in early 1945. RAF

Meteor III EE236 (YQ-H) is refuelled while operating with No. 616 Squadron at RAF Manston, Kent in early 1945. This was one of the 15 early Meteor III's powered by the Welland I engine of the Meteor I. After service with No.616 Squadron most of these early Welland powered Meteor III's were transferred to No. 1335 Conversion Unit at RAF Colerne. RAF

Chapter Eight

The Second Diver Campaign and Operations with Second Tactical Air Force - No. 616 Squadron Chronology, 1 February 1945 – August 1945

In February 1945, the 21st Army Group was involved in "Operations for the destruction of the enemy West of the Rhine." This was in preparation for the planned Rhine crossing operations, when Allied forces moved past this great natural water barrier into the heartland of Germany. When the No.616 Squadron detachment landed on the continent in early February, its task was not a combat role, but rather that of familiarisation of the area and for the ground, and to a lesser extent, allied air units to become used to the noise and sight of the new jet fighters. This plan was put in place in order to try and avoid fratricide incidents, whereby the Meteors might be attacked by Allied forces assuming the jet fighters were German.

The remainder of the Squadron was borrowed by Fighter Command and tasked to fly anti-Diver patrols from 1 March 1945 until 20 March 1945, but did not engage any flying bombs, which were being launched in very small numbers. Once released from anti-Diver patrols, the Squadron reverted back to Second Tactical Air Force and prepared to move to the continent where it was tasked with an operational role within Second Tactical Air Force, with the Meteors departing Britain on 31 March 1945, landing at the designated operating area that same day. Initially they were tasked with intercepting enemy aircraft over Allied held territory, but from 16 April they were tasked with Armed Reconnaissance missions, which quickly became a euphemism for ground attack missions, a role which they conducted until the war in Europe ended in early May 1945.

The following is a chronological listing of 616 Squadrons missions and activities from 1 February until August 1945, when the Squadron disbanded.

February 1945 - RAF Colerne

1-3.2 45: Training flights.

4.2.45: Four Meteors, followed by the communications Airspeed Oxford, left Colerne for Brussels/Melsbroeck/B.58. The aircraft and pilots were EE225 (YQ-P) flown by W/Cdr McDowall, DFM, EE239 (YQ-Q), S/Ldr Barry, EE240 (YQ-R), F/Lt Mullanders and EE241 (YQ-S), F/O Rodger. The Oxford, X7292 was flown by F/O Kistruck with F/O Stodhart as passenger. The aircraft refuelled at RAF Manston before proceeding to Brussels, landing at B.58 later that day.

5-6.2.45: Poor weather conditions prevented any Meteor flying at Colerne.

7.2.45: Weather remained poor, but some flying training was conducted.

8.2.45: Although weather was fair there was no Meteor flying at Colerne.

9.2.45: The fair weather remained allowing flying training to be conducted. W/Cdr McDowall returned to Colerne from B.58 in a Spitfire. The communications Oxford made another trip to Melsbroeck/B.58 flown by F/Lt Mackenzie with F/O Dean and F/O Wilson as passengers.

10.2.45: The communications Oxford returned from Brussels following a stop at Manston. Bright weather allowed some Meteor flying training at Colerne before snow rolled in later.

11-12.2.45: Poor weather. No Meteor flying at Colerne.

13.2.45: Another 3 Meteor III's, EE246 flown by F/O Miller, EE248 flown by W/O Wilkes and EE250 flown by F/Lt Cooper were collected from Moreton Valence. These were Derwent I engine aircraft.

14.2.45: Flying training at Colerne.

15-16.2.45: No flying.

17.2.45: Air test flight only.

18.2.45: This was the last day that the squadron flew Meteor I's, which were completely superseded by the more capable Meteor III. The OPREP for the day, reproduced below, shows the Meteor

I and III sorties. Note that although the Squadron was still based at Colerne on this date the OPREP was issued by 616 Squadron, stating Andrews Field as their base, therefore, suggesting that the OPREP was delayed a few weeks in being issued until the Squadron was at Andrews Field.

> **From: 616 Squadron, Andrews Field**
> **To: Headquarters Fighter Command (Operations Branch).**
> **19th February 1945.**
> **Ref: 616S/14/Air.** **SECRET.**
> **OPREP. A .49/m for 24 hrs. ending sunset 18.2.45.**
> A – H nil.   J – K nil.   L (i) Meteor Mk.I. 2. Meteor Mk. III   4 M (i) Meteor Mk.I. 1.05 hrs. Meteor Mk.III 2.30 hrs   N. nil. O (i) Meteor Mk.I 240 rounds ball. Meteor Mk.III 120 rounds ball.
>
> **for Wing Commander Commanding 616 Squadron. Andrews Field.**

The communications Oxford, piloted by F/Sgt Watts with F/Sgt Amor as passenger, left for Brussels/B.58 via Manston, arriving at B.58 on 20.2.45.

19-21.2.45: Flying training conducted at Colerne. From this date the Squadron flying was conducted on the Meteor III, the Meteor I having conducted its last training flights with the squadron the day before. The OPREP for this date is reproduced below.

> **From: 616 Squadron, Andrews Field**
> **To: Headquarters Fighter Command (Operations Branch).**
> **5th March 1945.**
> **Ref: 616S/14/Air.** **SECRET.**
> **OPREP. A .50/m for 24 hrs. ending sunset 19.2.45.**
> A – H nil.   J – K nil.   L (i) Meteor Mk.III   4 M (i) Meteor Mk.III. 1.50 hrs. N – O nil.
> **for Wing Commander Commanding 616 Squadron. Andrews Field.**

22.2.45: Meteor III EE253 was collected from Moreton Valence by F/O Miller, but landed at Filton as weather closed in.

23.2.45: Meteor III EE253 arrived at Colerne from Filton.

24.2.45: The Communications Oxford arrived back at Colerne from Brussels, flown by F/Lt Mackenzie with F/Lt Ritch as passenger.

25.2.45: A Squadron ground contingent left Colerne by road commencing the journey to Brussels/B.58. This echelon, which consisted of 221 Airmen and 38 vehicles was embarked at Gras the following day, arriving at Ostend on the continent on the 27th, but was not allowed to disembark and was returned to the UK arriving back in the UK on the 28th and proceeding to Andrews Field. The reason for this was that Fighter Command had requested the loan of 616 Squadron from Second Tactical Air Force as a counter to Flying Bomb attacks. The Squadron also moved seven Meteors from Colerne to Andrews Field.

February 1945 - Melsbroeck/B.58 (Belgium)

4.2.45: Four Meteors, followed by the communications Airspeed Oxford, left Colerne for Brussels/Melsbroeck B.58. The aircraft and pilots were EE235 (ORB states this aircraft was EE225, but this is obviously a mistake as EE225 was a Meteor I) flown by W/Cdr McDowall, DFM, EE239 (S/Ldr Barry), EE240 (F/Lt Mullanders) and EE241 (F/O Rodger). The four Meteors were painted an all over white colour scheme, coded P, Q, R and S. The Oxford, X7292 was flown by F/O Kistruck with F/O Stodhart as passenger. Other parts of the Squadron records state that F/Lt Clegg was the passenger of the Oxford and Stodhart arrived in a Spitfire. The aircraft refuelled at RAF Manston before proceeding to Brussels, landing at B.58 later that day. An advance party of 50 NCOs' and airmen had arrived at B.58 on 25 January under F/Lt Ellis to prepare the ground for the arrival of the first of the squadron's aircraft in early February.

5-7.2.45: Bad weather prevented any of the Meteors flying on these dates.

8.2.45: At around 14.30 hours the first Meteor flights out of B.58 were flown when the four aircraft flown by W/Cdr McDowall, S/Ld Barry, F/O Rodgers and F/Lt Clegg took off for a familiarisation flight of the local area. On this date the Squadron Intelligence Officer arrived at B.58 from Ostend.

As the Meteors were to conduct a training program before flying operational sorties six "training courses at 3000 ft, 300 IAS" were allocated to the Squadron B.58 detachment. These courses covered an area "bounded by Brussels, Louvain, Antwerp, Hilst Renzen and south of the Scheldt to Nieuport and Calais". As well as allowing the Meteor pilots to become familiar with the area, the training courses were mainly designed to familiarise ground based gunners with the Meteor jets as there was a real fear that they would be mistaken for German jets.

9.2.45: Clear weather in the afternoon saw 4 Meteors piloted by S/Ldr Barry, F/Lt Clegg, F/O Rodger and F/O Stodhart take off for a training flight which was completed without incident. W/Cdr McDowall returned to Colerne in a Spitfire on this date, therefore, S/Ldr Barry assumed command of the B.58 Detachment.

10.2.45: Only three of the Meteors were serviceable as one of the aircraft had electrical problems. At 15.00 hours the three serviceable Meteors flown by F/Lt Mullanders, F/O Wilson and F/O Dean took off for a training flight to the Antwerp area at an altitude of 3,000 ft and a speed of around 300 IAS. These flights were completed without incident.

11.2.45: In the afternoon three Meteors flown by S/Ldr Barry (Squadron records mistakenly state F/Lt Barry), F/O Rodgers and F/O Stodhart took off for a flight over training course No.4 to the Antwerp area. During this day German V.1 Flying Bombs were observed flying over B.58 at an altitude of 2,000 ft.

12.2.45: There was no flying due to heavy rain.

13.2.45: Four Meteors flown by S/Ldr Barry, F/Lt Clegg, F/O Rodger and F/O Dean took off at 12.00 hours to fly over training course No.2 to the Antwerp area at an altitude of 3,000 ft. North of B.58 the flight was cut short and the aircraft returned to base as cloud cover was 10/10 with base at 1,500 ft. Despite the fact that the Meteors aborted the training flight and returned to base, 25 Group Anti Aircraft (AA) telephoned the base to confirm that the 4 Meteors had been sighted in spite of the fact that there was cloud. There is confusion as to what aircraft 25 Group AA sighted if any at all. Later in the afternoon a Meteor was flown by F/O Wilson on an I.F.F. test flight.

14.2.45: Although weather was fine with excellent visibility there were no Meteor flights in the morning due to a "show by No.139 Wing". Only three Meteors were serviceable on this date. In the afternoon two Meteors flown by F/O Dean and F/O Wilson flew local flights west of B.58 and Brussels, which were completed without incident. In the afternoon the squadron communications Oxford arrived at B.58 from Colerne.

15.2.45: Only two Meteors were serviceable on this date. Mist prevented any flying.

16.2.45: Fog prevented any flying in the morning, but clearer weather in the afternoon allowed four Meteors flown by F/Lt Mackenzie, F/O Wilson, F/O Ritch and F/O Stodhart to fly over training course No.2. The Meteors encountered cloud in the Antwerp area and drifted off course when around 18 miles south of B.58 making then potential targets for allied AA units. No.84 Group concern for this incident led S/Ldr Watts to the conclusion that unless the weather was clear with perfect ground/air visibility then training flights would not achieve their purpose.

17-20.2.45: Low cloud and poor visibility resulted in no flying by the Meteor detachment.

21.2.45: The poor weather cleared in the afternoon. At 15.30 hours S/Ldr Watts flew a Meteor on a local flight in the area between B.58/Ghent/Courtrai at an altitude of 6,000 ft before landing back at B.58 without incident. The squadron Airspeed Oxford arrived from Colerne later in the afternoon.

22.2.45: Only three Meteors were serviceable on this date. At 10.05 hours three Meteors flown by S/Ldr Watts, F/O Wilson and F/O Stodhart took off on a training run over course No.4 North of Antwerp/Tervensen/Ghent/Base. The flight lasted 45 minutes before the aircraft landed back at B.58 without incident. With visibility of around 4 miles another training mission was flown in the afternoon when three Meteors flown by F/Lt Mullanders, F/Sgt Watts and F/Sgt Amor flew over course No.2. The aircraft were flown at an altitude of 3,000 ft.

23.2.45: A Meteor flown by F/O Wilson took off on a weather test flight at 10.00 hours. During the afternoon Air Chief Marshal Sir A Cunningham visited the squadron detachment at B.58. The ACM showed a particular interest in the Meteors. At 17.55 hours S/Ldr Watts took off in Meteor (code 'Q') for a 10 minute demonstration flight during which he flew over the squadron dispersal "at 500 feet, climbed and dived to and from 3,000 ft."

24.2.45: There were two separate "training runs", each of two sections of two aircraft, planned for the morning, but these were cancelled as the telephone system between B.58 and 25 Group AA was unserviceable. Four Meteors flown by F/O Dean, F/Sgt Watts, F/Lt Mullanders and F/Sgt Amor flew training flights locally. In the afternoon only three aircraft were serviceable. These aircraft took off around 14.00 hours flown by S/Ldr Watts, F/O Wilson and F/Sgt Amor on local flying over an area immediately west of Brussels.

Since the Meteors arrived at B.58 flying had been very limited due to the weather, which particularly if cloudy, reduced or even negated any benefit of the training flights as the missions were mainly for the benefit of ground based air defence units. The high tempo of operations by No.139 Wing which used B.58 airfield also limited the time available for Meteor flights as these operational flights often saw the runways in continuous use meaning the Meteors had to try and squeeze flights in between the priority operational flights by No.139 Wing.

Another pilot, F/Sgt Easy, arrived from Colerne to join the detachment.

25.2.45: Only three Meteors were serviceable on this date. Unfavourable weather conditions and the unserviceable telephone system between B.58 and 25 Group AA meant no runs were to be flown over the training courses. The three serviceable Meteors flown by F/O Wilson, F/Sgt Easy and F/Sgt Watts took off at 09.05 hours on local flying training.

26.2.45: With telephone contact with 25 Group AA still out no runs could be conducted over the training courses. Two Meteors flown by F/Lt Mullanders and F/O Stodhart were flown on local flying training. The squadron medical officer and seven airmen arrived by Dakota transport.

27.2.45: During the morning 10/10 cloud cover prevented flying, but clearer weather with the cloud base lifting to 3,000 ft in the afternoon and visibility of 4/5 miles allowed some local flights to be flown. Records show that four Meteors flown by F/O Dean, F/Sgt Amor, F/Sgt Watts and F/Sgt Easy took off on local flights. However, the squadron records also state that only three aircraft were serviceable on this date. If this is the case then the flights must have been staggered and not a four ship.

28.2.45: Unfavourable weather. No flying on this date. A BBC announcement on this date stated that "British Jet Fighters" were in action against the Luftwaffe. An announcement perhaps prompted by the anticipated operational employment of 616 Squadron on the continent, or perhaps prompted by the UK based elements of the Squadrons imminent employment against the renewed V-1 Flying Bomb threat.

March 1945 - RAF Andrews Field (UK)

1.3.45: From 1 March, 616 Squadron (Main) conducted 'Anti Diver' operations from Andrews Field, Essex. The Meteors had three patrol lines allocated covering the area between Southend and Wivenhoe, which included coverage of a part of the coastline in which V-1 Flying Bombs had previously made landfall. Two Meteors were held at readiness at dawn, but were not flown as no 'Diver' activity was reported on this day.

2.3.45: 2 Meteors held at readiness, but no 'Divers' reported.

3.3.45: At 14.40 hours F/O Miller scrambled in a Meteor III with take off in 2 minutes. He was vectored to the V-1 (Diver) and sighted the Flying Bomb, but was unable to intercept, landing back at base at 14.55. At 14.50 F/Lt Kistruck was scrambled in a Meteor III, but the scramble proved uneventful and he returned to base, landing at 15.20. A Meteor III flown by F/O Miller was scrambled at 16.05, landing back at 16.45 after an uneventful patrol. Another Meteor was scrambled at 16.55, flown by F/Lt Kistruck. This scramble proved uneventful and the aircraft landed back at 17.15. Operational sorties: 4

4.3.45: There were two Meteor III scrambles in the morning. F/Lt Gosling was scrambled at 10.45, landing back at 11.15 after an uneventful patrol. At 11.55 F/O Moon was scrambled. This patrol proved uneventful and the Meteor landed back at Andrews Field at 12.25 hours. There was no further Diver activity reported after 12.25 hours. Operational sorties: 2

5.3.45: At 12.25 hours 1 Meteor flown by F/O Dean was scrambled under control of North Weald, but the patrol was uneventful and Dean landed back at Andrews Field at 13.00. Some local flights were conducted during the afternoon. Operational sorties: 1

6.3.45: There were two Meteors held at readiness, two others on standby and two other aircraft available. There were two scrambles, one at 14.20, F/Lt Kistruck took off and returned at 14.40 after an uneventful patrol. F/O Hobson was scrambled at 17.40, landing back at 18.05 after an uneventful patrol. Operational sorties: 2

7.3.45: One Meteor flown by F/Lt Clegg was scrambled at 08.25 hours and landed back at Andrews at 08.40 hours after an uneventful patrol. Local flying training was conducted during the day. Operational sorties: 1

8-9.3.45: No operational flying. Local flying training.

10.3.45: No operation flying

11.3.45: No operational flying. Training flights flown.

12.3.45: No operational flying. Training flights flown and two more Meteor III's were delivered from Moreton Valence.

13.3.45: Two Meteors at 15 minutes readiness; 2 aircraft on standby and two aircraft available. No operational flying. Training flights.

14.3.45: The Squadron Form 540 suggests that there was only "flying Training flights" on this date, however, the Form 541 states that there was one operational 'anti-Diver' sortie. F/Lt

Clegg was scrambled at 13.45 and landed back at 13.00 after an uneventful patrol. Operational sorties: 1

15.3.45: No operational flying. Training flights.

16.3.45: There is conflicting information from the various squadron records for this date. The Form 540 states that there were two scrambles at 15.55 and 16.30 hours, both uneventful. However, the Form 541 states that only one scramble took place on this date. F/O Hobson was scrambled at 15.55 and landed back at Andrews at 16.30. This landing time is the same time as the Form 540 states the second scramble took place and could explain the confusion. Training flights continued on this date, which is another possible source of the confusion as one of the training flights may have been inadvertently put into the records as an operational flight. Correlating the squadron records with other available operational records suggests that there was only the single operational sortie on this date. Operational sorties: 1

17-18.3.45: No operational flights. Training flights only.

19.3.45: Two Meteors were on standby and three others at 15 minutes readiness. At 08.15 hours a Meteor flown by W/O Packer was scrambled and vectored to the area of Chelmsford, but did not make contact and returned to Andrews at 08.45 hours. Worsening resulted in no further flying on this date. Operational sorties: 1

20.3.45: The squadron was "released from state" at 13.30 hours effectively standing down from 'anti-Diver' operations. Such was the limited tempo of Flying Bomb operations that only 13 Meteor III sorties were flown during this phase off the campaign. Earlier in the day there were training flights flown.

21.3.45: During the afternoon four Meteors flown by W/Cdr McDowall, S/Ldr Watts, F/Lt Rodger and F/Lt Clegg were flown over Uxbridge "where the Royal Family were attending a Group Sports Day."

22.3.45: The squadron reported hearing V-1's during the night. There was no Meteor flying out of Andrews on this date, but one Meteor flown by S/Ldr Barry arrived at Andrews direct from B.58 near Brussels.

23.3.45: Weather was clear and sunny. W/Cdr McDowall led a 12 aircraft practise formation flight during the afternoon. The formation was flown over the local area at an altitude of 25,000 ft. The squadron reported "from early morning one continual hum of American 'Heavies' flying out on way to Germany."

24.3.45: No flying on this date. Echelon prepares to move to B.77 (84 Group).

25-30.3.45: No flying as squadron was stood down on the 25th to prepare for its move to the continent.

31.3.45: The Squadrons Meteors, with the exception of EE270 departed Andrews Field for the continent flying via Manston. The Meteors were EE252 (flown by W/Cdr McDowall), EE275 (S/Ldr Watts) EE272 (F/Lt Clegg), EE274 (F/Lt Hobson), EE248 (F/Lt Kilstruck), EE276 (F/Lt Rodger) EE271 (F/O Moon), EE253 (F/O Dean), EE273 (F/O Stodhart) and EE277 (F/O Miller).

March 1945 - Melsbroeck/B.58 (Belgium)

1.3.45: No flying due to adverse weather. There was an announcement published in all major daily news papers that Meter Jet Fighters were operating against the Germans, which although often criticised as being premature, was actually correct as from this date 616 Squadron elements at Andrews Field in the UK were tasked on 'anti-Diver' operations.

2.3.45: Three Meteors took off on local flying training in the afternoon flown by F/Lt Mullanders, F/O Stodhart and F/Sgt Amor. During the flight Amor's aircraft developed trouble with the starboard engine which went un-serviceable, although the aircraft was landed safely.

The communications Oxford arrived from the UK with S/Ldr Barry, F/Lt Cooper, and F/O Ridley and W/O Woodacre on-board. S/Ldr Watts, F/O Stodhart and F/O Wilson returned to Andrews Field in the UK.

3.3.45: Nothing reported for this date.

4.3.45: Two Meteors were serviceable, but there was no flying due to adverse weather.

5.3.45: Slightly improved weather allowed some local flying in the afternoon in Sections of 2 aircraft Flown by F/Lt Cooper, F/O Ridley, W/O Woodacre and F/Sgt Easy.

6-7.3.45: Bad weather. No Flying.

8.3.45: Bad weather cancelled out the flying program, but in the afternoon S/Ldr Barry took off in a Meteor to show the Meteor in flight to the Air Correspondent to the Daily Mail. The Meteor was flown for some 15 minutes.

9.3.45: Although weather had improved there was still 10/10 cloud cover at 2,000 ft cancelling out any flights over the training courses. Two Meteors flown by F/Sgt's Watts and Easy took off at 11.30 hours for local flying over an area covering B.58 and west to Ghent. In the early afternoon W/Cdr McDowall arrived at B.58 in a Spitfire V and the squadron Oxford returned carrying F/Lt Ellis, F/Sgt Epps, Mr Glover and Mr Cool (Special Duties). Later Two Meteors flown by F/Lt Cooper and F/O Ridley took off on local flying.

10.3.45: Local Flying.

11.3.45: Weather cleared up in the afternoon. One Meteor flown by W/O Woodacre took off on a local flight.

12.3.45: In the afternoon four Meteors flown by F/O Ridley, F/Lt Cooper, W/O Woodacre and F/Sgt Epps flew on practice flights.

13.3.45: "F/Lt Mullanders and W/O Woodacre on one practice flight," according to the ORB, although it is obviously assumed it was one flight each.

14.3.45: Adverse weather. No flying reported.

15.3.45: Two Meteors flown by F/O Ridley and F/Sgt Epps flew a "practice AA run Breskens/Nieuport/Ghent base.

16.3.45: Nothing reported for this date.

17.3.45: No flying.

18.3.45: Local Flying. Two Meteors were flown by F/Lt Cooper, F/Lt Mullanders (Belgian).

19.3.45: Two Meteors flown by F/O Ridley and F/Sgt Epps flew a practice Anti-Aircraft run over the Antwerp area. Around noon B.58 was bombed by two German aircraft which "zoomed out of heavy cloud and flew NE/SW at 6000 ft over airfield, some six fragmentation bombs" being dropped in the area in front of the 616 squadron hanger. There were no casualties, but one Meteor was damaged by bomb fragments. The enemy aircraft involved was confirmed to be a pair of Arado Ar.234 jet powered bombers from 6./KG76. However, post war; German records indicated that the raid involved 3 Ar.234's, each aircraft dropping two AB500 'container', each containing small SD15 fragmentation bombs. This raid was historic in the fact that it was the first time a jet powered aircraft was damaged by another jet powered aircraft in combat other than the Meteor I -V-1 engagements the previous summer. The Germans had drawn first blood against the RAF Meteors operating on the continent. There is no substance to suggestions that the German attacks were actually aimed at the Meteor detachment. On the contrary, post war records would suggest that the Germans were unaware of the fact that the Meteors were operating from B.58.

20.3.45: Clear weather allowed practice runs over the training courses to be resumed. Three Meteors sorties flown by F/Lt Mullanders, W/O Woodacre and F/Sgt Epps flew run No.5 Breskens/Nieuport/Ghent, and two Meteor sorties flown by F/Lt Cooper and F/O Ridley over Run No.3 Antwerp/Tenfusen/Base.

21.3.45: Favourable weather allowed practice runs to continue with two Meteor sorties flown on Run No.4 Breskens/Nieuport/Ghent. Local flights were flown by S/Ldr Barry and F/Lt Cooper.

22.3.45: During the course of the morning a two sortie practice AA run was flown over Run No.4 by F/Lt Mullanders and F/Sgt Epps. Later F/O Ridley flew on a local flight.

23.3.45: Four Meteors took off on local flying during the morning flown by F/Lt Cooper, W/O Woodacre, F/Sgt Epps and F/Sgt Easy.

24.3.45: Two Meteors flown by F/Lt Mullanders and W/O Woodacre flew an AA practice run over Run No.2.

25.3.45: No flying.

26.3.45: The squadron detachment at B.58 moved to B.77 Gilze-Rijen (84 Group). The Meteors were flown to the new base along with an Auster liaison aircraft.

27.3.45: The 616 squadron detachment at B.77 consisted of S/Ldr Barry, F/Lt Cooper, F/O Ridle, W/O Woodacre, F/Sgt Epps and F/Lt Ellis with a ground crew of 60 under an Engineering Officer.

At Andrews Field the squadron ground crew of 185 NCOs' and airmen with 32 vehicles departed at 08.00 hours under the squadron Adjutant, F/Lt E.P Howall and F/Lt Doughton the squadron Intelligence Officer. The convoy moved by road to Tilbury where it embarked, sailing to Ostend by LST.

28-29.3.45: preparations were made for the arrival of the squadron from the UK.

30.3.45: The convoy from the UK arrived at B.77 at 04.00 hours

31.3.45: Squadron settled in at B.77.

April 1945

Squadron records show that 17 Meteor III's departed Andrews Field on 31 March, leaving only a single aircraft, EE270, behind with engine trouble. Other unit records clearly record this figure as ten aircraft and even list serial numbers. The aircraft refuelled at Manston and then continued on to land at B.58 Melsbroeck near Brussels, Belgium. Among the aircraft and pilots were the following: EE252 (flown by W/Cdr McDowall); EE275 (S/Ldr Watts); EE272 (F/Lt Clegg); EE274 (F/Lt Hobson); EE248 (F/Lt Kilstruck); EE276 (F/Lt Rodger); EE271 (F/O Moon); EE253 (F/O Dean); EE273 (F/O Stodhart) and EE277 (F/O Miller). The Meteors remained overnight at Melsbroeck/B.58, but by midday on 1 April, 9 had taken off and landed at B.77. These aircraft were flown by W/Cdr McDowall, S/Ldr Watts, F/Lt Clegg, F/Lt Rodger, F/O Stodhart, F/Sgt Amor, F/Sgt Epps, F/Sgt Easy and F/Sgt Cartmel. Squadron records state that two Meteors were left behind at Melsbroeck with engine trouble. This leaves a shortfall of the expected numbers of Meteors, which should have been present at Melsbroeck on 31 March/1 April. Taking the figure of only ten aircraft arriving from the UK on 31 March, this would have brought the number of aircraft up to at least 13 as one of the original four aircraft detachment had been flown back to Andrews Field in the UK.

The nine Meteor III's which arrived at B.77 on this date were piloted by W/Cdr McDowall, S/Ldr Watts, F/Lt Clegg, F/Lt Rodger, F/O Stodhart and F/Sgt Amor, F/Sgt Epps, F/Sgt Easy and F/Sgt Cartmel.

Later on 1 April, the squadron communications Oxford and Spitfire V arrived at B.77 carrying F/Lt Gosling, F/O Miller and F/O Wilson respectively.

2.4.45: The squadron began to settle in at B.77, which was a forward airfield with the enemy lines around 10 miles to the North. During the night allied artillery could be seen and heard crashing into the enemy positions some ten miles distant.

616 Squadron was grouped into two Flights. 'A' Flight consisted of S/Ldr Watts, F/Lt's Rodger, Clegg, Gosling and Jennings, F/O's Stodhart, Wilson, Moon, Woodacre and Packer, F/Sgt's Cartmel, Amor and Epps. 'B' Flight consisted of S/Ldr Barry, F/Lt's Cooper, Kilstruck, Mullanders and Hobson, F/O's Dean, Ridley and Miller, P/O George, W/O Wilkes and F/Sgt's Easy and Watts.

3.4.45: At Dawn No.616 Squadron "took over" the duties of 'Pink Section', with two aircraft on standby on the runway for alert scrambles. At 16.50 hours Flying Control fired 'two Reds' signalling for the alert aircraft to scramble and the two Meteor III's, 'Blue 1' and 'Blue 2' were scrambled. This was the first operational mission flown by British Jet powered aircraft based on the European Continent. The aircraft, flown by F/Lt Cooper (Kenya) and F/O Dean were "vectored" to patrol in the Brussels area at an altitude of 15,000 ft. They landed back at base at 17.20 hours after an uneventful patrol. It later transpired from information received from 84 Group that the aircraft plots that prompted the scramble were "friendly".

At 19.15 hours 2 Meteor III's, Blue 1 and Blue 2, were scrambled, landing back at 19.55 hours after an uneventful patrol.

4.4.45: Two Meteors III's, 'Blue 1' and 'Blue 2' (squadron records are conflicting with some records stating that it was Blue Section and others stating that it was Pink Section) were scrambled at 10.25 hours; the pilots, W/O Wilkes and F/Sgt Easy, patrolling the Brussels area at 15,000 ft, landing back at 11.15 hours after an uneventful patrol. At 12.00 hours Blue 1 and Blue 2, F/Lt Cooper and F/Sgt Watts, were scrambled and patrolled the Brussels area at 10,000 ft, landing back at 12.55 hours after an uneventful patrol.

There was some local flying during the afternoon and one section that flew over the Nijimegen area was fired at by Allied AA guns, but the Meteors immediately departed the area and escaped without damage. After this incident it was stated that pilots were to avoid this area.

5.4.45: No operational flying due to rain, but some local flying later when the weather cleared up.

6.4.45: There was no operational flying on this date. There was some local flying, which again saw Meteors fired at by allied AA, this time over Eindhoven. There was a security breech at the squadron dispersal as a Dutch civilian wandered around the parked Meteors before being challenged by squadron personnel who then apparently set about him after he tried to take flight. He was then arrested and escorted away.

7.4.45: Two Meteors III's, 'Blue 1' and 'Blue 2', flown by F/O Ridley and F/O P/O George, were scrambled at 15.20 hours and were vectored to patrol the Brussels area at 20,000 ft, landing back at 16.05 and 16.10 hours respectively.

There was local flying during the day. The 616 Squadron Operations Room took effect from this date as No.135 Wing departed B.77 for B.91.

8.4.45: In the morning there was a "heavy ground mist" and one Section was at 30 minutes readiness. The mist cleared in the afternoon and at 14.10 two Meteors flown by F/Lt Clegg and F/Sgt Cartmel were scrambled and vectored by 84 Group G.C.C. to patrol the Antwerp/Brussels area at an altitude of 10,000 ft. Clegg's aircraft developed mechanical trouble and he returned, landing at 14.15. The other Meteor landed at 14.50 after an uneventful patrol.

9.4.45: With a squadron move to B.91 planned to keep up with the advance of the 21st Army Group, W/Cdr McDowall flew to this airfield to prepare for the move. Two Meteors III's, 'Blue 1' and 'Blue 2', flown by F/Lt Hobson and P/O George, were scrambled at 18.25 (squadron records show time for Blue 1 as 18.35 and Blue 2 as 18.25). A number of 149 Wing aircraft were still on the runway, which was detailed to "Pink Section" Meteors, causing the latter to be delayed a few minutes. After being airborne for around 5 minutes, P/O George, flying at 24,000 ft, observed "a single smoke trail at 30,000 ft, direction NE/SW". The Meteor was too far behind the smoke trail to for the pilot to see the aircraft, which was later reported by 84 Group as being thought to belong to a German Jet aircraft. Blue 1 landed back at 18.45 and Blue 2 landed at 18.55 hours. Patrol uneventful other than the smoke trail encountered. 2 Operational sorties

The 4 white painted Meteor III's were flown back to RAF Colerne by F/Lt's Gosling and Cooper, F/Sgt Easy and W/O Packer.

10.4.45: Two Meteors III's, 'Blue 1' and 'Blue 2' were scrambled at 10.30 hours, landing back at 11.15 hours. At 16.15 hours two Meteors, Pink 1 and Pink 2 were scrambled, landing back at 17.10 hours after an uneventful patrol. Two Meteors from Black Section, 'Black 1' and 'Black 2', were scrambled at 16.45 hours, landing back at 17.30 hours after an uneventful patrol. 6 operational sorties.

11.4.45: Two Meteors III's, 'Pink 1' and 'Pink 2' were scrambled at 10.10 hours, landing back at 10.25 and 10.40 hours respectively after an uneventful patrol. At 10.30 hours two Meteors from Black Section, 'Black 1' and 'Black 2', were scrambled landing back at 11.30 hours after an uneventful patrol. At 16.45 hours two Meteors from Blue Section, 'Blue 1' and 'Blue 2', were scrambled, landing back at 17.25 hours after an uneventful patrol. (Squadron record Form 540 states that only two sections were scrambled this day, while Form 541 states the three sections scrambled noted above). The scrambled Meteors patrolled the Brussels area at 15,000 ft. Throughout the day the squadron had one section at readiness on the runway and another section at 15 minutes readiness. 6 operational sorties.

12.4.45: Nothing reported other than that the squadron received notification to move to B.91 located a few miles north of Nijimegen.

13.4.45: The squadron moved to B.91. Ten Meteors, led by W/Cdr McDowall took off at 10.30 hours and flew in formation to B.91. The ground echelon left in a convoy for B.91 at 11.00 hours, arriving later that day and by evening the squadron was settling in to B.91, which consisted of a single 1,500 yard metal strip. Immediately upon its arrival No.616 Squadron assumed the "Pink Section" alert state. After dusk heavy gunfire could be heard from the direction of Nijimegen as First Canadian Army was attempting to smash trough the German positions into Northern Holland.

14.4.45: One section of Meteors was at readiness on the runway and another was at 15 minutes alert. No scrambles and no other operational flying on this date. Later in the day the squadron pilots were briefed on the possibility that Meteors may be used for armed reconnaissance missions over the North of Holland.

15.4.45: The weather throughout the day was overcast. There was no operational flying, but W/Cdr McDowall conducted a single non-operational sortie during the day. The rapid advance of the Allied Armies was pushing the enemy positions further away more or less with each passing day. This resulted in plans for another move and ground personnel were briefed accordingly.

16.4.45: This date saw the commencement of what would be termed offensive operations by the Meteors with the introduction of armed 'Recce' (reconnaissance) patrols over enemy territory; Western Holland, an area "bounded by Utrecht/Amsterdam/**illegible**/Wagingen". Four Meteors from Red Section, Red 1, 2, 3 and 4 (Sq/Ldr Watts, F/O Wilson, W/O Packer and F/Sgt Cartmel) were launched at 11.55 hours, landing back at 12.40 hours after an uneventful patrol. Four Meteors from Yellow Section, Yellow 1, 2, 3 and 4 (F/Lt's Rodger, Jennings, F/O Stodhart and W/O Woodacre) were launched at 12.55 hours, landing back at 13.30 hours after an uneventful patrol, interrupted only by some light flack. No aircraft sustained damage.

17.4.45: Two Meteors, Blue 1 and Blue 2, took off on an armed reconnaissance at 11.15 hours, landing back at 11.55 hours after an uneventful patrol. Green 1 and Green 2 took off on an armed reconnaissance at 11.15 hours, landing back at 12.05 hours after an uneventful patrol. Blue Section launched two aircraft, Blue 1 and Blue 2, on an armed reconnaissance at 12.45 hours, landing back at 13.25 hours after an uneventful patrol. Green Section launched two aircraft, Green 1 and Green 2, on an armed reconnaissance at 12.45 hours. This patrol encounter German motor transport, which was strafed with cannon fire by Green 1 with claims of 1 MT destroyed. "F/Lt Cooper attacked a large MT near Ijmuiden. Strikes were observed and the vehicle swung off the road and stopped". Green 1 and 2 landed back at 13.15 hours.

Red Section launched Red 1 and Red 2 at 14.15 hours along with Yellow Section, which launched Yellow 1 and Yellow 2 at 14.15. Red 2 had to abort and landed back at 14.20 with Red 1 landing back at 14.50 hours along with Yellow 1 and 2 after an uneventful patrol.

Red 1 took off on an armed reconnaissance at 15.45 hours, but Red 2, which was due to launch with Red 1, had engine trouble, with the engine failing to start. Yellow 1 and 2 also launched at 15.45 hours. Red 1 landed back at 16.00 hours, while Yellow 1 landed at 16.25 followed by Yellow 2 at 16.30 following an uneventful patrol.

Blue 1 and Blue 2 and Green 1 and Green 2 took off on an armed reconnaissance at 18.45 hours, with Green 1 and 2 landing back at 19.25 and Blue 1 and Blue 1 and 2 landing at 1930 hours after an uneventful patrol.

This was the busiest operational day so far since the squadron commenced operations with Second TAC. Nineteen sorties were flown, with one abort and another aircraft failing to launch. While results were meagre with only a single Motor Transport claimed destroyed, the increased tempo of operations was providing valuable operational flying experience in a contested air defence zone. Twenty Meteor sorties (including the abort) were flown, conducting searches of "All the roads in area Rotterdam/Ijmuiden/Amsterdam/Utrecht".

18.4.45: A ground haze prevented any flying until the afternoon. Blue 1 and 2 and Yellow 1 and 2 took off on an armed reconnaissance at 12.15, led by W/Cdr McDowall, with Yellow 1 and 2 landing back at 12.55 and Blue 1 and 2 landing at 13.00 after an uneventful patrol over Western Holland at 6,000 ft, with no road traffic observed.

At 12.50 hours Blue 1 and 2 took off on an armed reconnaissance, landing back at 13.35 after an uneventful patrol.

Green 1 and 2 took off on an armed reconnaissance at 13.25, landing at 14.00 after an uneventful patrol.

White 1 and 2 took off on an armed reconnaissance at 13.45, landing at 14.30 after an uneventful patrol.

Black 1 and 2 took off on an armed reconnaissance at 14.15, landing at 15.00 after an uneventful patrol.

Red 1 and Red 2 took off on an armed reconnaissance at 14.50, landing at 15.25 after an uneventful patrol.

Yellow 1 and Yellow 2 took off on an armed reconnaissance at 15.45, landing at 16.25 after an uneventful patrol.

Blue 1 and 2 took off at 16.20 on an armed reconnaissance. This patrol encountered enemy motor transport, which was strafed with cannon fire. Blue 1 (F/Lt Cooper -Kenya) claimed 1 MT destroyed and Blue 2 claimed a staff car destroyed. The two Meteors returned to base, landing at 17.00 hours. The squadron records state that "intense flak was encountered at 3 - 5000 ft. Flak was reported as bursting at the same height as the Meteors, but always well behind". The records go on to state the inference that this was "proving the Meteors speed is foxing the gunners".

White 1 and 2 took off on an armed reconnaissance at 16.50, but aborted and landed at 16.55.

Green 1 and 2 took off on an armed reconnaissance at 17.20, landing at 18.00 after an uneventful patrol.

Red 1 and 2 took off at 18.20, landing at 19.00 after an uneventful patrol.

A total of 24 Meteor sorties were flown throughout the day. The BBC made an announcement on this date about "British jets in action In Holland".

19.4.45: Blue 1 and Blue 2 took off on an armed reconnaissance at 09.50, landing at 10.30 and 10.25 respectively following an uneventful patrol.

Red 1and Red 2 took off on an armed reconnaissance at 10.30, landing at 11.05 following an uneventful patrol.

Green 1 and Green 2 took off on an armed reconnaissance at 10.55 hours. This patrol encountered enemy road traffic which was strafed by Green 1 (F/Lt Cooper - Kenya), with claims of an Armoured Car destroyed near Gouda. Only two of Blue 1's four 20-mm cannon worked during this attack. The pilot "fired a long burst and saw the turret fly off". The patrol then returned to base and landed at 11.25 hours.

Blue 1 and 2 took off on an armed reconnaissance at 11.50, landing back at 12.35 after an uneventful patrol.

Yellow 1 and 2 took off on an armed reconnaissance at 12.05, landing at 12.45 after an uneventful patrol.

Blue 1 and 2 took off at 12.55, landing at 13.35 hours after an uneventful patrol.

White 1 was launched on an armed reconnaissance at 14.00, landing at 14.30 after an uneventful patrol.

Green 1 and 2 (F/Lt's Hobson and Kilstruck) took off on an armed reconnaissance at 14.35. This patrol encountered German road traffic, which was strafed by both aircraft, with 1 MT claimed destroyed near Hoogewaard. Flak was encountered during this mission, but both aircraft returned without mishap.

Fifteen Meteor sorties were flown in Sections of two aircraft each, with the exception of one patrol of one aircraft.

20.4.45: The Squadron again moved to keep touch with the rapidly moving ground situation, which was pushing ever more eastwards. The ground echelon convoy moved in the early morning for Quakenbruck, Germany, located some 45 miles south west of Bremen. Thirteen Meteor III's took off about 11.00

hours led by W/Cdr McDowall, who then landed; the first British Jet Powered fighters to land on German territory.

21.4.45: Throughout the rest of the 20th and the 21st the squadron settled into the new base, which had a good condition airfield save the buildings, which were thoroughly demolished. No operational flying. Cloudy and rain.

22.4.45: Overcast with cloud base 1,000 ft. No operational flying on this date, but W/Cdr McDowall took off on a local flight, the first British Jet powered aircraft to take off from a base in Germany. By evening the Squadrons aircraft were ready for operations.

23.4.45: There is a confliction in squadron records about the number of Meteors involved in operations on this date. Form 540 states four Meteors and Form 541 states three Meteors. Further confusing is the fact that Form 540 names four pilots (S/Ldr Watts, F/O Stodhart, F/Lt Gosling and F/O Moon) as having participated, while Form 541 lists only (S/Ldr Watts, Red 1, F/O Stodhart, Red 2 and F/Lt Gosling, Red 3) as having participated. There is no mention in any Form about an abort. Red 1, 2 and 3 (and possibly Red 4) were launched on an armed reconnaissance at 09.45. This reconnaissance covered the area known as Area 2 "bounded by Bremen, the Frisian Islands/ Emden/Oldenburg". The mission encountered 10/10 cloud at 2,000 ft and the aircraft returned to base, landing at 10.25 after an uneventful patrol.

24.4.45: The squadron was briefed for an armed reconnaissance of Area 2, but was also tasked with a "beat up of Nordholt Airfield located a few miles to the south of Cuxhaven. Red 1, 2, 3 and 4 led by W/Cdr McDowall took off on an armed reconnaissance at 11.15. The Meteor III's conducted a "beat up" of Nordholt Airfield, "flying out of the Sun at 8,000 ft". W/Cdr McDowall claimed 1 damaged Ju-88 on the ground and 1 x M/T. P/O Wilson strafed two (illegible, possibly railway carriage), petrol tankers and buildings, F/O Moon strafed 12 x railway carriages, attacked a gun post and claimed to have silenced it with a long burst of 20-mm. A truck full of ground personnel was strafed by F/Lt Clegg. Red 1, 2 and 4 landed back at 12.05 hours and Red 3 landed at 12.10 on one engine.

Blue 1, 2, 3 and 4 took off on an armed reconnaissance at 11.35, landing at 12.15 following an uneventful patrol.

Red 1, 2, 3 and 4 took off on an armed reconnaissance; Red 1 and 2 at 14.15, Red 3 at 14.20 and Red 4 at 14.10. Red 3 aborted and landed at 14.30, but the three other Meteors continued and "beat up" Nordholt Airfield. Red 4 landed at 14.55 and Red 1 and 2 landed at 15.00. S/Ldr Watts claimed 1 x M/T destroyed and an airfield building damaged and F/O Rodger strafed a flak post. Flak was claimed as intense, one pilot stating "I could have put my wheels down and taxied across". Two of the Meteors received slight flak damage, but there were no casualties to aircrew.

Blue 1 and 2 took off on an armed reconnaissance at 15.20, landing at 16.05 after an uneventful patrol. Squadron records for this mission are conflicting with Form 450 stating that S/Ldr Barry, Blue 1 and F/O Dean, Blue 2 "damaged an M/T near Wittmund", while From 541 states that the mission was uneventful.

Red 1 and 2 took off on an armed reconnaissance at 17.25, landing at 18.00 after an uneventful patrol. 16 operational sorties.

25.4.45: Blue 1 and 2 took off on an armed reconnaissance at 09.45, landing at 10.25 after an uneventful patrol.

Red 1 and 2 took off on an armed reconnaissance at 10.45, landing at 11.30 and 11.25 respectively after an uneventful patrol.

Blue 1 and 2 took off on an armed reconnaissance at 11.50, landing at 12.30 after an uneventful patrol. 6 operational sorties.

A ground echelon moved to B.152/Fassburg, travelling during the night. Late on this date the squadron was moved from 84 Group control and attached to 122 Wing of 83 Group for operational reasons.

26.4.45: The Squadrons Meteors arrived at B.152.

27.4.45: Bad weather. No flying.

28.4.45: White 1 and White 2 were scrambled at 15.45, landing at 16.05 and 15.55 respectively after an uneventful scramble.

Yellow 1 and Yellow 2 were scrambled at 15.00, landing at 15.55 after an uneventful scramble.

Squadron Records Form 540 states that "2 Recces" were flown covering Area 2, but Form 541 states the mission noted above as all being scrambles. 4 operational sorties.

29.4.45: Green 1 and 2 were scrambled at 13.20, landing at 14.00 after an uneventful scramble.

Red 1 and 2 were scrambled at 14.10, landing at 14.45 after an uneventful scramble.

Green 1 and 2 took off on patrol at 15.20, landing at 16.15. Uneventful

White 1 and 2 took off on patrol at 14.50, landing at 15.35. Uneventful.

Red 1 and 2 took off on patrol at 16.30, but aborted and landed at 16.40.

Yellow 1 and 2 took off on patrol at 16.55, landing at 17.40. Uneventful.

Red 1 and 2 took off on patrol at 18.15, landing at 19.10. Uneventful.

Green 1 and 2 took off on patrol at 17.40, landing at 18.30. Uneventful.

Yellow 1 and 2 took off on patrol at 18.45, landing at 19.30. Uneventful.

Blue 1 and 2 took off on patrol at 19.20, but failed to return. The Squadron had suffered its first operational casualties as both pilots were killed. G.C.C. information indicated "that Spitfire pilots heard S/Ldr Watts calling F/Sgt Cartmel to come closer as he was going into cloud, shortly afterwards saw large explosion in air". The Meteors lost were EE252 (S/Ldr Watts) and EE273 (F/Sgt Cartmel).

Again there are conflicting reports between various squadron records, mainly on the basis of the times of some Sections flights. 20 operational sorties.

30.4.45: Patrols uneventful. Form 541 lists nothing for 30 April.

May 1945

1.5.45: Red 1 and 2 were scrambled at 10.45 hours, landing at 11.20 after an uneventful patrol

Yellow 1 and 2 took off on patrol at 11.20, landing at 12.20, after an uneventful patrol.

Blue 1 and 2 took off on patrol at 12.10, landing at 12.45 after an uneventful patrol.

White 1 and 2 took off on patrol at 12.35, but the patrol was aborted and they landed back at 12.50.

Red 1 and 2 took off on patrol at 13.10, but patrol was aborted and they landed at 13.35.

Yellow 1 and 2 took off on patrol at 13.25, landing at 14.20 after an uneventful patrol.

Blue 1 and 2 took off on patrol at 14.05, landing at 14.40 after an uneventful patrol.

White 1 and 2 were scrambled at 14.20, landing at 15.20 after an uneventful patrol.

Yellow 1 and 2 took off on patrol at 16.20, landing at 17.10 after an uneventful patrol.

Red 1 and 2 took off on patrol at 16.20, landing at 16.35 and 17.10 respectively.

Blue 1 (F/O Stodhart) and Blue 2 (F/Lt Jennings) and Green 1 (F/O Miller) and Green 2 (W/O Packer) took off for an armed reconnaissance at 18.55 hours. Blue Section attacked and claimed four M/T destroyed and 6 damaged. Blue 1 and 2 and Green 1 and 2 landed back at 19.45.

Red 1 (F/Lt Hobson) and Red 2 (F/Sgt Easy) took off on an armed reconnaissance at 19.20. Enemy road traffic was encountered and attacked with claims of 9 x M/T destroyed and 19 x M/T damaged. Aircraft landed at 20.10.

Yellow 1 and 2 took off on patrol at 20.25, landing at 21.05 after an uneventful patrol.

Red 1 and 2 took off on patrol at 20.45, landing at 21.20 after an uneventful patrol.

A total of 26 operational sorties were flown.

2.5.45: W/Cdr Schrader, DFC (formerly 496 Squadron and S/Ldr Gaze (formerly 41 Squadron) officially joined the squadron on this date. W/Cdr Schrader was scheduled to take over command of the squadron from Wing Commander McDowall.

Red 1 (F/Lt Rodger) and Red 2 (F/O Moon) along with Yellow 1 (F/Lt Kilstruck) took off on an armed reconnaissance at 05.50 hours. Enemy road traffic was encountered and attacked with claims of 4 x M/T destroyed and 18 x M/T damaged by Red 1 and 2. All three aircraft landed back at 06.40.

Pink 1 (W/Cdr McDowall), Pink 2 (F/Lt Clegg), Pink 3 (F/Lt Mullanders) and Pink 4 (F/Lt Hobson) took off at 07.10 hours. They encountered enemy road traffic, which was strafed with claims of 10 x M/T destroyed and 25 M/T damaged. Pink 1, 2 and 4 landed back at 08.00 and Pink 3 landed at 08.15.

Red 1 (F/O Ridle), Red 2 (F/Sgt Easy) and Red 3 (W/O Packer) took off on an armed reconnaissance at 08.25 hours. They encountered enemy road traffic, which was attacked, with claims of 4 x M/T destroyed and 22 M/T damaged. Red 1 and 3 landed at 09.05 and Red 2 landed at 09.10.

Red 1 (F/O Stodhart), Red 2 (W/O Wilkes), Red 3 (F/O Miller) and Red 4 (F/Lt Jennings) took off on an armed reconnaissance at 12.30 hours. The Section claimed a Fieseler Storch utility aircraft, which had just landed, destroyed on the ground, 1 x locomotive destroyed and 4 x railway trucks destroyed. They returned and landed back at 13.25.

Red 1 (F/Lt Kilstruck), Red 2 (W/Cdr Schrader), Red 3 (F/Lt Hobson) and Red 4 (F/O Moon) took off on an armed reconnaissance at 16.10 hours. They encountered enemy road traffic and attacked with claims of 2 x M/T destroyed and 15 damaged, landing back at 16.10.

Red 1 and 2 took off on patrol at 18.40 hours, landing at 19.25 hours after an uneventful patrol.

Yellow 1 and 2 took off on patrol at 19.05, landing at 19.45 after an uneventful patrol.

Red 1 and 2 took off on patrol at 20.15, landing at 20.50 after an uneventful patrol.

Yellow 1 and 2 took off on patrol at 20.30, landing back at 21.25 after an uneventful patrol. 25 operational sorties.

Again conflicting accounts in various squadron records for today's operations. Form 540 claims 22 M/T destroyed and 82 damaged, while Form 541 claims 20 M/T destroyed and 80 damaged. Furthermore, the detail in Form 540 then goes on to account for the 22 M/T destroyed, but only 70 damaged.

3.5.45: W/Cdr McDowall departed the Squadron for Colerne, with W/Cdr Schrader officially taking over command of the squadron. An advance party left the base at 23.00 for B.156 Luneberg also stated at times as Luneburg) in a convoy, arriving at 05.00.

Yellow 1 (S/Ldr Gaze), Yellow 2 (F/Sgt Easy), Yellow 3 (F/O Ridle) and Yellow 4 (F/O Miller) took off on an armed reconnaissance at 06.15 hours. Enemy road traffic was attacked with claims of 2 x M/T destroyed. Yellow 1 landed back at 07.00, while Yellow 2, 3 and 4 landed back at 07.05

Red 1 (W/Cdr Schrader), Red 2 (F/Lt Clegg), Red 3 (F/Lt Rodger) and Red 4 (F/Sgt Packer) took off on an armed reconnaissance at 05.55. They attacked enemy road traffic with claims of 2 x M/T destroyed and 4 x M/T damaged before landing at 06.40.

Red 1 (S/Ldr Gaze) and Red 2 (F/O Ridle) took off on an armed reconnaissance at 10.10. They attacked enemy road traffic with claims of 4 x M/T damaged, landing at 11.00.

Yellow 1 and 2 took off on an armed reconnaissance at 11.00, landing at 11.40 after an uneventful patrol.

White 1 (F/Lt Rodger) and White 2 (F/Sgt Easy) took off on an armed reconnaissance at 11.30. They attacked enemy road traffic with claims of 8 x M/T damaged and landed back at 12.10.

Blue 1 (W/Cdr Schrader) and Blue 2 (F/O Miller) took off on an armed reconnaissance at 12.25. They attacked enemy road traffic with claims of 2 x M/T destroyed and 4 x M/T damaged.

Red 1 (W/Cdr Schrader) in EE243 and Red 2 (F/Lt Jennings) took off for an armed reconnaissance at 18.35. They attacked landing ground at Schonberg with claims of 1 x Fieseler Storch, 2 x Ju-87, 2 x He.111 and 1 x Me.109 destroyed on the ground, before returning and landing at 19.15.

Yellow 1 (S/Ldr Gaze) and Yellow 2 (F/O Stodhart) took off on an armed reconnaissance at 19.05. They attacked enemy road traffic with claims of 2 x M/T destroyed and 10 x M/T damaged, landing at 19.50.

Red 1 (F/Lt Kilstruck) and Red 2 (W/O Wilkes) took off on an armed reconnaissance at 20.15. They attacked enemy road traffic with claims of 2 x M/T destroyed, landing back at 21.05. 22 operational sorties.

4.5.45: Red 1 (W/Cdr Schrader), Red 2 (F/Lt Jennings), Red 3 (F/O Stodhart) and Red 4 (W/O Wilkes) took off on an armed reconnaissance at 05.15. Red 1 and 2 aborted, Red 1 (W/Cdr Schrader) running out of fuel at 8,000 ft, making a dead stick landing back at base at 05.35, with Red 2 also landing at 05.35. The short duration of the fuel suggests a technical issue, but no details available in the unit records. Red 3 and 4 attacked enemy rail traffic with claims of 1 x locomotive destroyed and 1 damaged and 10 x railway trucks destroyed. Red 3 and 4 landed back at 06.05.

Red 1 and 2 took off on an armed reconnaissance at 07.45, landing back at 08.30 after an uneventful patrol.

Yellow 1 (S/Ldr Gaze) and Yellow 2 (F/O Ridle) took off on an armed reconnaissance at 10.00. They attacked enemy road traffic with claims of 1 x M/T destroyed, landing back at 10.45.

Blue 1 and 2 took off on an armed reconnaissance at 11.25, landing back at 12.05 after an uneventful patrol.

Red 1 ((F/Lt Rodger) and Red 2 (F/Lt Kilstruck) took off on an armed reconnaissance at 13.55. They attacked enemy road traffic with claims of 1 x M/T destroyed, landing back at 14.50.

Red 1 (S/Ldr Gaze) and Red 2 (F/O Ridle) took off on an armed reconnaissance at 16.20. They attacked enemy road traffic with claims of 1 x M/T destroyed, landing back at 16.45. This was the last operational mission flown by British Jet powered aircraft in World War 2.

There were 14 sorties on this date, including the two aborts. The squadron's aircraft were grounded at 17.00 hours and while the squadron records state. "END OF HOSTILITIES", while the war was still ongoing, it was in its closing days with much of the Allied effort in a holding pattern pending the imminent ceasefire, which was signed on 7 May, becoming effective on 8 May 1945.

5.5.45: There was no flying by the squadron on this date.

6.5.45: No flying. Squadron prepared for a move to Lubeck.

7.5.45: The squadron ground elements moved off from Luneburg in convoy at 13.00 hours, arriving at Lubeck at 17.00 hours.

8.5.45: No flying.

Resplendent in its overall white paint scheme, Meteor F Mk. I EE239 (YQ-Q) operating with No. 616 Squadrons four aircraft detachment at B-58-Melsbroeck near Brussels, Belgium in February or March 1945, is being manoeuvred to its dispersal. The detachment at B-58 operated four aircraft, all early production Meteor F Mk. III's powered by the Welland I engine of the Meteor I. RAF

Compared with the conditions existing on UK based airfields, the servicing and operational turnaround facilities available at B-58-Melsbroeck were somewhat austere. This Meteor III of the four aircraft detachment is being checked over and the 20 mm Hispano cannon barrels are being cleaned with a cleaning rod. RAF

RAF engine fitters conduct maintenance on a Rolls Royce W.2B/37 Derwent I engine of a Ni. 616 Squadron Meteor F Mk. III AT B-156/Luneburg in Northern Germany in the closing days of the war. The squadron flew its last operational sorties of the war at Luneburg on 4 May 1945, moving to Lubeck, Germany on the 7th, only hours before the official end of the European war. RAF

Chapter Nine

The End of the War in Europe and after - Formation of other jet fighter squadrons

With the European war over, No. 616 Squadron remained firmly grounded for the next few days. The following is a chronology of its operations from 9 May to 30 August 1945.

9.5.45: S/Ldr Gaze flew a captured Fw.190 from Luneburg.
10.5.45: No flying
11.5.45: The squadron conducted formation flying training.
12.5.45: Formation flying.
13.5.45: No flying.
14.5.45: Formation flying. The squadron C/O, W/Cdr W.E. Schrader "received Bar to his DFC."
15.5.45: Formation flying.
16.5.45: Local and formation flying.
17.5.45: Local and formation flying. W/Cdr Schrader "flew a Ju.34 from Schonberg".
18.5.45: Formation flying.
19.5.45: Flight formation flying during the morning.
20.5.45: Unfavourable weather; no flying.
21.5.45: 'A' Flight formation flying led by S/Ldr Barry.
22-23.5.45: No flying on these dates.
24.5.45: Seven Meteor III's took off at 10.20 hours on a cross country flight, which owing to favourable weather was conducted at "zero feet".
25.5.45: The good weather continued allowing more cross country flights to be conducted at "zero feet".
26.5.45: During the morning a low-level cross-country flight on the route Tagel/Wersen was conducted by four Meteors, while another two Meteors flew the Stade/Nordholt route with two other Meteors also flying on cross country flights.
27.5.45: No flying.

28.5.45: In the afternoon 22 sorties were flown on "formation, low level cross country, and aerobatics". This marked the beginning of an intensive flying program ordered by "Group".

29.5.45: There were 25 training sorties flown. A pair of Me.262's was flown in from Fassberg by W/Cdr Schrader and F/Lt Gosling. Schrader encountered problems in Me.262 'Yellow 7', making a flapless landing and the nose wheel did not come down and the aircraft caught fire at the side of the runway, although Schrader walked away without injury. This aircraft was repaired before going to RAE Farnborough in the United Kingdom for a series of trials. The second Me.262 was landed safely.

30.5.45: Squadron conducted 29 cross country, local, formation and aerobatic training sorties.

31.5.45: Training flights the same as the day before except that 30 flights were flown. This was noted as "probably, a record for the squadron".

1 June – 30 August 1945: The squadron continued its program of training flights. On 1 July, 12 Meteors took part in a flypast for the Soviet Commander in Chief, Marshall Zhukov, operating from Y.80 Frankfurt for the day. Training flights continued through July, including interception exercises for which the Meteors were tasked to intercept RAF Bomber Command Lancaster's escorted by Mustangs on 20 July.

Into August, training continued until the squadron was disbanded on the 30th. This was, however, little more than a squadron number plate change as the same day saw a Hawker Typhoon Squadron, No.263 from 146 Wing, disbanded and its number plate was allocated to the Meteor Squadron. Two days later the Meteor Squadron, under its new guise of 263 Squadron flew to its new base in the United Kingdom.

No. 616 Squadron was reformed in 1946, and in 1949 it began a new association with the Gloster Meteor, trading in its de Havilland Mosquito Night Fighters for Gloster Meteor F.3's, which were simply Meteor III's with a designation change, which came in post war.

In the last weeks of the war in Europe, plans were moving ahead to convert a second squadron to Meteor III's. At 16 March 1945, when the second Squadron was about to commence conversion to the Meteor III, No. 616 squadrons position in regards to aircraft was the following: Four x early production Meteor III's fitted with B.23 engines at B-57 airfield in Belgium and fifteen x Meteor III's fitted with B.37 engines at Andrews Field, UK. Three additional Meteors III's with B.37 engines were scheduled for delivery to Andrews Field that day or the following day, 16 March 1945.

Following a demonstration flight, apparently for the Brazilian Defence Minister, a trio of Gloster Meteor III's from No. 1335 Conversion Unit taxi to their dispersal at Molesworth, Huntingdonshire. The aircraft nearest is EE354 (XL-H). RAF

The second Meteor III squadron planned, No. 504 squadron was still operational with Spitfires at Hawkinge, operating in the bomber escort role. Its conversion to Meteor III's was delayed as the C in C Fighter Command (Air Defence of Great Britain had reverted back to Fighter Command on 15 October 1944) was unwilling to lose the squadron until 20 March, as he was short of squadrons for bomber escort work due to aircraft assets being utilised on 'Anti-Diver'/Flying Bomb and 'Anti-Big Ben'/V-2 Rocket operations.

At 15 March 1945, the schedule was for 504 squadron to move to No. 1335 Conversion Unit at Colerne on or about 20 March 1945. At 15 March 1945, 1335 Conversion was equipped with 7 x Meteor I's with B.23 engines and 8 x Meteor III's with B.23 engines. There was a single Meteor III with B.23 engines at the E.C.F.S., which was to be transferred immediately to the Conversion Unit.

At the time the planned establishment of the Conversion Unit was to have been 8 x Meteor I's with B.23 engines, 6 x Meteor III's with B.37 engines, 4 x Airspeed Oxford multi-engine trainers and 4 x Miles Martinet for target towing. This meant that the Conversion unit had one Meteor above planned establishment, but on the negative side its Meteor III's were all fitted with B.23 engines when it was planned that at least some should be B.37 powered.

At 16 March 1945, Fighter Commands plan was to equip 504 Squadron with B.37 powered Meteor III, while the squadron was at the Conversion Unit at Colerne. This meant that the B.23 powered Meteor III's would remain with the Conversion Unit until used up by natural "normal rates of wastage", the Conversion Unit then keeping up to strength with Meteor III's powered by B.37 engines "ex works". At this time it was planned to work up production to 30 B.37 powered Meteor III's per month. The only other Meteor III in service at 16 March 1945 was a B.23 powered aircraft with the C.F.E. (Central Fighter Establishment) based at RAF Tangmere.

The 15 March schedule proved to be accurate and 504 squadron moved to 1335 Conversion Unit at Colerne around 21 March 1945, where it commenced conversion to the Meteor. A number of pilots had undergone limited Meteor flying a few months before. On 8 May 1945, the war in Europe ended and any plans for deployment of 504 Squadron with 2nd Tactical Air Force had already been shelved. The Squadron had been allocated to RAF Fighter Command and its aircraft began appearing on Fighter Commands operational strength figures from the beginning of April 1945, with four aircraft on strength (all unserviceable) and at the beginning of May 1945, 16 aircraft were listed on Fighter Commands strength (7 serviceable and 9 unserviceable). On 10 August 1945, 504 Squadron was stood down and re-numbered No. 245 Squadron, a Hawker Typhoon Squadron serving with Second Tactical Air Force, which had disbanded in Germany on 10 August, and then re-formed the same day as the Meteor unit at Colerne.

The next Squadron to be equipped with Meteors was No. 74 Squadron, which was operating Tempest V's with the Second Tactical Air Force on the Continent. The Squadrons last operational mission prior to the German surrender was on 3 May, when four Tempests took off from ALG (Air Landing Ground) B.105 in Germany for an armed reconnaissance of the Wilhelmshaven area. On 10 May, the OC (Officer Commanding) informed the squadron that it was to return to the United Kingdom to be re-equipped with Meteor Jet fighters. On this date, the squadron flew its last sorties in support of the Allied occupation forces on the continent.

The squadron ground convoy departed B.105 on 11 May, arriving at Colerne in the UK on the 15th. To keep pilots proficient, a number of Oxfords were allocated to the Squadron in lieu of their Meteors. However, before the Squadron would be allocated Meteors, it would conduct training on the Conversion Unit aircraft. The first Meteors training flights were conducted on the 18th, when two training sorties were flown. Seven other pilots, including the Squadron Commanding Officer flew Meteors the following day. These early flights were conducted on Meteor I's, with further flights being conducted on early production Meteor III's powered by the lower thrust W.2B/23 Welland I. These aircraft had been transferred to the Conversion Unit from 616 Squadron once the latter unit had received W.2B/37 Derwent I powered Meteor III's.

The conversion process was hampered by the shortage of aircraft available. The Squadron records for 24 May 1945 states "Shortage of aircraft rather curtailed flying today, but there was quite a fair amount notwithstanding". It continued, "Now the whole Squadron has done at least one trip, and general consensus is they are 'dam fine aircraft'."

On 2 June 1945, the first of the squadrons own W.2B/37 powered Meteor III's was flown and by the 8th the Squadron was utilising a number of its own Meteors for training. A few No.74 Squadron Meteors were temporarily transferred to RAF Andrews Field on 12 September 1945, by which time the Japanese war in the Far East was over; the Japanese having accepted ceasefire terms on the 15th, with the Instrument of Surrender being signed on-board the USN Battleship, USS Missouri in Tokyo Bay on 3 September 1945.

In the immediate post war period the Meteor III equipped 74 Squadron was based at RAF Colerne along with the Meteors of 245 Squadron, while the RAF's premier jet fighter unit, 616 Squadron, but now re-numbered 263 Squadron, based at RAF Acklington, Northumberland, completed the RAF's first jet fighter wing.

The next Squadrons to begin conversion to the Meteor were No. 124 and 222 Squadrons. The former had been operating Spitfire IX's with RAF Fighter Command, conducting attacks on V-2 associated sites located in the Netherlands as well as flying some shipping reconnaissance missions, with its last operational sorties of the war being conducted on 24 April 1945. The Squadron commenced conversion to the Meteor III with No. 1335 Conversion Unit in July 1945 and was declared operational on 2 October that year, by which time the war in the Far East had ended. A few days later the Squadron moved to RAF Bentwaters.

No.222 Squadron had flown Tempests with 2nd TAC until the end of the war. In June 1945, 222 Squadron returned to the United Kingdom to commence conversion to the Meteor, which was conducted through the autumn, with the Squadron flying its own Meteors by October 1945.

APPENDICES

Appendix I

The following is a complete reproduction of a document relating to Meteor I and III performance and roles, dated 29 September 1944.

Top Secret

D.C.A.S.
       Copies to:- A.C.A.S. (Ops)
                    A.C.A.S. (T.R.)
                    D.O.R.

METEOR I

1. At Encl. 1A is a report on the operational and technical performance of Meteor I aircraft from C.C. No.616 Squadron which has been forwarded by Headquarters, A.D.G.B. without comment.

2. It will be seen that the Meteor I at present suffers from various technical limitations which considerably restrict its use operationally.

3. I understand from D.O.R. that the present technical limitations imposed on the Meteor I will not be removed, and the fitting of long range tanks to this Mark is not contemplated because production of the Mark I is limited to a total of 20. The Meteor I is therefore, operationally restricted to:-

    (a) 15,000 ft. in view of aileron overbalance above this height.

    (b) An endurance of 40/45 minutes.

4. The following figures of speed and rate of climb of Meteor I and other types are interesting:-

At 10,000 feet

	Meteor I	Spitfire XIV	Mustang III	Tempest V
Rate of climb in Ft. per minute	2,500	4,500	3,600	2,900
Speed. m.p.h.	430	405	403	402

At 15,000 feet

	Meteor I	Spitfire XIV	Mustang III	Tempest V
Rate of climb in Ft. per minute	2,250	3,700	3,000	2,750
Speed. m.p.h.	436	415	425	411

From these figures it will be seen that while the Meteor I is faster than the other types, it is considerably inferior in rate of climb.

5. With regard to the future use of the Meteor I, it would seem to be most suited for low attack and high speed photo reconnaissance, but its limited endurance is a disability in the later role.

6. Now that the flying bomb attacks are confined to air launchings at night the Meteors are no longer required in the anti-Diver role. Nor are they required in A.D.G.B. at present for interception. They might be useful in T.A.F. despite their present limitations. HANDWRITTEN PART

Authors Note: As can be seen from the above figures, in regards to operational speeds, the Meteor I was faster than the best of the piston engine fighters then available. At sea level the speed advantage was even more marked with the Meteor able to comfortably exceed 400 mph, with 410 mph being the norm, an achievement that none of the piston engine fighters were able to emulate. During the Anti-Diver campaign the Meteors superior speed at low altitude was demonstrated on a number of occasions when Meteor I's intercepted, overhauled and shot down V-1 flying bombs at speeds in excess of 400 mph, after Tempests and Mustangs had been forced to break off through an inability to overhaul the Diver. **End note.**

METEOR III

7.The first Meteor III is due to be produced in September 1944, while a further 2 are expected to be available in October. Thereafter production is at a rate of approximately 9 per month to the end of February when it increases. It is probable therefore, that one squadron could be equipped by the end of the year.

8.From the 50th aircraft onwards, these aircraft will be equipped with extra tankage amounting to 100 gallons, whilst from the 73rd onwards they will be capable of taking 180 drop tanks. Using this tank the operational endurance will be improved to 2.15 (hand written addition **2 ¼**) hours.

9.The first 40-45 Meteor III's will be equipped with W.2B/23 engines. Subsequent aircraft will be equipped with the W.2B/37. Which gives improved rate of climb and speed.

Authors note: Production plans were altered resulting in only the first 15 Meteor III's being equipped with the W2B/23. **End note.**

<u>Meteor III equipped with W.2B/37 Units – 1,600 lb. Static Thrust</u>
Authors note: The above should probably read W2B/23. **End note.**

	Rate of Climb	Speed
Sea Level	3,150 feet per min	410 m.p.h.
10,000 ft	2,500	430
20,000 ft	2,000	440
30,000 ft	1,300	445
40,000 ft	400	437

Meteor III equipped with W.2B/37 Units – 2,000 lb. Static Thrust

	Rate of Climb	Speed
Sea Level	3,975 feet per min	465 m.p.h.
10,000 ft	3,250	476
20,000 ft	2,500	483
30,000 ft	1,700	484
40,000 ft	750	466

10. As regards the employment of the Meteor III aircraft as far as can be foreseen at present, I suggest they could be suitably employed in the following roles:-

(a) High altitude interception against the Me.262 or other enemy jet or rocket aircraft.

(b) Low level ground attack, but it should be fitted to carry bombs.

(c) Photographic reconnaissance

(d) Short distance bomber support where opposition from enemy jet or rocket aircraft is likely to be encountered.

Signed

29ᵗʰ September, 1944   D.   Ops.
(A.D.)

Appendix II

TOP SECRET

Copies to: A.C.A.S. (Ops.)
D. of Ops. (A.D.)
D. of Ops. (Tac.)
D. of I. (R)

D.C.A.S.

METEOR III

With reference to the discussion at your Staff Conference this morning on the future development of No.616 Squadron, you may like to have the following maximum speed performance figures of the Meteor III when fitted with the various engines that will come off the production line in the near future. I quote the maximum speed at sea level and at 30,000 ft.

2. The first fifteen Meteor III's will be fitted with the W.2B/23 engines giving a static thrust of 1,600 lbs.

Sea level – 410 m.p.h.
30,000 ft. – 445 m.p.h.

The sixteenth and subsequent aircraft will have the B.37 engines at 1,800 lbs thrust

Sea level – 435 m.p.h.
30,000 ft – 465 m.p.h.

The B.37 engines giving an increased thrust of 2,000 lbs. will be introduced somewhere about the 40th aircraft.

Sea level – 465 m.p.h.
30,000 ft. – 485 m.p.h.

At some later date, at present unspecified, these same engines will give 2,200 lbs. thrust

Sea level – 485 m.p.h.
30,000 ft. – 503 m.p.h.

By about the 160th aircraft (June or July 1945), the B.37 engine will be developed to its maximum thrust of 2,400 lbs.

Sea level – 505 m.p.h.
30,000 ft. – 520 m.p.h.

3.　Until modified engine nacelles can be introduced (in August, according to present estimates); the Meteor III will be subject to a speed limitation of 500 m.p.h (Indicated) up to a height of 6,500 ft. reducing proportionately to 300 m.p.h. (indicated) at 30,000 ft. Every effort is being made to expedite the introduction of the new engine nacelles, but I think it is doubtful whether the firm will beat the estimated date of August.

4.　Owing to the absence today of most of the engine people in M.A.P., I have been unable to obtain their views as to whether the risk of losing one of these aircraft outweighs the obvious advantages of using them in the offensive role. (Next sentence had written on document) I hope to be able to report on this tomorrow.

(Sgd.) J.D. BREAKEY
A.C.A.S.(T.R.)

9/1/45

Authors Note: As can be seen from these various engine and performance figures, the first of the Derwent I powered Meteor III's were not capable of producing the 2,000 lb thrust that is often quoted. Correspondingly they were capable of 435 mph at sea level and 465 mph at 30,000 ft, significantly lower than the speeds of 450+ mph at sea level and 493 mph at 30,000 ft, often quoted.

Appendix III

Below is a reproduction of the conclusion of comparison tests of the Power Jets W2./700 Batch 3 Type engine and the Rolls Royce B.37 Series I engine fitted in test-bed Meteors.

The conclusions came from data from the following reports:

Power Jets report "Performance of Meteor I No. EE221 with W2. 700 Engines." DHW/RMJ/20.

Rolls Royce Hucknall Report "Preliminary Note on Level Speed Measurements on Meteor I No. EE/223/G with Derwent Engines Nos. 6 and 20. Dor/ChrDH. 1/MNH. 29.5.45.

The Rolls-Royce B.37 Series I engines compare favourably with the Power Jets W2. 700 engines. The B.37 production engines, however, give a flatter curve than the W2. 700, the speed increasing at altitude by only 5 m.p.h. against the 22 m.p.h. for the W2. 700. This suggests that their compressor efficiency falls off more than the W2. 700 at altitude. On the other hand, the B.37 engine curve with toroidal intake chutes rises steeply, indicating that the compressor efficiency in this case is well maintained. The speed in this case reaches 499 m.p.h. at 15,000 ft. with 2,160 lbs. of static ground level thrust.

Appendix IV

Description of Meteor III; extracts from Central Fighter Establishment documents:

Role

7. The Meteor III is a short range single seater interceptor fighter. With the addition of 180 gallon drop tank, a larger range is possible. (Note: drop tanks were not available during the period of operations in World War II).

Airframe

9. The airframe is of normal metal construction, with the tail-plane mounted on the fin to be clear of the jet blast. The pilot is seated in front alongside the guns which are in the fuselage, the fuel tanks are also in the fuselage.

10. Normal split flaps are fitted, strong enough to be put down to 20 deg at 225 m.p.h. to assist in slowing up, and to be fully deflected at 150 m.p.h. The air brakes extend from the middle of the chord of the stub wing between the fuselage and engine and are slotted plates. They are stressed to be used at all speeds, and are operated hydraulically to two positions only, fully extended or retracted.

11. The tricycle undercarriage is hydraulically operated from a pump on the starboard engine, with a hand pump in the cockpit and an hydraulic accumulator for emergency use. The accumulator will give one extension of the undercarriage flaps.

12. Owing to the nose wheel, the aircraft has a low resistance on the ground and wheel brakes are needed to slow up. No emergency brake system is fitted to provide for brake failure through break down or operational damage.

Engines

13. The aircraft is powered by two Rolls Royce Derwent I turbine jets. The characteristic power output, fuel consumption, and surging is dealt with in Appendix "D".

14. The true level speed is nearly the same at all altitudes at which the turbines will maintain full r.p.m. as their thrust decreases with altitude in nearly the same degree as the drag of the aircraft.

Fuel capacity

15. The fuel capacity is 330 gallons internally carried in one main fuselage tank which is divided into two compartments, the front one feeding the port engine and the rear one the starboard engine.

17. The two compartments of the main tanks can be inter-connected by a balance cock when the fuel will settle to the same level in the two tanks. This does not enable the two engines to be run off one tank.

Auxiliary Power

20. Electric power is supplied by a generator fitted on the port engine and a 40 ampere hour accumulator. The services operated are:- engine fuel pumps; compass, radio, gun firing, gyro gunsight, fuel, gauges, I.F.F., cockpit lighting and cockpit warning lights.

22. The hydraulic pump is driven by the starboard engine and serves undercarriage retraction, flap operation, and air brakes, An hydraulic accumulator will give an emergency extension of the undercarriage, and a cockpit hand pump is also fitted which lowers the undercarriage 130 strokes and raises in 150. Flaps are lowered in 52 strokes and are raised in 42 strokes.

23. A vacuum pump for instrument operation is fitted to each engine, with a vacuum transfer cock on the right of the pilot.

24. Pneumatic system which operates the brakes and cocks the guns is fed by air bottles which have to be refilled on the ground. (No engine driven compressor is fitted). The connection is in the port wheel bay.

Guns

25. The aircraft carried four Mk. II 20 mm. Hispano guns, two on each side of the cabin. They are mounted on diaphragms built out from the main webs. The fuselage structure is protected by metal blast tubes.

Ammunition

26. Ammunition is carried in four 150 round tanks mounted in pairs one above the other in the magazine bay. A rounds counter is fitted to the port side of the cockpit.

Gun Firing Control

27. The guns, which are fired electrically, are controlled by a wobble type button on the control column. When the flap is open the gun circuit is live and depressing any part of the finger plate fires all four guns and operates the camera.

28. If the guns are wired for selective firing, only two guns fire when the top of the finger plate is pressed, pressure on the bottom firing the other two. All four guns fire when the centre of the finger plate is pressed. The camera operates in all cases, but its harmonisation is disturbed by firing the guns.

29. A micro-switch is fitted to ensure that the gun circuit is broken when the undercarriage is down.

Gun Heating

30. The guns are heated by hot air, from a muff fitted round the port jet pipe, being blown on to the underside of the gun bodies. No control is provided.

Gunsight

31 ... Projector Type 1, Mk. 1. The sight, which reflects on the windscreen, is fitted to the mounting which is attached to the windscreen base. The gunsight dimmer switch is on the instrument panel and the master switch on the starboard switch panel.

Camera

33. A G.45 Camera, mounted in the fuselage nose fairing, operates with the guns through the wobble button, or can be operated independently by depressing the camera finger plate, which is visible when the safety flap is closed over the gun finger plate. An exposure and footage indicator is fitted on the port side of the cabin. The camera master switch is on the starboard switch panel.

Armour

35. 7.m.m. armour plate is fitted to the nose wheel and seat bulkheads. The windscreen panels and the rear view panels in the seat bulkhead are of armoured glass. The top skin forward of the windscreen is 10 SWG light alloy with 4 mm armour deflection plates fitted on the underside.

36. The rear nose wheel doors and the main webs forming the sides of the cabin are of 10 SWG light alloy to act as deflector panels. Other 10 SWG light alloy deflector panels are fitted to the outer structure at the sides of the cabin.

Ancillary Equipment

37. A TR.1143A V.H.F. set is fitted with the control box in front slightly above the throttle lever.

38. I.F.F. is fitted and a G.45 camera gun. No provision is made for reconnaissance camera.

39. A fire extinguisher is fitted to each engine. They are operated manually by pressing the two red buttons situated on the right hand side of the instrument panel next to the hood jettison handle.

Weights and Loadings.

47. The full loaded all up weight is 12,614 lbs., and the corresponding wing loading is 34 lbs/sq. ft. The wing loading of the Tempest V… is 38 lbs/sq. ft.

49. The maximum landing weight permitted is 12,000 lbs. This is reached with a clean aircraft when 250 gallons of fuel remains.

52. On the limited experience of this unit, the following times for typical servicing jobs have been found and are shown with similar jobs on the Tempest:-

	Tempest	Meteor
Mainplane Change	115 man hours	20 man hours
Engine Change	105 " " ex crate (75 man hours with components fitted)	48 " "
Minor inspections	105 man hours	70 " "
Daily Inspections		
Fitter	1.30 " "	.45 " "
Rigger	1.00 " "	.45 " "
Instruments	.10 " "	.10 " "
Electrical	.30 " "	.30 " "
Wireless	.05 " "	.05 " "
Armament	.30 " "	.30 " "
Refuelling (Oil and Fuel)	.15 " "	.20 " "
Reaming	.10 " " (2 airmen)	.15 " " (4 airmen)

(a) A delay of up to twenty minutes is caused in the daily inspection in removing and replacing the intake grill owing to the complication of the fastening.

(b) But in general it will be seen that the Meteor is much easier to service than the Tempest.

FLYING LIMITATIONS

54. (i) The maximum permissible speed on the Meteor III, imposed for structural considerations is 500 I.A.S.

(ii) The critical Mach number on the Meteor III is .74. (This is additional to the 500 m.p.h. I.A.S. restriction mentioned above). Therefore, it can be seen that at low altitude the structural limitation is

(iii) Intentional spinning is prohibited.
(iv) The undercarriage or flaps should not be lowered above 155 m.p.h. I.A.S.; if the undercarriage is down the aircraft should not be flown above 225 m.p.h. I.A.S.
(v) Aerobatics should not be performed at all up weights in excess of 12,300 lbs.
(vi) The aircraft should not be landed at all-up weights above 12,000 lbs.
(vii) The operational limitation are:-

Limit	r.p.m.	Jet Pipe Temp.	Time
Take-off	16,400/16,600	680	5 mins.
Climbing	16,000	650	30 "
Combat	16,400	680	5 "
Cruising	15,400	600	

<u>Handling in the Air</u>

62. … at normal service loadings

<u>Take-off</u>

63. To take-off, both the elevator and rudder trimming tabs need to be set at "Neutral". The engines are normally run up to a maximum r.p.m. against the brakes (16,500 + or – 100 r.p.m.), to ascertain whether full power is available, to check that the jet pipe temperature is not exceeding the maximum and the burner pressure is normal. One third flap can be used to shorten the take-off run. When the brakes are released the aircraft accelerates fairly slowly, with no tendency to swing. Using one third flap with no wind the aircraft becomes airborne in about 650 yards, approximately 105 m.p.h.

Landing

64. The Meteor III is a very straightforward and easy aircraft to land. Pilots do not find any difficulty in familiarising themselves with the tricycle undercarriage landing procedure and the brakes are good.

65. Even with the flaps down, the gliding angle is rather shallow and the speed without the use of dive brakes decreases very slowly. A normal gliding approach is recommended, flaps and wheels down, under 150 m.p.h., last turn in at 140 m.p.h. and the final approach at 115 m.p.h.

67. Landings have been made in cross winds without difficulty, the maximum being a wind of 30 m.p.h. at right angles to the runway. The Meteor is considered suitable for single runway operation.

Flying Controls

68. Rudder. The rudder is heavy, but effective. Owing, however, to the fact that use of the rudder tends to increase the snaking at medium and high speeds, this effectiveness is not an advantage.

69. Ailerons. The response to aileron movement is good but the stick force necessary to produce any particular movement is much heavier than on any modern fighter (at 1946, Author).

70. Elevator. The elevators are light and effective. Elevator and rudder trimmers are fitted. These are effective, especially above approximately 300 m.p.h., and provide adequate trim throughout the speed range. There is no change of trim on "unstuck" or when the undercarriage is retracted, and the slight tendency to sink when the flaps are raised can easily be corrected by elevators.

General Handling

71. On the whole, the aircraft is pleasant to fly in calm weather. At the lower end of the speed range the slightly greater care which has to be paid to the control movements suggests that the measure of longitudinal stability decreases with speed. Above 250 m.p.h., however, the balance between stability and elevator

stick force for manoeuvring is pleasant. At no time does the aircraft tighten in turns.

72. Due to the characteristics of the jet engine, the initial acceleration during take-off is moderate, and the climb is poor when airborne until the climbing speed is reached after which the best rate of climb is obtained at a comparatively high air speed and small angle of climb. The slow acceleration occurs at low speeds in all circumstances.

73. The great disadvantage of the Meteor III from a tactical and general viewpoint is the heaviness of the ailerons throughout the speed range. At medium and high speeds evasive action and even moderate turns are very tiring.

74. It is considered that the upright seating position and the low rudder pedals are a distinct disadvantage in combating the effects of "G".

75. The almost complete absence of change of trim on a typical fighter sortie relives the pilot a great deal.

76. Under "bumpy" weather conditions the aircraft becomes directionally unstable, the instability manifesting itself as moderate to bad "snaking". The only cure for this is to throttle back and reduce speed; the use of rudder only aggravates it.

<u>Search and Sighting View</u>

77. The view forward and to both sides is excellent. To the rear, however, immediately behind the pilots head, the metal armour-plate greatly restricts the view. Further considerable distortion is noted when objects are viewed through the rear canopy.

<u>Low Flying</u>

78. The Meteor III is a pleasant aircraft for low flying, having an excellent all-round view except that the original view forward and down is partly blocked by Gyro Gunsight (note this document dated 1946).

<u>Aerobatics</u>

79. The Meteor III would be an excellent aircraft for all aerobatic manoeuvres if the ailerons were not so heavy. It has the advantage that the turbines do not cut under conditions of negative "G" as provision is made for 15 seconds inverted flight

Formation Flying

80. Owing to the poor acceleration and deceleration of the Meteor aircraft, a little difficulty may be found to begin with in keeping a steady position. The normal fault is over-correction with the throttles, but with practise, this can be overcome. At speeds above 300 I.A.S. formation becomes simple, because the power of the engine increases, and it will be found that in the region of 350 I.A.S. any response to the throttle compares favourably with that of the conventional fighter.

81. For formation take-offs, the use of 16,000 r.p.m. by the Leader is recommended, thus allowing 400 r.p.m. for the rest of the section to use for correction.

82. The Leader should hold his aircraft on the ground longer than for a normal independent take-off, to enable the rest of the section to gain more speed before becoming airborne.

83. For formation flying, 15,000 r.p.m. allows sufficient reserve for keeping station and gives a suitable speed.

84. Formation landings are quite straightforward. Owing to the slow throttle response at low speeds it is essential for the Leader to give clear signals when he wants the wheels and flaps lowered.

Operational Ceiling and handling at altitude

85. The height at which rate of climb falls below 1,000 ft per minute was 31,000 ft. The handling qualities of the Meteor III at altitude are similar to lower down. Care must be taken to see that the burner pressure does not fall below 10 lbs/sq. in. As height is gained the r.p.m. have to be reduced to avoid surging.

Single Engined Flight

101. Single engine flying on the Meteor III presents no difficulties. The property of a normal propeller-engined twin aircraft to roll immediately an engine cuts is reduced on the Meteor.

102. The following approximate figures have been found from trials made at this establishment (Central Fighter Establishment) – N.B: In all cases the "dead engine" was stopped, not merely throttled back.

    (i)   <u>At 5,000 ft. – Starboard engine stopped</u>
            <u>Wheels and flaps up</u>
            15,400 r.pm. straight and level 250 I.A.S.
            16,500 r.p.m. "   " 284 I.A.S.

            16,000 r.p.m. climbing at 225 I.A.S. 450 ft/mins
            16,500 r.p.m. "   " "   " 600 "

    (ii)   <u>Port engine stopped</u>
            <u>Undercarriage down, flaps up</u>
            16,500 r.p.m. straight and level 168 I.A.S.
            16,500 r.p.m. climbing at 150 I.A.S. 80 ft/min.

At 16,500 r.p.m. with undercarriage and flaps down the aircraft does not maintain height. At 120 I.A.S. it losses height at approximately 100 ft/min. The minimum speed to control the aircraft and maintain height with the undercarriage down and quarter flap is 125/130 I.A.S. At this speed full opposite rudder is needed.

<u>Weapon Training</u>
116. <u>Towed Targets</u>.   Apart from its snaking qualities, the Meteor is a simple and straightforward aeroplane for firing against towed targets. Positioning for beam, quarter and shallow deflection attacks is especially easy due to the good forward vision.

118 <u>Ground Attack</u>.   The higher speeds which are unavoidable in diving attacks introduce a greater degree of snaking than in air to air gunnery. Although the speed can be kept down by the use of dive brakes, for the reasons given in

para. 127, this is undesirable if the pilots are to be trained in the operational use of their aircraft, and the use of dive brakes is not advised except prior to entry into the dive. The bumpy conditions which normally occur at low altitudes also aggravate snaking.

119. Two types of attack were found to be most effective:-

    (i) A dive well back from the target from 4,000 ft. flattening out until a height of 300 ft. is reached at a speed of 400 – 500 I.A.S. Opening fire at this height at a range of approximately 1200 yards and ceasing fire at 300 yards and breaking violently to right or to left at low altitude.

    (ii) A medium dive attack of about 15°, using dive brakes at entry.

120. Both these types of attack are designed to give plenty of time in which to get the sight steady on the target as it is essential to avoid violent manoeuvring. As with air-to-air firing, the rudder should not be used for aim corrections.

121. On occasions when carrying out ground attacks it was found that the debris thrown into the air from the target area has caused damage to the aircraft. Therefore, it is essential for the pilot to break off his attack by changing direction and keep from flying over his target. The Meteor is prone to damage from debris owing to its high speed and poor manoeuvrability.

Dive Brakes

122. The tactical use of dive brakes has been investigated with special reference to the following points:-

    (i) Escort evasion.
    (ii) Dog fighting.
    (iii) Ground attack dive.
    (iv) Quick circuit and landing.

<u>Escort Evasion</u>

123. For escort evasion, that is to say, diving through an escort of fighters and applying the brakes to attack the bombers, a number of trials established that if sufficient warning is given by the Leader for the brakes to be used, the aircraft stay in formation very well, and it is considered that with good briefing this would

apply to Squadron and even Wing formations. It is, however, considered that the serious loss of speed resulting would place the attacking aircraft at a tactical disadvantage.

Dog Fighting

124. For the tactical reason stated above, the use of dive brakes is advised only on selected occasions. Two such occasions are to avoid immediate attack by an overtaking aircraft and when overshooting oneself. At all other times the maintenance of high speed is necessary in case it is required to break off an engagement.

125. The use of dive brakes for controlling the speed in a half-roll and pull-out has been investigated. From 15,000 ft a half-roll and pull-out is completed by 10,000 ft without using brakes, from a starting speed of 200 I.A.S. The speed on reaching level flight is 380 I.A.S. When the brakes are used at the start of the dive immediately after rolling, level flight is regained at 10,000 (ft) also, at a speed of 320 I.A.S. As the brakes are extended the elevator becomes very light and insensitive, and it is considered probable that owing to this lack of "bite", there might be a tendency for pilots to pull back too far on the control column and flick into a spin.

Ground Attack Dive

126. Enough speed must be kept for get away and zoom when using dive brakes to slow up to a convenient speed for ground attack. The dive brakes should be taken off before putting the sight on as its retraction unsettles the aim.

PART III
Tactical COMPARISON WITH THE TEMPEST V

Level Speeds

128. The Meteor III is faster than the Tempest V at all heights. The following table gives the approximate comparative figures at various heights with full throttle:-

	Speed T.A.S.		
Height	Meteor	Tempest	Difference
1,000 ft.	465	381	84
15,000 ft.	471	416	55
30,000 ft.	465	390	75

Acceleration and deceleration in straight and level flight

129. Comparative acceleration trials have been carried out throughout the height range, and the results are similar, irrespective of height. At 8,000 ft. accelerating from a Meteor indicated speed of 190 the Tempest V has a slight initial advantage, but after approximately 30 secs., and as speed approaches 300 Meteor I.A.S., the Meteor III draws away rapidly and is out of range, i.e. 600 yards, in approximately 1½ mins. At 250/260 m.p.h. Meteor III I.A.S. their acceleration is identical at 8,000 ft.

13-. Comparative retardation trials at the Tempest V's maximum speed, shows that when the Meteor does not use its dive brakes, if the throttles of both aircraft are closed, the Tempest V will be behind the Meteor III in a position to shoot it down almost immediately at all heights. When the dive brakes are used, the position is reversed. After using them, however, it is necessary to retract to avoid dropping out of range.

Zoom climbs

132. In a pull-out and zoom climb at 40° with full throttle, from 500 I.A.S., during the pull-out the Tempest and Meteor are identical, but immediately the nose of the Meteor comes up to the horizon, it starts pulling away quite rapidly, and by the time its best climbing speed, i.e. 225 m.p.h. is reached, it is approximately 750 ft. above and 600 yards ahead of the Tempest. By steepening the angle of zoom the Meteor can convert this lead into a further height advantage. These facts apply at whatever height the zoom is commenced.

Turning Circles

133. The Meteor III which has a lower wing loading turns inside the Tempest V under all conditions, and can get on its tail in approximately four turns.

Rates of Roll

134. The Tempest V out rolls the Meteor III easily at all speeds, and the latter is therefore at a disadvantage in the initial manoeuvres of a combat.

Dive

135. If both aircraft are dived from any set level conditions up to the Meteor's limiting speed, and throttles are not opened during the dive, there is nothing to choose between the two. If, however, the throttles are fully opened in a dive from 12,000 feet, the Meteor is 500 yards ahead of the Tempest by the time its limiting speed of 500 m.p.h. is reached.

Conclusions

136. The Meteor III is superior to the Tempest V in almost all departments. If it were not for the heaviness of its ailerons and its consequent poor manoeuvrability in the rolling plane, and the adverse effects of snaking on it as a gun platform, it would be a comparable all-round fighter with a greatly increased performance.

PART IV
SUMMARY OF CONCLUSIONS

137. The Meteor has a high performance at low and medium altitude, its performance at high altitudes is moderate owing to the power output of the turbines being reduced by surging.

139. The Meteor has instability in yaw, ("snaking"), which makes it unsuitable as a gun platform at operational speeds.

140. It is pleasant to fly and handles satisfactorily except for the heaviness of the aileron control which is unsuitable for a fighter. This turbine jet engine gives slower acceleration at low speeds.

141. The dive brakes are valuable tactically on selected occasions and also for economical flying as they allow a steeper

dive at the limiting speed and curtail the time and space occupied when reducing speed before landing.

142. The forward view is normally very good, but is bad in rain as the front and front-side panels become entirely obscured. The clearness of vision to the rear is reduced by three transparent layers; and additionally it is difficult to clean the inner surface of the bubble canopy.

143. The position of the present cockpit lighting is not acceptable, but with the re-positioning as suggested… it becomes more satisfactory.

144. The armament of four 20 mm guns grouped in the nose is ideal… The duration of fire is limited to 15 seconds.

CALCULATION OF RADIUS OF ACTION
Meteor III with 330 Galls. Fuel

10,000 ft. Altitude

Conditions	r.p.m.	Consumption two turbines Gall/hr	Total	T.A.S. m.p.h.	Knots	Range - Miles Statute	Nautical
3 mins. take off power	16,500	640	32	-	-	-	-
5 mins. Climb to 10,000 ft.	14,500	-	30	-	-	19	17
5 mins. Combat	16,500	480	40	470	408	-	-
15 min. cruising	15,400	325	81	395	343	99	86
Balance at economical	M.E.C	210	147	328	285	230	200
Totals			330			348	303
Less 20%						70	61
						278	242
					Radius	139	121

CALCULATION OF RADIUS OF ACTION
Meteor III with 330 Galls. Fuel

20,000 ft. Altitude

Conditions	r.p.m.	Consumption two turbines Gall/hr	Total	T.A.S. m.p.h.	Knots	Range - Miles Statute	Nautical
3 mins. take off power	16,500	640	32	-	-	-	-
5 mins. Climb to 10,000 ft.	14,500	-	65	-	-	52	45
5 mins. Combat	16,500	360	30	472	410	-	-
15 min. cruising	15,400	240	60	385	334	96	83
Balance at economical	M.E.C	195	143	345	300	253	220
Totals			330			401	348
Less 20%						80	69
						321	279
					Radius	160	139

APPENDIX 'C'
FIG. 1

BEST HEIGHT FOR RANGE REQUIRED

METEOR III – DERWENT I

FOR MAX. RANGE, CLIMB TO SELECTED ALTITUDE
AT MAX. CLIMBING R.P.M.

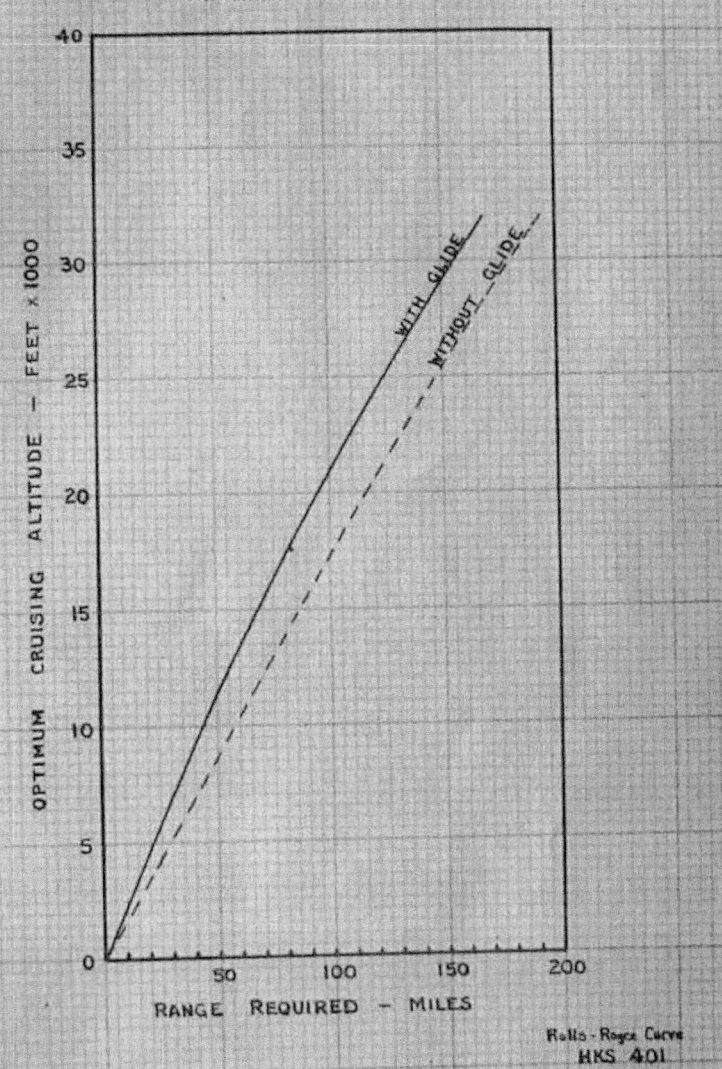

Rolls-Royce Curve
HKS 401
Copied 24.4.46

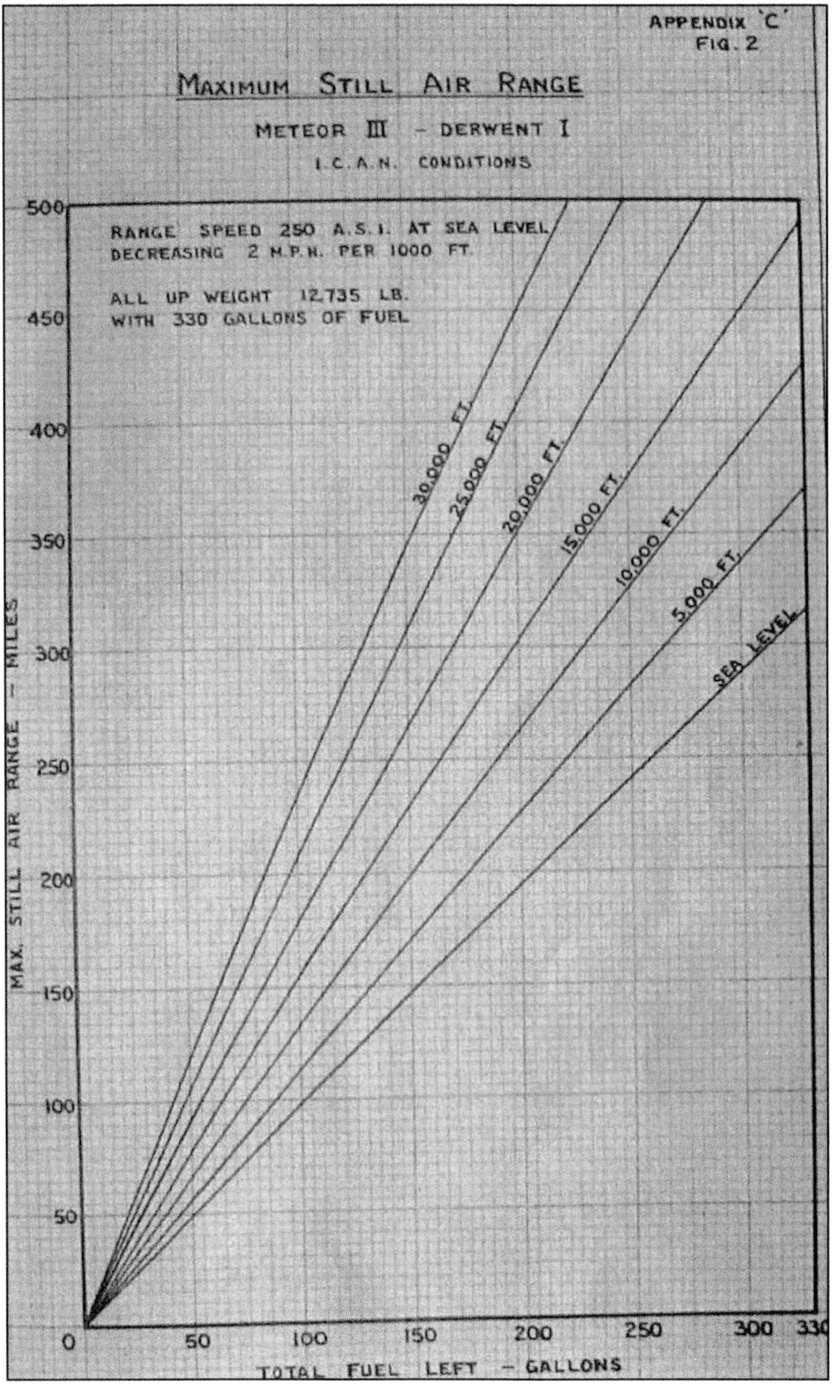

APPENDIX 'C'
FIG. 2
MAXIMUM STILL AIR RANGE
METEOR III - DERWENT I
I.C.A.N. CONDITIONS
RANGE SPEED 250 A.S.I. AT SEA LEVEL
DECREASING 2 M.P.H. PER 1000 FT.
ALL UP WEIGHT 12,735 LB.
WITH 330 GALLONS OF FUEL
30,000 FT.
25,000 FT.
20,000 FT.
15,000 FT.
10,000 FT.
5,000 FT.
SEA LEVEL
MAX. STILL AIR RANGE - MILES
TOTAL FUEL LEFT - GALLONS
0
50
100
150
200
250
300
350
400
450
500

Appendix V

The following three documents relate to concerns about disclosure of jet propelled aircraft developments in the press and the decision to release further information about Allied jet propelled aircraft developments in 1944.

Extract from:

W.M. (44), 98th Conclusions – Meeting of the War Cabinet held in the Cabinet War Room S.W.1, on Friday, 28 July, 1944, at 3 p.m.

On 28 July:

The Prime Minister said that he had been disturbed to see in the Daily Express a suggestion that jet-propelled fighters might be used against flying-bombs.

It was most important that newspapers should not speculate about future operations or about the development of new weapons, since even ill-informed guesses might lead the enemy to discover our plans.

The Minister of Information said that there was no question of disclosure of information in this case, but it was right that a warning should be given against speculation on topics of this kind. He undertook to convey a warning in the appropriate quarters.

Complete reproduction of W.P (944) 502. Concerning releasing further information on Allied Jet Propelled aircraft developments

TOP SECRET

W.P. (44) 502.
5th September 1944.

WAR CABINET.

PROPOSAL BY GENERAL ARNOLD FOR A SECOND JOINT ANGLO-AMERICAN STATEMENT REGARDING JET PROPELLED AIRCRAFT.

MEMORANDUM BY THE VICE CHIEFS OF STAFF

IN January 1944, when production of jet-propelled aircraft began, it became necessary to issue a joint Anglo-American statement in order to prevent speculations and unauthorised disclosures in the Press, more particularly in America, giving information to the enemy. It was feared that unofficial statements and articles by each side would tend through competitive publicity to prejudice security. It was therefore agreed between Sir Charles Portal and General Arnold that no further official statements would be made and that they would discourage, so far as they could any publicity in the Press on this subject.

2. Recently the Ministry of Aircraft Production recommended that, in the interests of production, this policy should be altered and that a statement should be issued by us revealing that British jet-propelled aircraft were operational. It was most unlikely that the Americans would agree to a one-sided public disclosure that in the development of these aircraft we were ahead of them. At the same time it was undesirable on security grounds to reveal to the enemy that we were operating jet-propelled aircraft against flying-bombs.

3. Speculation in the press about the use of jet-propelled aircraft against flying-bombs led the War Cabinet to rule that it was most important to prevent the enemy from discovering our plans about future operations and the development of our new weapons. Again, at the meeting of 31st July 1944, it was decided to discourage all references or speculations in the Press about the operational use of these aircraft.

4. The enemy has in the meantime brought a certain number of them into use against Allied, more particularly American aircraft. Several engagements have already taken place and a good deal of public interest has been aroused in America. The fact that the enemy is using this modern equipment against the American forces has increased the pressure upon General Arnold to issue some further statements reassuring the American public that the enemy has not been alone in developing this new weapon. Under this pressure General Arnold has proposed that a second joint statement on the subject should be made. The direction of the War Cabinet is desired as to what answer should be sent to General Arnold.

5. From the British point of view the Ministry of Aircraft Production would like a statement made for the encouragement of their work-people and as recognition of British enterprise in this field. No new technical information would be conveyed to the enemy by a general statement.

6. There are certain disadvantages in making a further statement at this time. The Germans are, in fact ahead of us in employment of this new weapon. We as yet are only using them in very small numbers and not against either the German or Japanese Air Force. It may be some months before they will be used in substantial numbers. It thus seems undesirable to make a claim which might later be found to have been lacking in substance.

7. On balance, the Vice-Chiefs of Staff are in favour of a public statement being made. This would be framed in general terms to show that British and American development of jet-propelled aircraft had reached the operational stage, and

would reassure the public while in no way suggesting that our development is in advance of the enemy's. Such a statement would be disconcerting rather than otherwise to the enemy and would no longer present any security objection. A draft of the kind of statement contemplated is attached.

    8.   The War Cabinet is asked to agree that a further statement should be made and that the chief of the Air Staff, after consultation with the Ministry of Aircraft Production, should have discretion to agree a joint text with General Arnold.

(Signed) A.E.NYE.
D.C.S. EVILL.
E.N. SYFRET.

Offices of the War Cabinet, S.W. 1,
    5th September 1944.

ANNEX
DRAFT ANNOUNCEMENT FOR DISCUSSION WITH GENERAL ARNOLD

Communiqués and correspondents' stories from the European theatre have recorded that allied aircraft have been in action against German jet-propelled aircraft.

The appearance of these new types had been expected and it is gratifying to note that their design, features and operational characteristics appear to follow closely the estimates which had been formed of them.

Our aircrews were not therefore surprised and in engagements to date have had satisfactory exchanges with them in combat.

A number of attacks have been successfully beaten off before they could develop. None of our own aircraft is known to have been shot down, while our aircrews have already destroyed some of them.

We must expect, however, that as their numbers increase and their crews gain more experience of handling them in action they will become more effective than they have so far proved to be.

Meanwhile, our own jet-propelled aircraft are also coming into operational service against the enemy. Details of these aircraft and their engines must still remain secret, but research scientists, aircraft technicians and workers in both Britain and America may take pride in their work and the speed at which this new weapon is going into the hands of our air forces.

Extract from:

C.O.S. (44) 298th Meeting (0).
WAR CABINET
CHIEFS OF STAFF COMMITTEE.

MINUTES of Meeting held on Tuesday, 5TH SEPTEMBER, 1944, at 10.30 a.m.
PRESENT
Lieut.-General Sir Archibald E. Nye,
Vice-Chief of the Imperial General Staff.

| Air Marshal Sir Douglas Evrill, | Vice-Admiral Sir Nevill Syfret, |
| Vive Chief of the Air Staff. | Vive-Chief of the Naval Staff. |

7. JOINT ANGLO-AMERICAN STATEMENT REGARDING JET-PROPELLED AIRCRAFT

The committee had before them a Memorandum by the Vice-Chief of the Air Staff requesting the Chiefs of Staff to agree that the Chiefs of the Air Staff should have discretion, after consultation with the Ministry of Aircraft Production, to agree with General Arnold the text of a joint Anglo-American announcement regarding jet-propelled aircraft.

SIR DOUGLAS EVILL said that before any such statement could be issued, it would be necessary to ask the War

Cabinet to alter their previous decision regarding reference in the press about the operational use of jet-propelled aircraft.

THE COMMITTEE:-

(a) Instructed the Secretary to submit the memorandum, as amended in discussion, to the War Cabinet over their signatures.

(b) Took note that, if the War Cabinet agreed to the proposals in the Memorandum, the Vice-Chief of the Air Staff would consult with the Ministry of Aircraft Production and signal to the Chief of the Air Staff the text of an agreed announcement.

Appendix VI

616 Squadron Record Sheet 'A' (Operational sorties with the Meteor F Mk. I)
27 July 1944 – 3 September 1944

Record Sheet 'A' July 1944

Date	Target or task	Effective	Hrs Flown	Aborts	Hrs Flown	Load carried	Expended (SAA by calibre)
\multicolumn{8}{l}{Day sorties (Aircraft)}
27	Intercept	8	5+5			9600	
28	Intercept	15	11.00			16000	
29	Intercept	4	2.05?			4500	
30	Intercept	2	1.40			2400	110
31	-	-	-			-	
Total		29	21.00			32500	110

Record Sheet 'A' September 1944

Date	Target or task	Effective	Hrs Flown	Aborts	Hrs Flown	Load carried	Expended (SAA by calibre)
\multicolumn{8}{l}{Day sorties (Aircraft)}
1	Intercept	21	....?			25200	....?
2	Intercept	4	2.15?			4800	
3	Intercept	3	2.30			3600	
Total		28	21.15			33600	...?

The total number of operational sorties flown during the Flying Bomb campaign in July, August and September 1944 is fraught with discrepancies between various records. The OPREP's list 327 sorties and the Record Sheet 'A' lists 323. The discrepancy between these two figures is small. The OPREP record for 19 August states 21 sorties, while the Record Sheet 'A' record for 19 August is a bit unclear. It appears to be 17, but may be a misprint or misinterpretation. The OPREP and Record Sheet 'A' figures conflict with other records such as the ORB form 540 and Air Ministry File D.D. Ops. (A.D.) 1., dated 16 March 1945, which states that the squadron flew "260 anti-flying bomb sorties, resulting in 11 claims." This figure is inaccurate as are the number of claims that the squadron submitted. The ORB Form 540/541 lists sortie numbers, which conflict with each other and other records such as the OPREP and Record Sheet 'A'. It is concluded that the OPREP figure of 327 is the most reliable and accurate.

Record Sheet 'A' August 1944

Record Sheet A August 1944

Day sorties (Aircraft)

Date	Target or task	Effective Sorties	Hrs Flown	Aborts	Hrs Flown	Load carried	Expended (SAA by calibre)
1	-	-	-			-	
2	F/B Patrol	3	2.30			3600	
3	F/B Patrol	10	6.45			12000	70
4	F/B Patrol	7	3.05?			8400	100
5	F/B Patrol	7	4.15			8400	
6	F/B Patrol	4	2.30			4800	
7	F/B Patrol	6	2.30			7200	120
8	-	-	-			-	
9	F/B Patrol	12	5.30			9600?	
10	F/B Patrol	19	11.00			20800	230?
11	F/B Patrol	4	2.15			4800	70
12	-	-	-			-	
13	F/B Patrol	1	0.45			1200	
14	F/B Patrol	8	4.15			9600	
15	F/B Patrol	8	3.15			9600	70
16	F/B Patrol	30	11.45?			36000	962
17	F/B Patrol	21	15.30?			25200	1336?
18	F/B Patrol	15	6.30			18000	
19	F/B Patrol	21	11.05			20400	1209?
20	F/B Patrol	5	3.15?			6000	
21	-	-	-				
22	-	-	-				
23	F/B Patrol	17	?			20400	
24	F/B Patrol	11	7.15			13200	
25	F/B Patrol	15	11.20			20400	1209?
26	F/B Patrol	2	1.00			2400	
27	F/B Patrol	6	3.15			7200	
28	F/B Patrol	23	17...?			30600	1360?
29	F/B Patrol	15	10.00			18000	614?
30	F/B Patrol	7	5.20			8400	
31	F/B Patrol	14	8.05?			16800	600?
Total		291					

Note 1: Where a '?' appears the record has been unclear or illegible.

Note 2: This record states three sorties for 2 August, which conforms with the OPREP for the period, however, other records suggest 4.

Note 3: This record states 21 sorties for the 17th, which conforms to the OPREP for that day, but conflicts with ORB Form 540, which records only 9 sorties.

Appendix VII

616 Squadron Record Sheet C (other Meteor flying - non operational)

21 July 1944 – 31 December 1944

July 1944

Record Sheet C July 1944
Other Flying – non Operational (Day Only)

Date	Sorties	Hours Flown	Practice Expenditure (20 mm)
21	2	1.30	
22	1	0.15	
23	10	5.45	
24	-	-	
25	18	6.30	
26	7	4.00	
27	3	2.00	
28	2	1.80	320
29	-	-	
30	7	4.45	165
31	8	3.45	1,789
Total	53	30.00+	2,274

August 1944

Record Sheet C August 1944
Other Flying – non Operational (Day Only)

Date	Sorties	Hours Flown	Practice Expenditure (20 mm)	
1	3	0.45	516	
2	1	0.45		
3	1	0.45	2125	
4	4	3.15	230	
5	10 or 11?	7.00		
6	8	5.10?	186	
7	4	2.30	1711	
8	3	1.00	320	
9	7	5.00		
10	2	1.30	165	
11	1	0.30	832	
12	-	-		
13	4	3.00	600	
14	13	5.15	2125	
15	16	....?		1,200
16	5?	1.15	130	
17	-	-		
18	1	0.25	1711	
19	2	1.00		
20	2	1.15		
21	-	-		
22	-	-		
23	5	4.45?	767	
24	1	0.30		
25	2	1.15		
26	10	8.00		
27	5	2.15?		
28	5	2.00	150?	
29	3	1.05		
30	2	1.15	240	
31	-	-		
Total	120	18.45?	9,720?	1,200

Note: The above figures are taken from documents that are in places illegible or partially illegible. The sortie numbers for example are clearly 120 in total, but there are some doubts on sortie numbers on certain dates. Where a '?' appears then the figures are either unknown, partially or completely assembled from other documents. Even when figures are clear there are some minor discrepancies with other documents. The figure of 1,200 in the bottom right corner relates to 20 mm ammunition wastage.

September 1944

Record Sheet C September 1944
Other Flying – non Operational (Day Only)

Date	Sorties	Hours Flown	Practice Expenditure (20 mm)
1	5	3.30	
2	2	1.15	
3	1	0.25?	810
4	2	1.25	1,200
5	-	-	
6	16?	11.15	2,215
7	-	-	
8	7	4.25	1,200
9	1	0.15	
10	19	12.15	2,100
11	22	20.30	832
12	23	14.15	
13	11	6.15	
14	8 or 9?	6.00	
15	(illegible, single figure)	2.45	1,200
16	15	8.30	1,780
17	12	6.15	1,200
18	-	-	
19	9	2.15	
20	-	-	
21	-	-	
22	1	0.30	
23	19?	11.30	1,200
24	-	-	
25	9	6.00	
26	10	9.00	
27	20	12.15	
28	10	6.15	2,610
29	12	2.10	
30	13	5.00	1,680
31	-	-	
Total	255		

October 1944

Record Sheet C October 1944
Other Flying (Day Only)

Date	Sorties	Hours Flown	Practice Expenditure (20 mm)
1	13	6.30	
2	12	9.00	
3	17	11.30	
4	6	2.30	
5	10	7.00	
6	19	10.15	
7	6	3.15	
8	-	-	
9	7	3.15	
10	4	0.45	
11	-	-	
12	2	0.45	
13	10	6.00	
14	7	4.15	
15	4	1.45	
16	1	0.15	
17	4	1.45	
18	11	6.15	
19	7	2.30	
20	2	1.30	
21	7	4.15	
22	6	2.45	
23	3	1.30	
24	6	2.00	
25	11	5.15	
26	2	1.30	
27	3	1.50	
28	7	3.00	
29	6	4.30	650
30	11	6.30	220
31	-	-	
Total	204	116.45	880

November 1944

Record Sheet C November 1944
Other Flying – non Operational (Day Only)

Date	Sorties	Hours Flown	Practice Expenditure (20 mm)
1	10	6.45	
2	14	8.45	
3	4	2.30	
4	10	5.15	840
5	14	7.45	
6	16	9.15	
7	19	9.45	
8	7	4.45	
9	7	5.00	
10	11	6.16	
11	12	6.00	360
12	8	3.30	
13	9	4.30	
14	9	5.00	
15	4	2.15	600
16	8	5.00	
17	-	-	
18	13	8.30	1,003
19	-	-	
20	14	8.00 or 9.00	260
21	15	10.45	
22	8	4.15	
23	7	6.45	
24	8	4.30	
25	11	6.00	
26	32	11.00	840
27	10	5.00	
28	-	-	
29	13	8.45	
30	16	5.00	460
31	-	-	
Total	309		4,363

December 1944

Record Sheet C December 1944

Other Flying – non Operational (Day Only)

Date	Sorties	Hours Flown	Practice Expenditure (20 mm)
1	9	3.00	120
2	16	9.00	227
3	5	3.00	
4	7	4.00	480
5	12	7.50	480
6	13	7.45	
7	12	7.50	
8	14	8.30	
9	9	6.00	
10	8	6.10	
11	20	12.30	460
12	1	0.15	
13	-	-	
14	10	3.45	
15	7	4.30	
16	7	4.30	
17	-	-	
18	18	12.45	
19	7	4.00	
20	-	-	
21	-	-	
22	-	-	
23	7	8.15	
24	12	9.15	360
25	-	-	
26	1	0.30	240
27	-	-	
28	16	13.45	480
29	9	2.45	660
30	-	-	
31	29	19.30	720
Total	249	155.30	4127

Appendix VIII

Identified No.616 Squadron Meteor deliveries based on Squadron Record Sheets B1, B2 and Operations Record Book Form 540

July 1944

12   Meteor I's EE213/G and EE214/G, both non-operational, were delivered from RAE Farnborough, Hampshire to RAF Culmhead, Somerset for No. 616 Squadron.
21   The two aircraft mentioned above were delivered to RAF Manston, where 616 were to operate from.
23   The first operational Meteors I's arrived at Manston when the five aircraft were flown in from Farnborough.
28   Two Meteor I's were delivered to 616 Squadron in the evening

August 1944

6   Record Sheet B S2 shows 1 Meteor delivered
7   Record Sheet B S2 shows 1 Meteor delivered
10   Record Sheet B S2 shows 1 Meteor delivered
14   Record Sheet B S2 shows 1 Meteor delivered
24   Record Sheet B S2 shows 1 Meteor delivered
27   Record Sheet B S2 shows 1 Meteor delivered

September 1944

2   Record Sheet B1 shows 1 Meteor, probably EE229, but possibly EE219 delivered or re-delivered

October 1944

27   Record Sheet B S1 shows 1 Meteor delivered or redelivered
28   Record Sheet B S1 shows 1 Meteor delivered or redelivered
31   Record Sheet B S1 shows 1 Meteor delivered or redelivered

November 1944

12 Record Sheet B S1 shows 1 Meteor delivered or redelivered

December 1944

9   Record Sheet B S1 shows Meteor I EE217 was received
18 Record Sheet B S2 shows 1 Meteor III delivered; EE231 was the first Meteor III for 616 Squadron
24 Record Sheet B S2 shows 3 Meteor III's delivered including EE233 (possibly EE232)
28 Record Sheet B S1 shows 1 Meteor received, serial number part illegible (could be EE22? or EE21?, but was probably the aircraft damaged on 29 November 1944 being re-delivered
28 Record Sheet B S2 shows 3 Meteors III's delivered.

January 1945

1   Meteor III's EE240 and EE241 delivered
16 Meteor serial part illegible; possibly EE234 or more likely Meteor I EE224 being re-delivered after repairs to accident on 3 January
19 Three Meteor III's delivered

February 1945

13 Three Meteor III's EE246, EE248 and EE250 collected from Moreton Valence. These were Derwent I powered aircraft
22 Meteor III EE253 was collected from Moreton Valence, but landed at Filton as weather closed in
23 Meteor III EE253 arrived at RAF Colerne from Filton

March 145
12 Two Meteor III's were delivered from Moreton Valence

Appendix IX

Identified No.616 Squadron aircraft lost or damaged based on Squadron Record Sheets B1, B2 and Operations Record Book Form 540, for period August 1944 to January 1945

August 1944

15	B S2 1 Meteor damaged or destroyed F/A (Flying Accident) EE224
19	B S2 1 Meteor damaged F/A
28	B S2 1 Meteor damaged or destroyed other cause, not EA (Enemy Action)
29	OPREP NO.19/M states that 1 Meteor Cat. H "crash landed near base when returning from anti-Diver patrol. Pilot escaped with only slight injury."

October 1944

1	BS1 1 Meteor	Flying Accident
15	BS1 1 Meteor	Flying Accident

November 1944

20	BS1 EE217	Flying Accident
29	BS1 EE215?	Flying Accident

January 1945

3	EE229 or EE239 damaged in a flying accident

Appendix X

Official Air Ministry Statement – "RAF Jet Fighters in Action" - Released early in 1945. (Note: This statement has been reproduced from several copies, all of which had the occasional word here and there and sometimes full or part sentences illegible; hence there are several breaks.)

The first and so far the only jet-propelled aircraft of the United Nations to go into action against the enemy is the Gloster 'Meteor'... These 'Meteor' jet-propelled fighters were first employed by No.616 Squadron of the R.A.F. Fighter Command against flying bombs employed by the Luftwaffe last summer from France; so the first combats... British jets were not against conventional aircraft. The R.A.F. 'Meteor' proved to possess a greatly superior speed to the pilotless German flying bombs, and many tactical lessons were learned...

Like the Gloster E.28/39, the first turbine jet aircraft in the world to fly in May 1941, the 'Meteor' is a product of the Gloster Aircraft Company (Hawker Siddeley Group). The Meteor... powered with Rolls-Royce engines manufactured to the basic design of Air Comdre Frank Whittle, R.A.F., in collaboration with Power Jets Ltd and the British Thomson-Houston Co. Ltd. The... (probably first) engine was supplied to the U.S. Army Air Force in October,... was built by Power Jets Ltd. Air Comdre Whittle visited the U.S.A. in order to assist our allies to initiate their development programs.

In addition to the 'Meteor', Great Britain has another jet-propelled fighter in an advanced stage of development. This has been designed by... the de Havilland... These engines are all manufactured on the basic principle used by Air Comdre Whittle.

One built by this company was supplied to the U.S.A.A.F. in July 1944, and was used by the Lockheed Company as the power unit of... prototype aircraft which was built by that firm. The prototype... developed into the Lockheed P-80A.

Other research and development work in active progress with a view to progressive increase of the performance of British-built aircraft using jet propulsion units. These are of a highly secret nature.

Just as full information was provided to the United States... of the original Whittle design, so in conformity with... policy of the

British Government to make all technical information immediately available to our American ally, and details of the progress made by British aircraft firms in developing jet aircraft and engines have been freely communicated to the United States. Information on American developments is similarly being made available to us.

The original British turbine jet aircraft was a single-engined aircraft, but the 'Meteor' is a twin-engined monoplane of very clean design. It first flew experimentally in March 1943, and since then the production... has been considerably improved.

There are several immediate advantages to be found in the jet engine, or gas-turbine. First and foremost; it is simpler in almost every respect than the piston engine; it is lighter; it is far more easily serviced; and it possesses a rotary as distinct from a reciprocating movement. It is known that the Rolls-Royce engine of this type is more efficient and of longer life than the Jumo engine of the German Me.262.

The turbines emit no flame, as did the jet-propulsion units of the flying-bombs, and only under certain rare conditions do they leave any smoke trail. The passage of a jet plane on the ground leaves in its wake the typical smell given off by a hot paraffin oil stove or a hurricane lamp.

The Gloster designers, chief of whom is Mr. W. G. Carter had to take account of a new crop of dynamic problems in order to... with safety at the high speeds at which the 'Meteor' flies, but in spite of this the aircraft is highly praised by the R.A.F. as being very manoeuvrable... Its excellent smoothness of running... and simplicity of the engine controls are welcomed by pilots.

The first R.A.F. squadron to be equipped with "Squirts" as they call their jet planes was a squadron which had previously been flying Spitfires.

The squadrons pilots, not specifically selected in any way and representing an average... of any fighter unit in the Royal Air Force, began their jet training by converting from single-engine aircraft to 'twins', learning the multi-engine technique in Oxfords, standard R.A.F. twin-engine training aircraft.

.... they went solo on 'twins'... and after an average of six hours multi-engine flying time they were judged ready to pass on to the next stage-the jet aircraft.

Travelling secretly, and in small batches, pilots and key ground (crew) went to an R.A.F. experimental establishment. Where jet fighters fresh from the factory assembly lines were awaiting collection.

While the pilots, fortified with a few hours ground instruction from test pilots and experimental personnel, flew their first solo jet flights... added a few hours practise flying on the new type, the ground crews (learned) the care and maintenance of the prototypes.

Then, after a few days, the pilots flew the jet aircraft back to their base, where the aircraft were guarded every minute... by special security police.

The first R.A.F. operational jet patrol was flown during the Battle of the Flying-bomb and had its first success on August 4, 1944. Subsequently, the 'Meteor' shot down a substantial number of flying-bombs.

"They are really beautiful aircraft, and I should hate to return to normal flying," said a pilot. "When they start up and taxi, our 'Squirts' make a noise rather like an oversize vacuum cleaner but when they take off or fly at full throttle, they sound almost like a normal aircraft.

"The cockpit layout differs very little from the conventional type, and it is very comfortable, with good visibility all round.

"The 'Squirts' have plenty of power, and if you open the throttle suddenly you get a kick in the back of your seat. They're sweet to handle even at high speed..."

Appendix XI

British Jet Aircraft of World War 2 significant first flight dates

Gloster E.28/39	
W4041/G	15 May 1941
W4046/G	1 March 1943 (lost 30 June 1943)
Gloster F.9/40	
DG202/G	24 July 1944
DG203/G	9 Nov 1943
DG204/G	13 Nov 1943 (lost 1 April 1944)
DG205/G	23 June (12 June) 1943 (lost 27 April 1944)
DG206/G	5 March 1943
DG207/G	24 July 1945
DG208/G	25 January 1944
DG209/G	18 April 1944
Gloster Meteor I	
EE210/G	12 January 1944
Gloster Meteor III	
EE230/G	September 1944
Gloster Meteor IV	15 August 1945
de Havilland E.6.42	
L2548	20 September 1943
de Havilland Vampire F Mk. I	20 April 1945

Appendix XII

RAF Meteor Strength (aircraft in Squadron service only) from document 'RAF Strength in Squadron' 1944-45.

	Serviceable	Unserviceable	Total
Fighter Command			
Start of			
Nov 1944:	6	2	8
Dec 1944:	6	1	7
Jan 1945:	12	4	16
April 1945	0	4	4
May 1945:	7	9	16
Second Tactical Air Force			
Feb 1945:			21
March 1945:			26
April 1945:	17	5	22
May 1945:	8	5	23

Note 1: The figures for Meteors serving with the Second Tactical Air Force in January 1945; the month that it was transferred (on paper) are not reproduced in the above table. While the Squadron was nominally on the strength of the Second Tactical Air Force from 21 January 1945, it remained in the UK and was loaned to Fighter Command and conducted Anti-Diver patrols beginning on 1 March 1945, until released on 20 March 1945. Although the table shows 21 aircraft on the strength of Second TAC in February 1945 and 26 in March 1945, the only Meteors operating with the Second TAC on the continent during this time were four early production Welland I engine aircraft, which landed at B.58 near Brussels on 4 February 1945. The rest of the Squadron flew out on 31 March 1945.

Note 2: The figures for Second TAC in May 1945 read a total of 23 aircraft, which is close to squadron establishment. The figures of 8 serviceable and 5 unserviceable aircraft add to only 13. It is possible that the figure for serviceable aircraft should read 18 as it is more realistic for the squadron to have had an establishment of more than 13 aircraft at the beginning of May. Other Squadron records bear this out.

Appendix XIII

RAF Fighter Strength excluding Meteors (aircraft in Squadron service only) Fighter Command and Second Tactical Air Force.

Fighter Command	Serviceable	Unserviceable	Total
Start of month			
Spitfire			
Nov 1944:	402	75	477
Dec 1944:	382	142	524
Jan 1945:	327	77	404
Tempest			
Nov 1944:	16	4	20
Dec 1944	16	4	20
Jan 1945:	16	3	19
Mustang			
Nov 1944:	153	42	195
Dec 1944:	148	60	208
Jan 1945:	172	53	225

The following table shows the relative figures for Spitfire, Tempest, Mustang, Typhoon and Mosquito's serving with the Second Tactical Air Force at the beginning of February and the Beginning of May 1945.

Second Tactical Air Force	Serviceable	Unserviceable	Total
Spitfire			
Feb 1945:	457	78	535
May 1945:	414	61	475
Tempest			
Feb 1945:	84	21	105
May 1945:	95	22	117
Mustang			
Feb 1945:	11	8	19
May 1945:	8	1	9
Typhoon			
Feb 1945:	321	56	377
May 1945:	275	51	326
Mosquito			
Feb 1945:	80	18	98
May 1945:	65	20	85

As can be seen from the relative figures for the Meteor III's period of service with the Second Tactical Air Force; February, March, April and May 1945, there were more Meteors serving with this force than there were Mustangs.

Appendix XIV

Flying Bombs Claimed by No. 616 Squadron in August 1944.

4 August 1944	1 x Flying Bomb	F/O Dean
4 August 1944	1 x Flying Bomb	F/O Rodger
7 August	1 x Flying Bomb	F/O Dean
10 August 1944	1 x Flying Bomb	F/O Dean
16 August 1944	1 x Flying Bomb	F/O McKenzie (RCAF)
16 August 1944	1 x Flying Bomb	F/O Mullander (Belgian)
17 August 1944	1 x Flying Bomb	F/O Ritch
17 August 1944	1 x Flying Bomb	W/O Woodacre
17 August 1944	1 x Flying Bomb	F/Sgt Easy
19 August 1944	1½ x Flying Bomb	F/O Hobson
(The half kill is from a kill shared with a Hawker Tempest)		
19 August	1 x Flying Bomb	F/Sgt Watts
28 August 1944	1 x Flying Bomb	F/O Hobson & F/Sgt Epps (Shared)
29 August 1944	1 x Flying Bomb	F/O Miller

Although several documents list the total claims as 12 and a half, the totals listed above amount to 13 and a half claimed kills, which corresponds with the Squadron Operation Record Book and OPREP's to H.Q.A.E.A.F. and 11 Group.

In addition to Flying Bombs claimed destroyed, the Squadron also had claimed a number of engagements, which resulted in Flying Bombs being damaged or possibly destroyed, although in the latter case their demise was not recorded. Some of the more notable of these claims are listed below.

3 August 1944: A 'Diver' was intercepted and engaged with unobserved results. This interception it was claimed was impeded by a Mustang III, also trying to intercept said Diver.
16 August 1944: Two 'Divers' attacked by Wing Commander Wilson.
27 August 1944: A 'Diver' escaped after being intercepted when the Meteors guns jammed.

Appendix XV

Meteors Lost during operational flying with 616 Squadron July 1944 – May 1945.

15 August 1944: 1 x Meteor I EE224 crashed while flying to High Halden to take up readiness alert. Pilot killed.
29 August 1944: 1 x Meteor I destroyed when it crash landed. Pilot suffered only slight injury.
29 April 1945: 2 x Meteor III's, EE252 and EE273 destroyed in the air, while on an armed reconnaissance. Assumed to have collided in cloud. Both pilots killed.

Appendix XVI

Anti-Diver Operations 1 March 20 March 1945

March 1945 Andrews Field

Date	Sorties
3.3.45	4
4.3.45	2
5.3.45	1
6.1.45	2
7.3.45	1
14.3.45	1 (Form 450 states no sorties on this date while Form 541 states one sortie)
16.3.45	2 (Form 540 states 2 sorties on this date, while Form 451 states 1 sortie)
19.3.45	1
Total	14

Air Ministry File D.D. (Ops.) 1. Stated "Since the renewed flying bomb activity 616 squadron, stationed at Andrews Field, has carried out up to last night (15th March) 15 anti-flying bomb sorties with no claims." This figure is regarded as being inaccurate.

Appendix XVII

Operational Sorties with the Second Tactical Air Force 1 April – 4 May 1945

April 1945

Date	Operational Sorties	Additional Sorties
3.4.45	4 (Interception)	
7.4.45	2 (Interception)	
8.4.45	2 (Interception)	
9.4.45	2 (Interception)	
10.4.45	6 Interception)	
11.4.45	6 (Interception)	
13		10 transfer to B.91
15.4.45		1 non operational
16.4.45	8	
17.4.45	20	
18.4.45	24	
19.4.45	15	
20.4.45		13 transfer new base
23.4.45	4 (Form541 states 3)	
24.4.45	16	
25.4.45	6	
26.4.45		transfer to B.152
28.4.45	4 (Interception)	
29.4.45	20 (4 Interception)	
30.4.45	Records unclear if patrols were flown	
1.5.45	26	
2.5.45	25	
3.5.45	22	
4.5.45	14	
Total	216	

Note: The 216 operational sorties listed above included 30 Interception and 186 armed reconnaissance sorties. As records are unclear for some dates, additional sorties may have been flown. In addition there were a number of other flights including no less than 40 transfer sorties between bases and at least one non operational flight.

Bibliography

1. 616 Squadron ORB Summary of Events July 1944
2. 616 Squadron Record of Events July 1944
3. 616 Squadron Summary of Events August – September 1944
4. 616 Squadron Summary of Events 1 October 1944 – 31 March 1915
5. 616 Squadron Record of Events March 1945
6. 616 Squadron Summary of Events April 1945
7. 616 Squadron Record of Events April 1945
8. 616 Squadron Summary of Events May 1945
9. 616 Squadron Record of Events May 1945
10. 616 Squadron ORB Appendices April 1944 – 1957 (included Squadron Record Sheets A, B & C until December 1944.)
11. 616 Squadron OPREP's TO: H.Q.A.E.A.F. an 11 Group, 12 July 1944 – 19 January 1945 and H.Q.A.E.A.F. and 84 Group T.A.F. from 19 January 1945, with specific reference to the following:
12. OPREP. A.6/M for 24 hrs. ending sunset 27.7.44.
13. OPREP. A.7/M for 24 hrs. ending sunset 28.7.44.
14. OPREP. A.6/M for 24 hrs. ending sunset 2.8.44.
15. OPREP. A. 13/M for 24 hrs. ending sunset 3.8.44.
16. OPREP. A-14/M for 24 hrs. ending sunset 4.8.44.
17. OPREP. A. 20/M for 24 hrs. ending sunset 10.8.44.
18. OPREP. A. 26/M for 24 hrs. ending sunset 16.8.44.
19. OPREP. A. 27/M for 24 hrs. ending sunset 17.8.44.
20. OPREP. A. 29/M for 24 hrs. ending sunset 19.8.44.
21. OPREP. A. 38/M for 24 hrs. ending sunset 28.8.44.
22. OPREP NO. 19/M.
23. OPREP. 44/m FOR 24 HRS. ENDING SUNSET 3.9.44.
24. OPREP. A. 128/M for 24 hrs. ending sunset 25.11.44., Operation Exercise "Bemould One"
25. OPREP. A .49/m for 24 hrs. ending sunset 18.2.45.
26. OPREP. A .50/m for 24 hrs. ending sunset 19.2.45.
27. 616 Squadron Record Sheets A, B and C 1 July 1944- 28 February 1945

28. 616 Consolidated Diver Reports, with specific reference to the following:
29. CONSOLIDATED DIVER REPORT, F/O J.K. RODGER
30. CONSOLIDATED DIVER REPORT, F/O RITCH (R.C.A.F.), 17th August 1944.
31. CONSOLIDATED DIVER REPORT., F/SGT R. EASY., 17th August 1944.
32. CONSOLIDATED DIVER REPORT., W/O Woodacre T.S., 17th August 1944.
33. CONSOLIDATED DIVER REPORT., F/SGT. EPPS, 28.8.44
34. CONSOLIDATED DIVER REPORT., F/O Hobson, 28.8.44
35. D.C.A.S., Meteor I and III performance and roles, dated 29 September 1944
36. 74 Squadron Summary of Events 1 May – 31 December 1945
37. 74 Squadron Record of Events May 1945
38. 616 Squadron Record Sheets A, B and C 1 July 1944- 28 February 1945
39. Official Air Ministry Statement – RAF Jet Fighters in Action (Released early in 1945)
40. D.C.A.S., METEOR III, 9/1/45
41. W.P. (44) 502., 5th September 1944., WAR CABINET. PROPOSAL BY GENERAL ARNOLD FOR A SECOND JOINT ANGLO-AMERICAN STATEMENT REGARDING JET PROPELLED AIRCRAFT
42. C.O.S. (44) 298th Meeting (0)., WAR CABINET, CHIEFS OF STAFF COMMITTEE., MINUTES of Meeting held on Tuesday, 5TH SEPTEMBER, 1944, at 10.30 a.m. JOINT ANGLO-AMERICAN STATEMENT REGARDING JET-PROPELLED AIRCRAFT
43. Ministry of Supply, Aeronautical Research Council Report No.2222
44. J.R.D.P. (44) 7. (Final.), WAR CABINET, Joint Committee on Research and Development Priorities, 21ST JULY 1944

45. J.I.C. (44) 316 (0) (REVISED FINAL) (LIMITED CIRCULATION), WAR CABINET JOINT INTELLIGENCE SUB-COMMITTEE, NEW WEAPONS IN RELATION TO GERMAN STRATEGY, 28TH JULY, 1944

46. Report No. F-TR-1133-ND by US Air Material Command on performance of the Me.262

47. Aeronautical Research Council Technical Report R & M No. 2791

48. Meteor III performance card dated 21.3.45

49. Air Ministry and MAP document dated August 1942

50. C.B.C. (44) 22, 15TH JULY. 1944

51. C.B.C. (44) 31 (0), WAR CABINET, CROSSBOW COMMITTEE, 24TH JULY, 1944

52. C.B.C. (44) 69, 28TH AUGUST, 1944, WAR CABINET, CROSSBOW COMMITTEE, FIFTEENTH REPORT BY THE CHAIRMAN, FLYING BOMB

53. C.O.S. (44) 298th Meeting (0)., WAR CABINET, CHIEFS OF STAFF COMMITTEE., 5TH SEPTEMBER,, 1944, at 10.30 am.

54. Marshall of the Royal Air Force, Sir Charles F.A. Portal, Chief of the Air Staff's reports to the War Cabinet, Chiefs of Staff Committee on various dates during July, August and September 1944

55. Aircraft and Armament Experimental Establishment, Bascombe Down Report No. A&AEE/819,a, Vampire F Mk. I TG.274 (Goblin I), Level Speed and Position Error Trials, 9 April 1946.

56. RA.E. Tech. Note No. F.A. 235/5

57. LXV Corp z.v. Report dated on scale of attack of V-1 and V-2, dated April 1945

58. The Employment of V-Weapons by the German During World War II, Department of the Army, September 1954

59. Report signed by General Heinmann on 14 June 1944 on authorised and actual strength of V-1 units.

60. RAF Strength in Squadrons report, 1945

61. Notes on the Operations 2^t Army Group, 6 June 1944 – 5 May 1945

62. Rolls Royce Derwent I turbine engines in a Gloster Meteor III aircraft EE 291,

63. Air Ministry File D.D. (Ops.) 1

64. Air Ministry and Ministry of Defence: Central Fighter Establishment: Reports and Papers. Night flying trials in Meteor III EE 232: (F.I.D.S. report No.277) Report No. 44

65. Aircraft Data Sheets and Photographs. Meteor III: Fighter, Records created or inherited by the Ministry of Supply and successors, the Ordnance Board, and related bodies

66. War Cabinet Chiefs of Staff Committee (C.O.S. (44) 247th Meeting (0) on 25 July 1944

In addition to the documents listed above many pages from operational, production, development and governmental documents were used as source material.

Glossary

AA	Anti-Aircraft
A&AEE	Aeroplane & Armament Experimental Establishment
ACM	Air Chief Marshal
ADGB	Air Defence of Great Britain
ALG	Air Landing Ground
AOC	Air Officer Commanding
Ar	Arado
A.W.	Armstrong Whitworth
CAS	Chiefs of Staff
CFE	Central Fighter Establishment
CO	Commanding Officer
DCAS	Deputy Chief of the Air Staff
DFC	Distinguished Flying Cross
Diver	V-1 Flying Bomb
E	Experimental
F	Fighter
Fi	Fieseler
GAF	German Air Force
GCI	Ground Controlled Interception
GL	Gun Laying
HAA	Heavy Anti-Aircraft
He	Heinkel
IAS	Indicated Air Speed
IFF	Identification Friend or Foe
Kg	Kilogram
KM	Kilometre
KM/H	Kilometres per Hour
LAA	Light Anti-Aircraft
lb	Pound
LST	Landing Ship Tank
MAP	Ministry of Aircraft Production (formerly Air Ministry)
Me	Messerschmitt

MPH	Miles per Hour
MT	Motor Transport
N.W.	North West
OC	Officer Commanding
OPREP	Operational Report
OR	Operational Requirement
P	Pursuit
RAE	Royal Aircraft Establishment
RAF	Royal Air Force
ROC	Royal Observer Corp
RPM	Revaluations per Minute
S.E.	South East
TAC	Tactical
TAF	Tactical Air Force
TAS	True Air Speed
UK	United Kingdom
US	United States
USAAF	United States Army Air Force
V-1	Vengence-1
WU	Whittle Unit
XP	Experimental Pursuit

Centurion Publishing

ISBN: 978-1-903630-22-8